The NEUROSCIENCE of RISKY DECISION MAKING

BRONFENBRENNER SERIES ON THE ECOLOGY
OF HUMAN DEVELOPMENT

Chaos and Its Influence on Children's Development: An Ecological Perspective
Edited by Gary W. Evans and Theodore D. Wachs

Research for the Public Good: Applying the Methods of Translational Research to Improve Human Health and Well-Being
Edited by Elaine Wethington and Rachel E. Dunifon

The Neuroscience of Risky Decision Making
Edited by Valerie F. Reyna and Vivian Zayas

The NEUROSCIENCE of RISKY DECISION MAKING

Edited by
Valerie F. Reyna and Vivian Zayas

American Psychological Association • *Washington, DC*

Published by
American Psychological Association
750 First Street, NE
Washington, DC 20002
www.apa.org

To order
APA Order Department
P.O. Box 92984
Washington, DC 20090-2984
Tel: (800) 374-2721; Direct: (202) 336-5510
Fax: (202) 336-5502; TDD/TTY: (202) 336-6123
Online: www.apa.org/pubs/books
E-mail: order@apa.org

In the U.K., Europe, Africa, and the Middle East, copies may be ordered from
American Psychological Association
3 Henrietta Street
Covent Garden, London
WC2E 8LU England

Typeset in Goudy by Circle Graphics, Inc., Columbia, MD

Printer: Edwards Brothers Inc., Ann Arbor, MI
Cover Designer: Naylor Design, Washington, DC

Library of Congress Cataloging-in-Publication Data

The neuorscience of risky decision making / edited by Valerie F. Reyna and Vivian Zayas. — First edition.
pages cm
Includes bibliographical references and index.
ISBN 978-1-4338-1662-8 — ISBN 1-4338-1662-8 1. Risk-taking (Psychology)
2. Decision making. I. Reyna, Valerie F., 1955- II. Zayas, Vivian.
BF637.R57N48 2014
153.8'3—dc23
2013034272

British Library Cataloguing-in-Publication Data

A CIP record is available from the British Library.

Printed in the United States of America
First Edition

http://dx.doi.org/10.1037/14322-000

This series is dedicated to the personal memories and lasting theoretical insights of our friend, colleague, and mentor, Urie Bronfenbrenner. His thinking about human development has profoundly influenced so many students and colleagues in multiple areas of enquiry. We hope this series will provide another vehicle through which Urie's ideas on the bioecology of human development can continue to flourish.

CONTENTS

Contributors .... *ix*

Foreword .... *xi*
Colin F. Camerer

Preface .... *xv*

Introduction to *The Neuroscience of Risky Decision Making* 3
Valerie F. Reyna and Vivian Zayas

I. Neuroeconomics 9

Chapter 1. Reward, Representation, and Impulsivity: A Theoretical Framework for the Neuroscience of Risky Decision Making 11
Valerie F. Reyna and Scott A. Huettel

Chapter 2. Behavioral and Neuroscience Methods for Studying Neuroeconomic Processes: What We Can Learn From Framing Effects 43
Irwin P. Levin, Todd McElroy, Gary J. Gaeth, William Hedgcock, and Natalie L. Denburg

II. Neurodevelopment **71**

Chapter 3. Risks, Rewards, and the Developing Brain in Childhood and Adolescence 73
Barbara R. Braams, Linda van Leijenhorst, and Eveline A. Crone

Chapter 4. The Adolescent Sensation-Seeking Period: Development of Reward Processing and Its Effects on Cognitive Control 93
Beatriz Luna, Aarthi Padmanabhan, and Charles Geier

Chapter 5. Reward Processing and Risky Decision Making in the Aging Brain 123
Gregory R. Samanez-Larkin and Brian Knutson

III. Neuropsychology **143**

Chapter 6. Mind and Brain in Delay of Gratification.................... 145
Vivian Zayas, Walter Mischel, and Gayathri Pandey

Chapter 7. The Neuroscience of Dual (and Triple) Systems in Decision Making 177
Samantha M. W. Wood and Antoine Bechara

Index 203

About the Editors.................... 213

CONTRIBUTORS

Antoine Bechara, PhD, Department of Psychology and Brain and Creativity Institute, University of Southern California, Los Angeles; Department of Neurology, University of Iowa, Iowa City

Barbara R. Braams, MS, Department of Developmental and Educational Psychology, Leiden University, Leiden, The Netherlands

Colin F. Camerer, PhD, Department of Behavioral Finance and Economics, Division of Humanities and Social Sciences, California Institute of Technology, Pasadena

Eveline A. Crone, PhD, Department of Developmental and Educational Psychology; Institute for Brain and Cognition, Leiden University, Leiden, The Netherlands; University of Amsterdam, Amsterdam, The Netherlands

Natalie L. Denburg, PhD, Department of Psychology, University of Iowa, Iowa City

Gary J. Gaeth, PhD, Department of Marketing, University of Iowa, Iowa City

Charles Geier, PhD, Department of Human Development and Family Studies, Pennsylvania State University, State College

William Hedgcock, PhD, Department of Marketing, University of Iowa, Iowa City

Scott Huettel, PhD, Department of Psychology and Neuroscience, Duke University, Durham, NC

Brian Knutson, PhD, Departments of Psychology and Neuroscience, Stanford University, Stanford, CA

Irwin P. Levin, PhD, Departments of Psychology and Marketing, University of Iowa, Iowa City

Beatriz Luna, PhD, Departments of Psychiatry and Psychology, University of Pittsburgh, Pittsburgh, PA

Todd McElroy, PhD, Department of Psychology, Appalachian State University, Boone, NC

Walter Mischel, PhD, Department of Psychology, Columbia University, New York, NY

Aarthi Padmanabhan, MS, Departments of Psychiatry and Psychology, University of Pittsburgh, Pittsburgh, PA

Gayathri Pandey, MS, Department of Psychology, Cornell University, Ithaca, NY

Valerie F. Reyna, PhD, Departments of Human Development and Psychology, Human Neuroscience Institute, Cornell Magnetic Resonance Imaging Facility, Cornell University, Ithaca, NY

Gregory R. Samanez-Larkin, PhD, Department of Psychology, Yale University, New Haven, CT

Linda van Leijenhorst, PhD, Department of Education and Child Studies, Leiden University, Leiden, The Netherlands

Samantha M. W. Wood, Department of Psychology, University of Southern California, Los Angeles

Vivian Zayas, PhD, Department of Psychology, Cornell University, Ithaca, NY

FOREWORD

COLIN F. CAMERER

The topic of risky decision making is important for both personal decisions and for measurement and control in complex social institutions. (Think of pricing the mysterious "systemic risk" hidden in our highly interlocked financial systems, or avoiding pandemics.)

Risky decision making is studied by researchers in a wide variety of disciplines. This book represents a current snapshot of what is known and a rough guide for future research on how to make sense of the complexity of risk. The editors' recipe: Create as much coherence across evidence from different disciplines as possible, and measure as much about underlying neural mechanisms as you can; then get top researchers working on their respective frontiers to say what they know in general language that makes shared understanding easy.

A striking feature of this volume is how risk taking can be construed as fundamentally different, according to discipline. For traditional economists, risk is simply variance of outcomes, with no regard to their sign. Psychologists have shown the additional importance of loss, compared with gain—losses are often valued about 1.5 to 2 times as much as equivalent gains (unless you have amygdala damage, in which case traditional economics applies to you; DeMartino et al., 2010).

Much more speculative, and interesting, are the roles emotion and memory play in risky decision making (see Chapter 1). There is good meta-analytic evidence that insula cortex encodes financial uncertainty, and other interocepted discomforts such as pain and disgust. Experienced risks are clearly encoded dually by verbatim and gist (distilled) memories (e.g., Reyna & Farley, 2006), a distinction that is just now migrating to decision neuroscience.

The economists' view is that how much risk you take is a personal matter: Who are we to condemn either cave diving or college cheerleading (which is more dangerous than you think, Amber!)? But many risks *aren't* just personal, because they expose others to harm (e.g., reckless driving, unsafe sex) or expose oneself to unknown harm.

But how can we say *scientifically* that somebody took "too much" risk or took an "unnecessary" risk? To do so, a concept of inhibitory control becomes useful. In this mechanistic view, healthy risk takers know when to stop and can inhibit the last throw of the dice. Shannon et al. (2011) reported a remarkable finding about youths: In the most impulsive incarcerated youths, premotor areas were positively connected with "default network" areas and negatively connected with attention and control areas. These struggling adolescents are always ready to act, and "don't attend and control"—adequately.

Regardless of how much you know, something in this book will surprise you. For example, if you know that basic psychological performance on simple attention, sensory, and memory tasks slowly degrades beginning in one's 20s, you might then be surprised to find that there are no reliably established differences in risk taking between young and old people. Happily—for this 50-something scientist—as people age, they show muted neural response to anticipated loss, and other "positivity" biases, along with weakened frontostriatal connectivity (see Chapter 5).

Do you know what the default network is (Raichle & Snyder, 2007)? It's a circuit including prefrontal and parietal cortex that is reliably active during rest or "doing nothing special." You might be surprised by a recent finding that the default network is activated when one is simply judging the probability of a state occurring, independent of reward (d'Acremont et al., 2013). A string of findings like these are interesting clues that the default network is *not* doing nothing . . . instead, it is probably doing some evolutionarily important low-effort work (perhaps thinking about the risky world or the social world).

As a proud neuroeconomist, I credit the contents of volumes like this one as the source of much of my optimism. When there is genuine eagerness to think about the brain computing a wide variety of psychological and economic constructs (preferably numbers, please), and to treat all kinds of different evidence seriously, progress will be rapid. Of course, rapid progress will make us wince over time, because it means we will know, hopefully within a decade or two, which half of what we now think is true is false.

REFERENCES

d'Acremont, M., Fornari, E., & Bossaerts, P. (2013). Activity in inferior parietal and medial prefrontal cortex signals the accumulation of evidence in a probability learning task. *PLoS Computational Biology, 9,* e1002895. doi: 10.1371/journal.pcbi.1002895

De Martino, B., Camerer, C. F., & Adolphs, R. (2010). Amygdala damage eliminates monetary loss aversion. *PNAS, 107,* 3788–3792.

Raichle, M. E., & Snyder, A. Z. (2007). A default mode of brain function: A brief history of an evolving idea. *NeuroImage, 37,* 1083–1090.

Reyna, V. F., & Farley, F. (2006). Risk and rationality in adolescent decision-making: Implications for theory, practice, and public policy. *Psychological Science in the Public Interest,* 7(1), 1–44. doi:10.1111/j.1529-1006.2006.00026.x

Shannon, B. J., Raichle, M. E., Snyder, A. Z., Fair, D. A., Mills, K. L., Zhang, D., . . . Kiehl, K. A. (2011). Premotor functional connectivity predicts impulsivity in juvenile offenders. *PNAS, 108(27),* 11241–11245.

PREFACE

Risky decision making occurs in many domains of life, such as eating, sexual activity, crime, drugs and alcohol use, finances, warfare, and health care. In each of these domains, crucial outcomes—developing diabetes, HIV infection, a terrorist attack, going to jail, being pulled over for drunk driving, losing one's lifetime savings in a high-risk investment, or dying from a preventable cancer—are uncertain. Research on the neuroscience of risky decision making has surged in recent years, reflecting the intersection of interests in the brain, decision processes, and the welfare of people—often young people—who suffer or die needlessly as a consequence of their actions. A goal of this book is to delineate the precise neural mechanisms that affect risky decision making and how the brain is affected by momentary tempting situations, chronic dispositional differences, and developmental periods.

Exciting new discoveries suggest that the neural mechanisms underlying decision making across domains are simultaneously empirically and theoretically similar but also meaningfully different depending on the domain. Fundamental constructs such as self-control, sensitivity to reward, and preference for risk predict risky decision making across drastically different domains, and similar areas of brain activation have been associated with each construct across domains. New constructs are being introduced to explain and predict risky behavior in multiple domains, such as neural representations of the gist of risky options. From a developmental perspective, risky decision making changes from childhood to old age, with the greatest risky behavior occurring during adolescence and young adulthood, and these behavioral changes map onto massive changes in brain structure. And, individual differences that were first observed in childhood manifest in differences in brain activation 40 years later. Moreover, the differences in risky decision making across ages and individuals that are assessed in laboratory behaviors and in brain scanners correlate with real-world outcomes ranging from income to incarceration.

Despite consistency in brain function and structure across domains, risky decision making also differs from one domain to another behaviorally and neurally. The cultural condemnation attached to overeating, smoking, and crime varies, as does the availability of different kinds of rewards, and the brain distinguishes among them. People who take seemingly unreasonable risks with sex can be careful with money, and vice versa—in spite of the fact that neurobiological factors such as sensation seeking predict risk taking in both domains.

Research in the neuroscience of risky decision making has now reached that productive state in which there is sufficient evidence to take stock and present frameworks to integrate the seemingly inconsistent, conflicting, and contradictory findings in this literature. It seems remarkable that this would be the first book to do so in such an active area of research. However, this makes sense when one considers that the first study of any kind using functional magnetic resonance imaging occurred as recently as the 1990s.

Research on risky decision making has benefited from the fact that scholars from diverse disciplines have been brought together by a shared fascination with these amazing new technologies, such as magnetic resonance imaging, which allow them to study the functioning brain without disruptive or invasive methods. For example, the Society for Neuroeconomics, which had its inaugural meeting in the early 2000s, fosters interaction "among scholars from the psychological, economic, and neural sciences" (http://www.neuroeconomics.org/society). Advances in the neuroscience of risky decision making are also presented increasingly at other national and international meetings, such as the Society for Neuroscience, the Society for Research in Child Development, and the American Psychological Association (APA).

This book, the third in the APA Bronfenbrenner Series on the Ecology of Human Development, traces its inspiration to Urie Bronfenbrenner's 1996 book entitled *The State of Americans*, coauthored with Peter McClelland, Elaine Wethington, Phyllis Moen, and Stephen Ceci. The 1996 book presented a compilation of statistics on crime, poverty, family well-being, education, and the like, with the goal of using "hard facts" to translate social scientific insight into a form that would influence policy and practice. Although this research is still in its infancy, neural processes of risky decision making (as discussed in the current volume) have been shown to be related to these kinds of important social and health statistics.

One assumption of Bronfenbrenner's 1996 book was that the adoption of policies and practices based on scientific evidence would improve the well-being of Americans (and others). A second assumption was that social scientists should be at the table with policymakers in solving practical social problems because research has practical implications for improving health and development in the population. Nowhere is that potential more evident than for research on risky decision making.

In his final book in 2004 (*Making Human Beings Human: Bioecological Perspectives on Human Development*), Bronfenbrenner combined biological perspectives with his ecological framework for human development, paying particular attention to the different contexts in which biological and brain development take place—at individual, family, institutional, and societal levels. In recognition of his lifetime contributions to applied psychology as a founder of Head Start and to understanding critical social problems, Bronfenbrenner received the James McKeen Catell Fellow Award from the Association for Psychological Science (previously the American Psychological Society) in 1993. In 1996, the APA Award for Lifetime Contribution to Developmental Psychology in the Service of Science and Society Award was renamed, in honor of Bronfenbrenner, the Urie Bronfenbrenner Award for Lifetime Contribution to Developmental Psychology in the Service of Science and Society.

Urie Bronfenbrenner continues to influence his colleagues at Cornell University and around the world. In particular, this volume was inspired by a meeting supported by the Bronfenbrenner Center for Translational Research at Cornell University focused on this topic that gathered leading scholars from around the world. To see their talks and be similarly inspired, access http://mediasite.video.cornell.edu/Mediasite/Catalog/catalogs/BCTR_review.aspx. The meeting was also a project of the Cornell Judgment, Decision Making, and Social Behavior interdisciplinary group and the Center for Behavioral Economics and Decision Research (http://socialsciences.cornell.edu/judgment-decision-making-and-social-behavior/). We gratefully acknowledge the assistance of John Eckenrode, The Bronfenbrenner Advisory Committee, Carrie Chalmers, Karene Booker, and Thomas Craig.

The current book emerges at a key time in understanding the basic mechanisms underlying risky behavior, a focus of this volume, which is an essential step in the process of translation of research findings into policy and practice. Without this understanding, policymakers and practitioners can misapply research and waste precious resources, while important problems are left unaddressed. We hope that this trend of increasing research on basic mechanisms of risky decision making continues and that this volume contributes to efforts to translate basic science about the neuroscience of risky decision making into policy and practice.

This area of research is evolving rapidly, and so is the audience for it. At this moment, we anticipate that the target audience for this book includes scholars approaching risky decision making from multiple perspectives: neuroscientists, neuropsychologists, clinicians, psychologists (developmental, social, and cognitive), economists and other social scientists, legal scholars and criminologists, and professionals in public health and medicine. May science continue to supplant superstition when human welfare is at stake.

The NEUROSCIENCE of RISKY DECISION MAKING

INTRODUCTION TO *THE NEUROSCIENCE OF RISKY DECISION MAKING*

VALERIE F. REYNA AND VIVIAN ZAYAS

The processes by which individuals make decisions under uncertainty has important implications for real-world outcomes in law, medicine, economics, clinical psychology, and public policy, to name a few. Despite the explosion of research on risky decision making over the past four decades, many questions remain: What are the neurobiological, psychological, and sociocultural factors that influence risky decision making either in isolation or in combination? How do the effects of these processes on decision making differ across development? And, what are their implications for problematic behaviors and health? The primary goal of this book is to address these questions, thereby advancing basic understanding and scientific theory about the brain mechanisms underlying risky decision making across the life span.

Understanding the mechanisms—from brain to behavior—of risky decision making is essential in paving the way for translation of basic science into policy and practice. A second goal of this book is to encourage intellectual integration of existing diverse approaches. To date, the factors that influence

http://dx.doi.org/10.1037/14322-001
The Neuroscience of Risky Decision Making, by V. F. Reyna and V. Zayas (Editors)

risky decision making have been studied from a number of perspectives that span the spectrum of neuroscience, psychology, and behavioral economics. These approaches address the same general topic. However, each focuses on a different level of analysis (neural, individual, and societal, respectively), different units of analysis (behaviors, cognitions, affective states, neural patterns of activation), different domains (e.g., problematic behaviors, financial decision making, medical and health-related decisions), and different types of questions (e.g., normative processes to individual differences to developmental changes). Despite significant scientific advances, researchers in each area have remained relatively isolated from one another.

The speed of scientific advances, especially in neuroscience, calls for integrating findings from various levels of analysis to provide a more comprehensive view of the process underlying risky decision making as they operate over the lifespan. This intellectual integration is another goal of the book. Building on the recent surge of research on the neuroscience underlying risky decision making, the book brings together scholars with expertise that blends approaches from multiple disciplines to promote the development of a comprehensive and contextually sensitive model of risky decision making across the life span.

In the chapters that follow, leading neuroeconomists, neuroscientists, and social scientists discuss the latest findings and theoretical perspectives on risky decision making, reviewing such topics as the changing impact of rewards and punishments at different ages (from early childhood through old age); the role of emotional regulation and self-control abilities as well as individual differences in personality in contributing to chronic difficulties in risky decision making; and the social, cognitive, biological, and developmental factors that shape risky behavior.

The book is organized into three sections that reflect active areas of research on the neural underpinnings of risky decision making: neuroeconomics, neurodevelopment, and neuropsychology. Neuroeconomics is the study of the brain making economic judgments and decisions. We lead off the book with interdisciplinary approaches to neuroeconomics because of the foundational role that economics has played in defining the basic phenomenon of risky decision making. Hence, from the outset, we compare tenets of psychology and economics that have provided the context for neuroscience research on risky decision making over the past decade.

The second section on neurodevelopment describes a special focus of research on risky decision making, namely, how risky decision making changes dramatically from childhood to adolescence to adulthood to old age as a function of maturational and experienced-based changes in the brain. The third section presents influential research in neuropsychology and individual differences, including the famous paradigms known as the "marshmallow test" (that incorporates the economic notion of temporal or delayed discounting) and the Iowa Gambling Task. Both tasks call on overlapping neural systems and elicit behavior that predicts risk taking in the real world. Throughout the book, many of the authors weave elements of neuroeconomics, neurodevelopment, and neuropsychology together.

Specifically, in Part I on neureconomics, fundamental economic phenomena such as risk preferences and framing effects (i.e., shifting from risk-seeking to risk-avoiding when options are equivalent but worded differently as gains versus losses) are discussed. In Chapter 1, Reyna and Huettel describe the implications of risky decision making for law, medicine, and public health and contrast the definitions of risky decision making in economics versus psychology. They explain that economists focus on risk in the sense of variance in outcomes (hence, by this definition, *risk takers* are people who tolerate uncertainty in outcomes), whereas psychologists focus on risk in the sense of the particular case in whice uncertain outcomes are bad and detrimental to well-being (e.g., financially, legally, or medically) and highlight the effects of emotion and immaturity. Reyna and Huettel then summarize neuroscientific evidence ranging from ventral striatal reward circuitry to involvement of the default network in impulsivity. Grounded in this evidence, they introduce a preliminary integrative theoretical framework encompassing neural substrates of emotional salience, memory representations of options, and decision conflicts as people experience internal clashes between competing strategies for making risky decisions.

In Chapter 2, Levin, McElroy, Gaeth, Hedgcock, and Denburg summarize research on framing effects, which challenge axiomatic principles of economic theories of risk preference. Levin et al. present a process-oriented perspective that explains why people take risks and why their risk preferences shift in different circumstances. Summarizing and integrating research using behavioral and biological/neurological measures, such as neuroimaging, eye-tracking, circadian rhythms, and life span developmental techniques, they characterize the cognitive and emotional underpinnings of risky decisions across tasks and individuals.

In Part II on neurodevelopment, the authors address how developmental differences in brain functioning—from childhood to old age—are associated with risky decision making. In Chapter 3, Braams, van Leijenhorst, and Crone review the conditions under which developmental differences in risky behaviors are found among children, adolescents, and adults and how neuroscience elucidates the neural underpinnings of these differences. They also describe important neurodevelopmental frameworks of risk and reward processing, including the dual-processing network, the imbalance model, and the social information processing network approaches. They explore such issues as why the striatum is sometimes overactivated and other times underactivated in adolescents; the role of hormones and individual differences; and the role of social factors, such as peer relations and peer pressure. They conclude with a new working model that explains how the striatum is influenced by environmental context and how it connects to other regions in the brain, which ultimately influence risk-taking behavior. This model is informative for policymakers and educational practitioners because it identifies what can be expected of people depending on their age.

In Chapter 4, Luna, Padmanabhan, and Geier focus on sensation seeking in adolescence, which is known to increase during the pubertal period across different societies and different species and often results in risk-taking behaviors that undermine survival. Despite being a period of peak physical health, adolescence is a time of increased mortality rates due in great part to risky behaviors such as substance abuse, unprotected sex, and extreme sports. To account for the paradox of heightened fitness and increased mortality during adolescence, Luna et al. propose that increased sensation seeking in adolescence is an adaptive mechanism. Sensation seeking affords the ability to explore the environment and expose the individual to information, thereby modeling the maturing brain. Sensation seeking may also underlie motivation for seeking independence, which supports an adolescent's transition to adult levels of maturity and responsibility.

Drawing on evidence from animal models and human studies, Luna et al. propose that developmental changes in neurotransmitter availability (along with pubertal changes) are a possible mechanism underlying the heightened propensity for sensation seeking in adolescence. Like Braams et al., they explore discrepancies in neuroimaging studies of engagement of reward-related brain systems in adolescence, drawing on developmental differences during stages of reward processing and age-related differences in value assessment. Luna et al.'s model of increased sensation seeking in adolescence has implications for juvenile law and education. Concluding the section on neurodevelopment, in Chapter 5, Samanez-Larkin and Knutson discuss emerging research on risky decision making in the aging brain. Despite the aging of the world population and the importance of decision competence in old age (e.g., retirement and end-of-life decisions), remarkably little research has focused on how aging might influence risk and reward processing. Samanez-Larkin and Knutson review studies that examine how age influences psychological and neural responses to financial incentives and risks. Early findings from this literature suggest that aging may influence the structure and function of neural circuits implicated in incentive processing and risky decision making (e.g., the ventral striatum, the anterior insula, the prefrontal cortex) and that the consequences of these changes for choice apply to both laboratory and real-world settings. In addition to informing theory about the impact of affect and cognition on choice, these novel findings imply that understanding how the aging brain processes incentives may eventually inform the design of more targeted and effective decision aids for individuals of all ages.

In Part III on neuropsychology, Zayas, Mischel, and Pandey provide a compelling review of 40 years of research on delay of gratification. By age 4, children differ in the ability to delay gratification, and such individual differences predict risky decision and problematic behaviors across development, such as higher social competence, higher academic achievement (SAT scores), and lower substance abuse and body mass index (BMI). Recent findings provide empirical evidence that the remarkable long-term continuity in delay of gratification is rooted in individual differences in prefrontal cortical activity as well as affect-related brain circuits—a proposition consistent with a growing body of neuroscientific work in risky decision making.

Specifically, differences in preschool delay of gratification ability were observed most clearly in adulthood in tasks that involve inhibiting responses to rewarding stimuli (e.g., smiling face indicating approval) but not to neutral stimuli. Moreover, in imaging work, the preschool delay predicted greater activation of the inferior frontal gyrus, a structure in the prefrontal cortex (PFC) recruited when resolving conflict between representations and motor responses, on trials that required inhibiting a response. Preschool delay ability also predicted less activation of the ventral striatum in response to the rewarding stimulus. These authors conclude by arguing that a key benefit of enacting effortful self-control is that it lessens the tempting aspects of the cues to be inhibited and thus makes the very act of delaying gratification easier, essentially lessening the need to exert effortful self-control.

In the final chapter on neuropsychology, Wood and Bechara weigh in on the debate about "single system" versus "dual system" models for valuation in risky decision making. Using clinical evidence, they argue that not only are the traditional two processes supported by the clinical facts, but, in addition, the evidence points to a third process, thus calling for the notion of "triple process" models. This third system, involving the insula, translates homeostatic, bodily signals into feelings of craving.

That is, Wood and Bechara present evidence that many clinical conditions associated with poor impulse control and poor decision making are the product of an imbalance between two separate but interacting neural systems: (a) an impulsive, amygdala and striatum-dependent, neural system that promotes automatic and habitual behaviors and (b) a reflective, PFC-dependent, neural system for decision making. These neural systems map onto the psychological systems named "System 1" and "System 2," respectively. System 1 is defined as quick, automatic, and associative in its response, while System 2 is slow, effortful, reflective, and "rational." The reflective system controls the impulsive system via several mechanisms. However, this control is not absolute; hyperactivity within the impulsive system can override the reflective system. The impulsive system is reminiscent of the described properties of System 1, which require a long time to build associations, but once those associations are made, they are rapid and difficult to override.

However, critically, going beyond standard dual-processes models, Wood and Bechara suggest that the insula plays a key role in modulating the dynamics of these two systems. While most prior research has focused on the impulsive versus reflective or System 1 versus System 2, they suggest that the insula plays a key role in modulating the dynamics of these two systems. More specifically, the insula or "craving" system potentiates the activity of the impulsive system, weakens the goal-driven cognitive resources that are needed for the normal operation of the reflective system, or does both. Thus, when physiological states that involve deprivation, withdrawal, stress, anxiety, or any condition associated with homeostatic perturbation are considered, a third process (the insula) comes to the fore with direct impact on the functionality of the traditional dual systems.

As a whole, the book provides a comprehensive and up-to-date overview of major approaches to the neuroscience of risky decision making. The authors summarize cutting-edge research on the neuroeconomic, neurodevelopmental, and neuropsychological factors that explain and predict risky decision making. Diverse findings from structural and functional neuroimaging, as well as behavioral and neurophysiological studies, on populations ranging from young children to old age, are integrated to provide a scientific framework for understanding causal mechanisms underlying risky decision making across the life span. This work has important implications not only for reconceptualizing and reforming the next phase of research on the neuroscience of risky decision making but also for informing practice and policy in law, medicine, and public health.

I

NEUROECONOMICS

1

REWARD, REPRESENTATION, AND IMPULSIVITY: A THEORETICAL FRAMEWORK FOR THE NEUROSCIENCE OF RISKY DECISION MAKING

VALERIE F. REYNA AND SCOTT A. HUETTEL

We provide an overview of neuroscience research on risky decision making, organizing findings in an integrative theoretical framework aimed at elucidating mechanisms that drive behavior. The concept of risk has been used to describe a variety of influences on decisions—including both the variance of outcomes and the potential for a negative outcome—each of which may have a distinct influence on neural processing. Armed with these distinctions, we examine neural substrates of reward and valuation, reviewing evidence that the ventromedial prefrontal cortex (vmPFC) computes a common currency signal that allows comparison of rewards across domains (e.g., food and money). This common currency signal is modulated by the variables that shape decision making, such as gains, losses, and their probabilities. We review evidence that subjective feelings about the uncertainty and valence of outcomes (e.g., risk and loss aversion) follow from signals in the insula and that signals associated with uncertainty

Preparation of this manuscript was supported in part by the National Institutes of Health under award number R21CA149796 and R01NR014368-01 to the first author. The content is solely the responsibility of the authors and does not necessarily represent the official views of the National Institutes of Health.

http://dx.doi.org/10.1037/14322-002
The Neuroscience of Risky Decision Making, by V. F. Reyna and V. Zayas (Editors)

can be distinguished from signals of emotional salience in the amygdala. Representations of options in vmPFC/medial orbitofrontal cortex serve as inputs to a comparison process in anterior cingulate cortex (ACC)/ dorsomedial prefrontal cortex (dmPFC), which reflects decisional conflict. Activation in ACC/ dmPFC is greater when choices conflict with otherwise dominant strategies, such as gist-based simplification versus verbatim-based trading off, triggering cognitive control mechanisms in dorsolateral PFC. When value signals are translated into actions, prefrontal signals influence processing of neurons in the posterior parietal cortex whose activity is consistent with drift-accumulator models of choice. This tentative process model differentiates several independent contributors to risk-taking behavior and identifies levers of behavioral change that could be used to prevent unhealthy decisions.

People often die from risky choices. Choices to initiate smoking, take illicit drugs, eat unhealthy foods, drive recklessly, and drink excessively contribute to cancer, heart disease, and trauma from traffic accidents (Reyna & Farley, 2006). Lifetime prevalence of alcohol dependence alone approaches 20% (Bloom, 2010). Crime is less a phenomenon of psychopathy (although psychopaths commit a disproportionate percentage of crime) than of age-related risk taking, peaking in adolescence and young adulthood. Indeed, homicide is the second leading cause of death among 15- to 19-year-olds, after unintentional injury; firearms are the instrument of death in 85% of cases (Centers for Disease Control and Prevention, 2012). Therefore, the "burden of illness"—the severity and prevalence of harm to oneself and others—produced by risky decision making is enormous (Arnett, 1992; Reyna & Rivers, 2008).

Risky decision making is a major public health problem, as illustrated by this brief litany of statistics, but it is also a problem of law, medicine, social relations, and personal finance. In the domain of personal finance, for example, people commit errors of risk aversion and risk seeking, avoiding riskier investments with better lifetime returns and spending down reserves rather than saving enough for retirement (Benartzi & Thaler, 1995; Rick, Cryder, & Loewenstein, 2008). Although risky behaviors can differ across domains of life, they also correlate with one another, peak at roughly similar ages, and activate a common neural circuitry of risk and reward valuation (Jessor, 1991; D. J. Levy & Glimcher, 2011; Porcelli & Delgado, 2009; Reyna, Chapman, Dougherty, & Confrey, 2012). As we discuss in this chapter, understanding the risk and reward mechanisms in the brain, and their development, is key to unraveling the mystery of irrational risk taking in real life.

Laboratory experiments are an essential element in this understanding. Risky decisions made in the laboratory predict real-world decisions, although far from perfectly (e.g., Galvan et al., 2006; Galvan, Hare, Voss, Glover, & Casey, 2007; Lejuez, Aklin, Zvolensky, & Pedulla, 2003; Parker & Fischhoff, 2005; Pleskac, 2008; Reyna et al., 2011; Steinberg, Cauffman, Woolard, Graham, & Banich, 2009; Stout, Rock, Campbell, Busemeyer, & Finn, 2005). Alternatively, using real-world behaviors for prediction of different risky behaviors does not solve the problem of imperfect prediction, and typically such relationships are difficult to interpret because they are confounded (i.e., multiple correlated factors contribute to risky behaviors). (Using some real-world risky behaviors to "predict" other risky behaviors is satisfactory for actuarial purposes, but it sheds little light on causation or mechanisms.) Consequently, when the proper methodological controls are used, laboratory tasks provide crucial insight into the mechanisms of risky decision making. The main challenge in developing effective practice and public policy is *understanding* these mechanisms of risky decision making to determine (a) whether they apply in a given context and (b) how they combine to produce behavior.

Progress in this endeavor hinges on distinguishing among related concepts such as impulsivity, reward sensitivity, risk perception, risk preference, sensation seeking, and how rewards are represented and remembered; many tasks used in research conflate these concepts. One thesis of our broader argument is that behavioral evidence that distinguishes these concepts is essential to inform the design of tasks and analyses, and, hence, the interpretation of neuroscience data. Despite generally impressive rigor, the amount of neuroscience data regarding any one question is relatively limited, and what data there are is sometimes not sufficiently theoretically grounded to be interpreted unambiguously. In addition, neuroscience research can be enhanced through a greater emphasis on hypothesis testing and by experimental designs that complement correlational approaches, as found in relevant behavioral research (e.g., see Huettel, Song, & McCarthy, 2009).

Furthermore, although it is possible to wait until more data arrive, research on both brain and behavior will progress more expeditiously if they are brought together. More fundamentally, the functions of the brain cannot be understood without a process analysis of the behavioral tasks they support, and a deep understanding of behavior cannot be achieved in ignorance of the rich new world of neuroscience research. In short, this chapter is a prolegomenon to a fully verified theoretical framework for the neuroscience of risky decision making. The interpretations we offer are preliminary, but they respond to the challenge of developing a functional taxonomy that maps decision behavior onto its underlying processes, both psychological and neuroscientific (Huettel, 2010; Poldrack et al., 2011).

DEFINITIONS AND DISTINCTIONS

There are two main approaches to defining risky decision making: economic and psychological. For economists, risk is about variance of known outcomes (i.e., uncertain events, not uncertainty in the epistemic sense). Within the expected utility framework of economics, *risk preference* (sometimes called *risk attitude*) refers to the shape of the utility function estimated from a series of risky choices, with the choice between a sure versus a risky option of equal expected value being a canonical example (von Winterfeldt & Edwards, 1986). Expected utility is a nonlinear transformation of expected value into subjective value.

For example, consider a choice between (a) winning $1,000 for sure versus (b) a .50 probability of winning $2,000 and .50 probability of winning nothing. Risk-averse people would prefer the sure thing (a) over the risky gamble (b). Comparison of option (a) with option (b) indicates that the second option has more variance in outcomes than the first. (It may be useful to think of the sure option as .50 × $1,000 + .50 × $1,000, illustrating that outcomes do not vary when they are sure.) When the expected values of each option are equal to one another, as in this example, sure options ($1,000) are mathematically closer to the origin (i.e., closer to zero) than non–zero gamble outcomes ($2,000). Thus, if people prefer the sure option, their "utility" function for money is assumed to have a concave curvature—$2,000 deviates more (in a downward direction) from its objective value than $1,000 does from its objective value.

In neuroscience research on decision making, the values of decision options are talked about in at least two ways: the value of the outcomes ($1,000 and $2,000 in our example) and the value of the whole option, known as *expected value*, which is a weighted average of outcomes and probabilities (i.e., $1,000 × 1.0 = $1,000 or .5 × $2,000 + .5 × 0 = $1,000) (e.g., D. J. Levy & Glimcher, 2012; Zhang & Hirsch, 2013). When outcomes are positive, they are referred to as *rewards;* expected value captures the idea that probability and reward trade off to produce overall value (e.g., stocks have greater expected value but greater risk than bonds).

Expected value corresponds roughly to people's intuitions about probabilities and outcomes. If people did not weight outcomes by their probabilities, they would feel the same way about a lottery ticket that paid off with a $1,000 prize for sure and one that paid off $1,000 with a .50 probability. Even if a person has never heard of the concept of expected value, she would not prefer a .5 chance (e.g., flipping a coin) to win $1,000 over a sure $1,000. Animals and children who have not yet learned to multiply also make such trade-offs of risk and reward intuitively (Reyna & Brainerd, 1994). Thus, the formal concepts of variance and expected value have some psychological reality.

For economists, none of the outcomes need to be "bad" for an option to be considered risky. The second option (or gamble) in our example could be a .50 chance of winning $1,200 and a .50 chance of winning $800, and it would still be riskier in the economics sense compared with a sure $1,000. For psychologists, however, behavioral choices that lead to the possibility of loss or harm are referred to as *risky* (Fox & Tannenbaum, 2011). As in the economists' definition of *risky,* these bad outcomes (losses or harms) are *uncertain:* Crimes go unpunished, most people who drink never become alcoholics, unprotected sex does not necessarily result in HIV infection, and many pieces of pie do not necessarily produce death or disease. Individuals differ in their willingness to tolerate this uncertainty.

Taking undue risks can be considered pathological and, thus, classified in the *Diagnostic and Statistical Manual of Mental Disorders* (4th ed.; *DSM–IV–TR*; e.g., eating disorders or antisocial personality disorder; American Psychiatric Association, 2000) or the *International Statistical Classification of Diseases and Related Health Problems* (10th ed.; ICD–10; World Health Organization, 2010). However, risky choices can also be socially approved, for example, when football players risk serious injury, or they can be an ordinary part of daily life, as in high-risk jobs such as logging or washing windows of skyscrapers. A question that has guided neuroscience research is how the brain processes this variance or uncertainty, in particular, how brain systems support compensatory tradeoffs between a safer, lower value option and a riskier, higher value option (De Martino, Kumaran, Seymour, & Dolan, 2006; Huettel, 2006; Tom, Fox, Trepel, & Poldrack, 2007; Venkatraman, Payne, Bettman, Luce, & Huettel, 2009). Given the uncertainty inherent in risk taking, it can be difficult to draw a clear line between healthy and unhealthy risk taking, but that distinction is the crux of adaptive behavior (Reyna & Farley, 2006).

The psychological definition of risky behavior conflates two aspects of decision making, however, that are separable theoretically and functionally in the brain: risk and loss attitudes (e.g., Yechiam & Telpaz, 2013). The example of the type that we have discussed (a sure gain vs. a gamble of equal expected value) is frequently used to illustrate *risk aversion* because most people prefer the sure option to the gamble of equal expected value. People find the uncertainty in the gamble aversive despite its mathematical equivalence over repeated trials (i.e., if the gamble were enacted repeatedly, the average winnings or expectation would be $1,000). However, risk aversion is not the same as loss aversion.

Loss aversion does not just mean that losses (e.g., losing money, people dying rather than being saved) are negative, but that losses hurt more than gains of similar magnitude feel good (Kahneman & Tversky, 2000; there is also evidence that people pay closer attention to losses; see Yechiam & Telpaz, 2013). So, most people will not accept a bet on the flip of a coin in which the amount to win is equal to the amount to lose (e.g., win $10 if heads, lose $10 if tails). They usually require about a 2:1 ratio of wins to losses to accept the bet (e.g., win $20 if heads, lose $10 if tails). Loss aversion refers to an asymmetry in the impact of gain versus loss outcomes, rather than risk or uncertainty (Willemsen, Böckenholt, & Johnson, 2011).

In sum, risk aversion can be defined as preferring a sure thing to a roughly mathematically equivalent (or superior) gamble, and risk taking as the opposite preference. Economists focus on people's taste for variance, which classic theories identify with nonlinear functions of outcomes, such as money. In the economists' view, two gambles can differ in risk if one has higher variance in outcomes than another. Psychologists focus on tolerance for uncertain bad outcomes, such as losses, and the implications of risk attitudes for life outcomes. However, risk and loss aversion can be distinguished empirically—and loss aversion can be demonstrated when options are certain. Both economists' and psychologists' definitions of risk attitude have influenced neuroscience research (e.g., Schonberg, Fox, & Poldrack, 2011).

According to either economists' or psychologists' definitions, most people have an aversion to uncertainty. When people demonstrate a high tolerance for uncertain outcomes, whether inside or outside of the laboratory, what are the brain processes that underlie their risk preferences? Do they process risk or reward differently, fail to trade them off properly, or lack the ability to control their attraction to rewards? Moreover, are the nature of thinking and underlying brain processes qualitatively different among those who seek versus avoid risks, especially in ways that go beyond traditional dichotomies between sensation seeking and self-control (Chick & Reyna, 2012; Reyna et al., 2011)? With these definitions and distinctions in mind, we can begin to assemble the neural building blocks of risky decision making.

NEURAL SUBSTRATES OF REWARD AND VALUATION

The neural substrates of reward have been well characterized, building on carefully controlled research with animals (Platt & Huettel, 2008). The reward circuit of the brain consists of the midbrain dopamine areas (the ventral tegmental area and substantia nigra) and the basal ganglia structures to which they project (the ventral striatum, where the nucleus accumbens is located, and the dorsal striatum). Axons from the midbrain areas also project broadly to the prefrontal cortex, but particularly to the ventromedial prefrontal cortex (vmPFC; Galvan, 2012). Dopaminergic activity in these areas has been linked to current and anticipated rewards (e.g., Glimcher, Camerer, Fehr, & Poldrack, 2009).

Rewards are often appetitive in studies of animals (e.g., juice or food), but studies of humans have shown generalization of value signals to include monetary, social, and other rewards (Delgado, Nystrom, Fissell, Noll, & Fiez, 2000). The idea that there is a common currency of rewards in the brain is consistent with economic notions of utility in which the subjective values of different types of rewards all project onto a dimension of reward value (Montague & Berns, 2002; Smith et al., 2010). (We initially focus on rewards, such as appetitive stimuli, but discuss aversive stimuli below.)

To test the common-currency hypothesis, D. J. Levy and Glimcher (2011) mapped neural circuits for reward valuation by scanning subjects who made choices for money, food, and water (see also Chib, Rangel, Shimojo, & O'Doherty, 2009; FitzGerald, Seymour, & Dolan, 2009; Kim et al., 2010). For example, a subject might choose between a sure win of five M&Ms versus a risky option offering a 38% chance of winning 20 M&Ms (and a 62% chance of winning nothing). Subjects also received trade-off trials in which they chose between a sure win of a small amount of money ($0.50) versus some probability of either winning a fixed amount of food or water (or getting nothing).

D. J. Levy and Glimcher (2011) found that risk preferences across reward types were correlated: The level of risk aversion when choosing among monetary options predicted risk aversion for food and water. In other words, a subject who was more risk averse for money was generally also more risk averse for food and water (although substantial variation among individuals was observed). The common areas of neural activation that varied with valuation across domains were the vmPFC and striatum. These results are reminiscent of those of other studies implicating the vmPFC and striatum in representing values in risky choice tasks (Daw, O'Doherty, Dayan, Seymour, & Dolan, 2006; De Martino, Kumaran, Holt, & Dolan, 2009; Huettel, Stowe, Gordon, Warner, & Platt, 2006; Kable & Glimcher, 2007; Knutson, Fong, Bennett, Adams, & Hommer, 2003; I. Levy, Snell, Nelson, Rustichini, & Glimcher, 2010).

Interestingly, vmPFC is close to, or part of, the default mode network, which is more active at rest than during task performance (Raichle & Snyder, 2007). This suggests that task-related activations in vmPFC might correspond to different degrees of deactivation, relative to rest (Rushworth, Noonan, Boorman, Walton, & Behrens, 2011). However, traditional default mode activation is anterior to the posterior region of the vmPFC most often linked to common-currency activation.

In addition to common areas of activation in vmPFC, D. J. Levy and Glimcher (2011) found that distinct neural networks represented monetary and food rewards: the dorsal hypothalamic region responded mainly to the reward value of food, whereas the posterior cingulate cortex responded mainly to the value of money. Within the vmPFC itself, there were overlapping but also distinct areas of activation for money and food (see also Clithero, Carter, & Huettel, 2009, for similar conclusions from pattern classification of brain activation). However, only the vmPFC represented the value of money and food on what appeared to be a common scale, as predicted by expected utility and neurobiological approaches (Glimcher, Dorris, & Bayer, 2005; Glimcher, 2011; von Neumann & Morgenstern, 1944). That is, the relative levels of activity in vmPFC to food and money rewards reflected the relative values of food and money rewards to that individual and predicted trade-off choices between these different types of rewards.

In contrast to this common-currency hypothesis, Weber, Blais, and Betz (2002) and others have argued that an individual's risk taking in one domain, such as finances, need not be reflected in her risk taking for health or other outcomes. Weber et al.'s Domain-Specific Risk-Taking (DOSPERT) scale assesses risk-taking separately for decisions about monetary gambling and investment, ethical, health/safety, social, and recreational domains (for an updated scale, see Blais & Weber, 2006). As in classic expected-utility approaches, they distinguish between perceptions of risks and benefits (i.e., rewards), and relate those to risk taking.

More specifically, the updated DOSPERT's items include "Having an affair with a married man/woman" (*Ethical*), "Investing 10% of your annual income in a new business venture" (*Financial*), "Engaging in unprotected sex" (*Health/Safety*), "Disagreeing with an authority figure on a major issue" (*Social*), and "Taking a weekend sky-diving class" (*Recreational*). Weber et al. (2002) and other studies show that risk attitudes are not the same across these domains within individuals (which seems to contradict D. J. Levy & Glimcher's, 2011, results, but see below). Content varies across items, which makes them rich descriptors of real-life behavior, but they do not isolate risk preference per se. In other words, each item taps factors unrelated to risk preference, such as moral compunctions or athletic interests, as well as risk preference.

Despite finding domain differences, Weber et al. (2002) reported that sensation seeking (and its various subscales) correlated significantly with risky behavior in all five domains of the DOSPERT scale, with the highest correlation between the thrill-and-adventure-seeking subscale and recreational risk taking ($r = .56$), echoing decades of similar results in which sensation seeking predicts a broad spectrum of risky behaviors (e.g., Arnett, 1990a, 1990b; Hoyle, Fejfar, & Miller, 2000; Zuckerman, 1994). In addition, Weber et al. found that scores on each domain's risk attitudes scale significantly predicted frequency of risky behaviors for the other domains (with the exceptions of the social subscale and social risk taking). Thus, D. J. Levy and Glimcher (2011) used a common procedure to elicit risk attitudes across reward domains, rather than comparing apples to oranges (i.e., noncommensurate financial vs. health risk preferences), but Weber et al.'s results nevertheless confirm that preferences across reward types that reflect realistic decisions are correlated within individuals. That is, a person who is more risk averse in a given reward type is likely be more risk averse in another reward type. A recent meta-analysis using data from 13 different functional magnetic resonance imaging (fMRI) studies corroborated the conclusion that this common reward representation is located in a subregion of the vmPFC and adjacent medial orbitofrontal cortex (mOFC; D. J. Levy & Glimcher, 2012).

NEURAL SUBSTRATES DIFFERENTIATING GAINS, LOSSES, AND PROBABILITY

Consistent with research that we have reviewed, the vmPFC/mOFC blood oxygen level dependent (BOLD) signal has been shown to be correlated with the reward value of choices in multiple studies (e.g., Rushworth et al., 2011). For example, Plassmann, O'Doherty, and Rangel (2007) presented subjects with a series of pictures of food items and asked them how much they were willing to pay for each item. They used a Becker–DeGroot–Marschak method to ensure that subjects had an incentive to provide their true valuation; if their valuation exceeded a randomly drawn number, they forfeited money and accepted the food instead. The vmPFC/mOFC signal increased with participants' valuation of the food.

The balance of evidence suggests that the vmPFC/mOFC signal responds to losses as well as gains, decreasing proportionately to the magnitude of anticipated losses or negative outcomes (Rushworth et al., 2011; Tom et al., 2007). For example, Plassman, O'Doherty, and Rangel (2010) showed that willingness to pay to avoid eating an unpleasant food inversely correlated with signal in this region. The signal also decreases with other dimensions of choice that lower the overall value of an option, such as lower probability of gains or greater delay to receive gains (Kable & Glimcher, 2007; Peters & Buchel, 2009; Prévost, Pessiglione, Me´te´reau, Cléry-Melin, & Dreher, 2010). Hunt et al. (2012) advanced a plausible model of neuronal activity in this region in which signals initially correspond to the sum of the values of potential choices, but, later in the trial, reflect the value difference between choices. Using magnetoencephalography, Hunt et al. found that such a sequence of signals occurred in vmPFC/mOFC and also superior parietal cortex near the intraparietal sulcus. Thus, conflicting results supporting both the presence of overall value and value-difference signals in vmPFC/mOFC can be reconciled by assuming that these outputs occur at different points in time (Rushworth, Kolling, Sallet, & Mars, 2012; Wunderlich, Rangel, & O'Doherty, 2010).

Therefore, across studies, neural valuation subsumes both the reward value of outcomes and overall expected value, which includes probability (or risk) and outcomes. However, little consensus exists about the neural substrates of probability or risk (Huettel, 2010). Indeed, information about probability or risk has no meaning without information about outcomes; the probability must refer to the probability of some outcome to elicit preferences or choices. (This psychological reality about probability does not imply that probability cannot be varied orthogonally to outcomes; see d'Acremont, Fornari, & Bossaerts, 2013; Reyna et al., 2011).

D'Acremont et al. (2013) varied probability independently of outcome value using a probability learning task (subjects learned the probabilities of stimuli representing various payoffs through repetitive sampling). They found that activation in the medial prefrontal cortex and parietal cortex (angular gyri) increased linearly with the probability of the currently observed stimulus. Connectivity analyses during rest and task revealed that these regions were part of the default mode network. (Outcome values were encoded outside of the default network, in the striatum, when net rewards were realized at the end of the decision phase.)

Thus, contrary to the usual characterization, the default mode network was active during a task requiring attention to external stimuli (see also Spreng, 2012). Neuroimaging studies have identified these areas of the network, parietal cortex and medial prefrontal cortex, as involved in successful recognition (Cabeza, Ciaramelli, Olson, & Moscovitch, 2008; Wagner, Shannon, Kahn, & Buckner, 2005). D'Acremont et al. (2013) argue that a major function of the default mode network is to represent memory strength for traces of past events, consistent with contemporary memory-based theories of decision making (Reyna & Brainerd, 2011; Weber & Johnson, 2009). As we discuss in greater detail below, activation in dorsal anterior cingulate cortex (ACC) was related to *choice* uncertainty (i.e., uncertainty in making a choice, or decisional conflict). When choices were made but outcomes were unknown (the risky phase of the task), the right anterior insula and bilateral caudate were activated; the insula signaled *outcome* uncertainty.

To evaluate the evidence about neural substrates of probability (or risk), Mohr, Biele, and Heerkeren (2010) conducted a quantitative meta-analysis of fMRI experiments on risk processing. Mohr et al. examined how risk processing is influenced by emotions, how it differs between choice and nonchoice situations, and how it changes when losses are possible. Over a range of paradigms, risk was consistently associated with activation in the anterior insula, a brain region known to process aversive emotions, such as anxiety. The anterior insula was predominantly active in the presence of potential losses. The authors interpreted these results as evidence that risk processing is influenced by emotions and as indicating that potential losses modulate risk processing.

Reflecting the nature of the literature, Mohr et al.'s (2010) conclusion spans the concepts of risk and loss aversion, which, as we have already discussed, are distinct (e.g., Kahneman & Tversky, 2000). However, these results raise the interesting question of whether risk and loss aversion share an underlying commonality—a subjective feeling of aversion—despite the fact that this feeling is elicited by different causes (i.e., uncertainty vs. loss, both of which many people find distasteful; Reyna & Brainerd, 2011; Willemsen et al., 2011). This subjective feeling of aversion, in turn, is one avenue through which risk taking can be inhibited (Clark et al., 2008).

An interpretation of Mohr et al.'s (2010) meta-analysis, then, one that is consistent with studies cited by Wood and Bechara in this volume, is that the insula signals the phenomenology of aversion, common to risk and loss aversion. In other words, the insula provides an interoceptive signal of subjective feeling, not only of aversion (or disgust) but also of cravings and other homeostatic signals, as well as more abstract feelings such as admiration, love, and indignation (Chapter 7, this volume). Physiological states activated in the posterior insula seem to be re-represented in the anterior insula, the latter mapping onto subjective feelings. Craig, Chen, Bandy, and Reiman (2000), for example, found that activity in the posterior insula was linearly related to the actual temperature of a stimulus (applied to the hand), but activity in the anterior insula correlated with subjective ratings of temperature. Thus, processing of the magnitudes of potential losses in vmPFC/mOFC should be distinguished from subjective twinges associated with feeling those losses in the insula, which may help people avoid risk (Kuhnen & Knutson, 2005).

The function of the insula should also be distinguished from that of the amygdala, although they are connected reciprocally (the anterior insula is also connected to the ventral striatum, vmPFC, and ACC). As Wood and Bechara (Chapter 7, this volume) explain, "Although the amygdala is responsible for associative learning and emotions, the insula governs the conscious feeling of those emotions" (p. 189). Some patients with amygdala lesions do not show loss aversion, which is consistent with other research showing such patients' impaired processing of negative stimuli (De Martino, Camerer, & Adolphs, 2010; Murray, 2007). However, other patients with amygdala lesions have shown impairments for risky decisions involving gains rather than losses (Weller, Levin, Shiv, & Bechara, 2007). Basten, Biele, Heekeren, and Fiebach (2010) found that ventral striatum activated more in response to expected rewards or benefits in a decision task, whereas amygdala activated more to expected losses (and cost–benefit differences were correlated with an inferred comparison region in the vmPFC). As suggested above, results for vmPFC were consistent with computing expected reward by trading off amygdalar "costs" and ventral striatal "benefits."

Although stimulating the amygdala produces fear, anxiety, and vigilance (Phillips, Drevets, Rauch, & Lane, 2003), the amygdala activates more in response to positive, negative, and unusual or interesting stimuli than in response to neutral stimuli (Cunningham & Brosch, 2012). Therefore, the amygdala may signal emotional salience, with riskiness and losses being among those features of decision options that have functional significance (Cunningham, Van Bavel, & Johnsen, 2008; De Martino et al., 2006; Roiser et al., 2009). De Martino et al. (2010) speculated that an initial negative anticipatory response is generated in the amygdala to potential losses, which influences the striatal computation of the gamble's net value, and consequently leads to loss aversion. Thus, in this view, the amygdala is not the locus of memory or choice, and its effect on loss aversion is indirect. Although patients with amygdala lesions would be less likely to be loss averse, those with an intact ventral striatum and vmPFC/mOFC—and especially insula—might be able to avoid disadvantageous (in the sense of lower expected value) gambles involving losses (Weller et al., 2007).

These areas of the brain are dynamically connected, as seen when people regulate emotional affect. Studies of emotion regulation suggest that activation of the vmPFC and the amygdala are related, and coupling of the amygdala and vmPFC is related to trait anxiety in both task-related and resting-state studies (Burghy et al., 2012). For example, individuals high in trait anxiety exhibit reduced amygdala-vmPFC resting-state connectivity (Kim, Gee, Loucks, Davis, & Whalen, 2011), as though the lack of connectivity reflected habitual inability to down-regulate anxiety (but see Poldrack, 2006, for caveats regarding "reverse inference").

COMPARISON AND CONFLICT

As we have discussed, the evidence suggests that values of gains, losses, and their probabilities are represented in the vmPFC/mOFC, informed by the striatum and the rest of the reward circuit. The options also give rise to subjective feelings and are infused with emotional significance, reflected in the insula and amygdala. At some point in the decision process, the representations of options are input to another comparison process that takes place in dorsal ACC or adjacent (e.g., Hare, Schultz, Camerer, O'Doherty, & Rangel, 2011).

In contrast to signals in the vmPFC/mOFC, the ACC/dmPFC BOLD signal increases when the difference between the values of potential choices decreases. For example, Pochon, Riis, Sanfey, Nystrom, and Cohen (2008) had subjects choose between two attractive faces; activity in the ACC/dmPFC was higher when faces were similar in attractiveness, provoking decisional conflict. Similarly, De Martino et al. (2006) observed greater ACC/dmPFC activation when subjects made choices that were inconsistent with their dominant preference of framing effects. Increased activation in the dmPFC seems to represent a conflict between the generally preferred gist-based response and a compensatory analytical choice. In other words, the difficulty of a comparison between options varies with signal in the ACC/dmPFC as though this area captures disparity detection (e.g., error monitoring), cognitive conflict, or decisional conflict (e.g., Brown & Braver, 2008; Taren, Venkatraman, & Huettel, 2011; Venkatraman et al., 2009; see Venkatraman & Huettel, 2012). The output of this comparison process then determines activation in the motor system, guiding which response should be made to satisfy the reward goal, and culminating in the response (Cai & Padoa-Schioppa, 2012; Rushworth et al., 2012). Hence, the vmPFC/mOFC can be thought of as "choosing" (or favoring) a reward goal, whereas the ACC/dmPFC adjudicates potentially antagonistic actions or rules for decision making (Brown & Braver, 2008; Rushworth et al., 2012; Venkatraman & Huettel, 2012).

REPRESENTATION AND RESPONSE PREFERENCE

While the vmPFC/mOFC signal increases with the difference in value between possible choices, the BOLD signal in the parietal cortex and some other motor association areas increases as the choice selection becomes more difficult, as indexed by reaction time. The parietal signal, therefore, often has characteristics that are the opposite of the vmPFC/mOFC signal. Like the ACC/dmPFC, the size of the parietal signal (e.g., posterior parietal cortex, the medial intraparietal sulcus) is negatively correlated with the difference in value between choices (Basten et al., 2010; Rushworth et al., 2011). According to Basten et al. (2010), for example, a neural representation of the difference between rewards (ventral striatal benefit signal) and losses (amygdalar cost signal) is evaluated in the vmPFC and then accumulates in the parietal cortex (intraparietal sulcus) until a decision threshold is reached.

Thus, one way to think of the accumulator is as an index of response preference; difficult choices are those for which the difference in value between response options is small. The accumulator can operate within trials, as people process information about risks and rewards, or costs and benefits, with longer response latency and lower confidence for difficult choices. The accumulator can also be thought of as operating across trials, as information becomes acquired through experiencing outcomes of risky decisions. As examples of learning from experience, one can have unprotected sex and either experience pregnancy or not over the course of a year; one can leave a car unlocked each night for a month and find out each morning whether items in the car have been stolen or not (e.g., Yechiam, Barron, & Erev, 2005). Alternatively, one can read about the probability of pregnancy given unprotected sex over a year on a contraceptive label or look up the rates at which cars are broken into in a neighborhood, learning from description as opposed to experience (Reyna & Adam, 2003; Reyna & Farley, 2006).

Many of the decision paradigms we have cited involve learning about outcomes and probabilities through experience rather than direct description, as in the Iowa Gambling Task (IGT). In the IGT, subjects select cards from "good" and "bad" decks, discovering that some decks yield small rewards and losses but net gains, whereas other decks yield large rewards but still larger losses (e.g., Hochman, Yechiam, & Bechara, 2010). Therefore, subjects learn to anticipate outcomes by virtue of experience, a process that relies heavily on memory for outcomes and their probabilities (Stout et al., 2005). Developmental differences in risk taking in the IGT, for example, virtually disappear when children are provided with ongoing tallies of frequencies of outcomes (Van Duijvenvoorde, Jansen, Bredman, & Huizenga, 2012; see also Reyna & Brainerd, 1994). As we discuss, in addition to the medial temporal lobe (MTL), encompassing the hippocampus and parahippocampal regions, the parietal cortex plays an important role in memory representation and retrieval (Cabeza et al., 2008).

Memory Representations

Memory representations are generally encoded simultaneously in two formats: verbatim (e.g., the number of dollars to be won) and gist (e.g., the categorical or ordinal qualitative essence of the amount to be won, such as "some money" or "a lot of money"; Kühberger & Tanner, 2010; Reyna & Brainerd, 1995, 2011). Verbatim representations support precise processing (e.g., trading off the magnitudes of risk and reward, as in expected value or utility), but gist representations support the fuzzy, impressionistic processing of intuition (Reyna, 2013). Although neuroscience research has focused on representing quantitative valuation of rewards or expected value (even when options are nonnumerical, such as food; Hare et al., 2011), behavioral research demonstrates that qualitative, fuzzy gist representations of decision options, along with retrieval of associated broad mores (e.g., that saving lives, gaining money, or helping family is good), often govern risk preferences (Reyna, 2012; Reyna et al., 2011).

Specifically, consistent with neuroscience research, decision makers appear to estimate expected value or expected utility (e.g., Glimcher, 2011; Hare, Camerer, & Rangel, 2009), a conclusion that, at first blush, contradicts the literature ruling out expected value or utility as viable descriptive theories of behavior (e.g., Tversky & Kahneman, 1986). However, these views can be reconciled by positing parallel systems that process both verbatim (symbolic, but superficial) values of options and their qualitative gist. Qualitative gist, in turn, is responsible for effects of meaning and context that can be said to "bias" decisions, such as framing effects, used as evidence against expected value and utility theories (Reyna & Brainerd, 2011).

Furthermore, these verbatim–gist parallel systems are required to account for predicted double dissociations and nonmonotonic effects in the behavioral literature, and they are supported by mathematical models tested for goodness-of-fit with behavioral data (e.g., see Brainerd, Reyna, & Howe, 2009; Brainerd, Reyna, & Mojardin, 1999; Reyna, 2012; Reyna & Brainerd, 1995; Singer & Remillard, 2008). Evidence that people encode both verbatim (literal) and gist (simple meaning) representations comes from research on memory, reasoning, and decision making, and has been studied across the life span (e.g., for reviews, see Reyna, 1995, 2012; Reyna & Mills, 2007).

In particular, many experiments have compared verbatim-based true memory to so-called false memory, the latter usually based on memory for the gist of experience (Kim & Cabeza, 2007; Slotnick & Schacter, 2004). While true recollection (verbatim memory is vivid or recollective) has been associated with neural activity in the MTL (hippocampus and posterior parahippopcampal gyrus), medial prefrontal cortex (mPFC), lateral parietal cortex, and posterior cingulate, vague familiarity has been associated with activity in lateral PFC regions, the MTL (anterior parahippocampal gyrus and rhinal cortex), and the superior parietal cortex (e.g., Daselaar, Fleck, & Cabeza, 2006; Spaniol et al., 2009; Yonelinas, Otten, Shaw, & Rugg, 2005; for reviews, see Diana, Yonelinas, & Ranganath, 2007; Eichenbaum, Yonelinas, & Ranganath, 2007; Eichenbaum, Sauvage, Fortin, Komorowski, & Lipton, 2012).

These memory studies provide clues about the neural basis of gist versus verbatim representations and processing that explain risky decision making, as we presently discuss. However, many of the memory studies confound phenomenology—vivid recollection versus vague familiarity—with verbatim or gist representation. Although verbatim representations (e.g., memory for frequencies of outcomes of draws in the IGT) are vivid, gist representations can be either vague (experienced as global similarity or familiarity) or vivid (experienced as "phantom recollection"; Brainerd, Payne, Wright, & Reyna, 2003).

Using a recognition task with pictures, Dennis, Bowman, and Vandekar (2012) separated recollection from familiarity by asking subjects to judge recognition-test pictures as "remember," "know," or "new" ("remember" responses were designated as recollection and "know" responses as familiarity). Test items were previously presented pictures (true), semantically similar but not identical pictures (false or gist-consistent), or unrelated pictures.

Directly comparing true with false recollection revealed that true recollection uniquely involved hippocampus and early visual cortex, consistent with verbatim memory supporting remember responses to presented pictures (remember hits; Brainerd et al., 2003). Gist memory is assumed to be common to both true and false recollection and thus may be reflected in conjunction results for true and false recollection (e.g., precentral gyrus and superior parietal cortex).

Dennis et al. (2012) also assessed whole brain functional connectivity for an MTL region in the anterior parahippocampal gyrus that was activated for true (true remember > true know) and for false recollection (false remember > false know). For true recollection (compared with false recollection), the anterior parahippocampal gyrus showed greater functional connectivity with inferior regions, including the bilateral hippocampus, the ACC, the orbitofrontal cortex, and the occipital cortex. In contrast, false recollection (compared with true recollection) showed greater functional connectivity between the anterior parahippocampal gyrus and superior regions including the bilateral pre- and post-central gyrus, the superior PFC, and the bilateral parietal cortex. This inferior–superior dissociation may support a distinction between bottom-up, lower-order verbatim processes in true recollection and top-down, higher order gist and control processes in false recollection (Cabeza, 2008).

Memory Representations of Risk Preference in Decision Making

In decision making as in other information-processing tasks, people encode verbatim and gist representations of options, and in experiential paradigms (e.g., IGT), they encode both types of representations of the probabilities and outcomes of choices. People extract multiple gist representations of options but typically rely on the simplest (categorical) gist, distinguishing between some quantity versus nothing, outputting a decision if the choice is not contradicted by parallel verbatim processing. For example, the simplest gist of the example presented earlier is (a) winning some money versus (b) either winning some money or winning nothing. Because most people value money, some money is generally preferred to nothing, favoring the sure option.

The same kind of categorical (some–none) gist applies to choices involving losses: Thus, a choice between (c) losing \$1,000 for sure versus (d) a .5 probability of losing \$2,000 and .5 probability of losing nothing boils down to (c) losing some money versus (d) either losing some money or losing nothing. Because most people value losing nothing more than losing money, they generally prefer the risky option. The shift from risk avoiding for gains to risk seeking for losses is an example of a framing effect (Kahneman & Tversky, 2000). Critical tests have been conducted showing that categorical gist accounts for a variety of framing effects and ruling out expected utility and prospect theory as explanations for these effects (e.g., Kühberger & Tanner, 2010; Reyna, 2012; Reyna & Brainerd, 1991, 1995).

To take one example, removing the mathematically redundant zero complement of the gamble (.5 probability of winning/losing nothing = 0) removes the categorical some–none contrast and eliminates framing effects, although all of the causal elements of framing effects, according to utility and prospect theory, remain. These and other empirical results, such as larger framing effects when numbers are removed, experimentally manipulating attention to the zero outcome to increase framing effects, and the growth of framing effects from childhood to adulthood, all support a fuzzy-trace theory account of verbatim and gist processing in risky decision making (e.g., Kühberger & Tanner, 2010; Reyna & Brainerd, 1991, 1995; Reyna & Ellis, 1994; Reyna et al., 2011; Reyna & Farley, 2006). Although framing effects themselves divulge the use of categorical gist (per the explanation above), parallel verbatim processing is revealed through people's sensitivity to expected value: People are usually indifferent between options when their expected values are equal—provided that the zero complement is removed—but they favor the option with the larger expected value when options are unequal (e.g., Reyna & Brainerd, 1995; Weller et al., 2007).

Venkatraman et al. (2009) explored the use of these alternative strategies of verbatim trading off of expected value versus categorical some–none gist processing by presenting subjects with a series of five-outcome gambles containing gain and loss outcomes (probabilities are shown in parentheses), such as $80 (.20), $40 (.25), $0 (.20), –$25 (.15), –$70 (.20). However, subjects could improve the gambles, for example, by adding $15 to either the $0 outcome (changing that outcome to $15) or to the –$70 (changing that outcome to –$55). The choices subjects made to change gambles diagnosed their information-processing strategies.

Altogether, Venkatraman et al. (2009) assessed three strategies: increasing the magnitude of the highest gain (Gmax), decreasing the magnitude of the worst loss (Lmin), or improving the probability of winning something by adding money to the middle outcome (e.g., by eliminating the categorical possibility of winning nothing; Pmax). The Gmax and Lmin choices represent a compensatory verbatim analytical strategy consistent with standard models of risky choice, whereas Pmax represents a simplifying gist-based strategy. Thus, the tasks used by Venkatraman et al. (2009), like those used by Kühberger and Tanner (2010); Mills, Reyna, and Estrada (2008); and Reyna (2012), make it possible to discriminate between gist- and verbatim-based strategies in risky decision making.

Activation in the posterior parietal cortex and dorsolateral prefrontal cortex (dlPFC) predicted gist-based, simplifying choices, whereas activation in the vmPFC and anterior insula predicted verbatim analytical, compensatory choices, maximizing gains (i.e., Gmax) and minimizing losses (i.e., loss aversion or Lmin), respectively (see also, Hedgcock, Denburg, Levin, & Halfmann, 2012). Functional connectivity (psychophysiological interaction) analyses showed positive correlations between the dmPFC and the dlPFC for simplifying choices and between the dmPFC and insula for compensatory choices. Although many scholars assume that compensatory strategies are more adaptive, research has shown that gist-based simplifying strategies are associated with greater development (from childhood to adulthood), greater expertise in adulthood, and better health outcomes (e.g., Reyna et al., 2011; Reyna & Farley, 2006; Reyna & Lloyd, 2006).

Consistent with our earlier discussion of the ACC/dmPFC, activation in this area was greater when subjects made choices that conflicted with their dominant strategy, such as when people who generally preferred the gist-based, simplifying choice made a compensatory choice and vice versa. Greater ACC/dmPFC activation occurs for higher decisional conflict even when subjects do not have to respond overtly on a given trial and when decision and response phases are separated (Pochon et al., 2008; Venkatraman et al., 2009). Further, Venkatraman et al. (2009) showed, using resting state connectivity analyses, that the dmPFC was connected to the dlPFC, the latter associated with response selection, in an anterior to posterior organization (e.g., anterior dmPFC to rostral dlPFC; posterior dmPFC to caudal dlPFC and premotor cortex; Bunge, Hazeltine, Scanlon, Rosen, & Gabrieli, 2002; Taren et al., 2011). Venkatraman and Huettel (2012) argued that the anterior dmPFC regulates activity in the anterior dlPFC when control demands are highly abstract (e.g., choosing among conflicting strategies), but the posterior dmPFC regulates the posterior dlPFC and premotor cortices when control demands merely choose between conflicting motor responses.

Impulsivity/Inhibition of Responses

The dlPFC, often in conjunction with the ACC, has long been associated with cognitive control, which can be manifested as response inhibition, cognitive distraction (distancing), or reappraisal of the meaning of a stimulus (Ochsner & Gross, 2008; Venkatraman & Huettel, 2012; see also Chapter 6, this volume). The dlPFC modulates the value signal encoded in the vmPFC, and dlPFC activity is correlated with successful self-control (e.g., in go/no-go tasks; Casey et al., 2011; or when choosing between healthy and unhealthy foods; Hare et al., 2009).

Several studies have reported a link between higher dlPFC activity and lower risk taking. For example, Gianotti et al. (2009) found a negative correlation between tonic activity in the dlPFC (i.e., cortical hypoactivity) as measured using electroencephalogram at rest and risk-taking propensity in a laboratory task. These results are consistent with findings from patients with lesions in this area and healthy subjects with "virtual lesions" (created using transmagnetic cranial stimulation, or TMS), who showed increased risk taking relative to controls (Knoch et al., 2006). Conversely, Fecteau et al. (2007) reduced risk taking in a laboratory task by increasing dlPFC activity using transcranial direct current stimulation. Schonberg et al. (2012) interpreted their results showing increasing dlPFC activation as risk mounts in a repeated sampling task as reflecting the increased engagement of self-control, which prompts subjects to terminate the trial.

Finally, Hutcherson, Plassman, Gross, and Rangel (2012) instructed subjects to down-regulate ("distance") or up-regulate ("indulge") their desire for foods (or react naturally) while being imaged. During down-regulation, activation *decreased* in the dlPFC but not in the vmPFC, and the relative contribution of the two value signals to behavior shifted toward the dlPFC. The opposite pattern was observed during up-regulation; activation increased in the vmPFC but not the dlPFC, and the relative contribution to behavior shifted toward the vmPFC. Although the direction of activation seems to contradict other research on cognitive regulation of emotion, the authors interpret the reduction in activation in the dlPFC as indicating value modulation (see Hutcherson et al.'s, 2012, discussion), a finding consistent with recent research on emotional value in vmPFC (Winecoff et al., 2013). However, in both regulation conditions relative to "natural" responding, Hutcherson et al. observed significant activation in the ventrolateral PFC and the posterior parietal cortex, areas also found in other studies. Taken together, these studies suggest that dlPFC (and other areas') activity reflects cognitive control that reigns in risk taking, generally through inhibition or reevaluation of emotional, rewarding, or prepotent responses.

Going beyond the influence of a single area or region such as the dlPFC, Shannon et al. (2011) correlated resting state connectivity with a measure of impulsivity for adolescents incarcerated in a high-security facility. The impulsivity measure included "need for stimulation" (e.g., "I enjoy gambling for large stakes"). Shannon et al. showed that prediction of impulsivity peaked using premotor (i.e., motor planning regions) functional connectivity (i.e., selecting or adding other brain regions of interest degraded prediction of impulsivity). A typical young adult sample displays positive correlations between the premotor area and both the dorsal attention and executive networks, and negative correlations with the default mode network. A similar pattern was observed in less impulsive incarcerated youth as well as normal controls; premotor areas were connected to networks involving attention and executive processes.

In contrast, premotor areas were positively correlated with the default network among the impulsive incarcerated youth, parts of which (e.g., vmPFC), as we have discussed, are involved in task-related reward valuation and probability learning in normally developing adults. Premotor areas were negatively correlated with attention and control networks. Hence, impulsive incarcerated youth displayed the opposite pattern shown with normal adults. Moreover, functional connectivity varied with age among another sample of normal controls ranging in age from 7 to 31. As age increased, functional connectivity with the premotor area migrated from the default network (significantly decreasing with age) to the attention and control networks (significantly increasing with age). Thus, the relationship of the networks to impulsivity, though stronger in incarcerated youth, was recapitulated by age, as though impulsive offenders were developmentally delayed.

OVERVIEW AND IMPLICATIONS FOR RISKY DECISION MAKING

Our review of the literature on the neuroscience of risky decision making has ranged from reward circuitry to response inhibition. We have reviewed activations in different brain regions, but also the interconnections among areas, for example, between the amygdala and the vmPFC (e.g., the input of the amygdala to vmPFC valuation comparisons). The hypotheses offered about function represent an effort to make sense of neuroscientific findings, but they can only be tentative as the necessary process models remain underspecified.

In particular, the simultaneous and countervailing interactions among different brain processes challenge interpretation (e.g., Shannon et al., 2011, which demonstrates network-level interactions). For example, if the dlPFC downregulates the global valuation of a risky option, then activation of the vmPFC might appear misleadingly small. By misleading, we mean that the causal pathway for risky behavior differs for an individual who has mastered self-control (but for whom self-regulation is imperfect) versus someone who was never tempted to begin with (DeYoung, 2010). Understanding these causal pathways is crucial for designing interventions and public policies to reduce unhealthy risk taking.

For example, the levers for behavioral change include shaping the encoding of the *functionally significant* features of decisions (e.g., consequential financial losses or major health threats; Reyna, 2008). Very little is understood about "salience" and how the amygdala categorizes features of decisions, such as their riskiness, as significant or not. The presence of risk, by itself, is not a contraindication to choosing an option; driving in most cities represents a nonnegligible risk. (Phobias about driving, flying, or otherwise engaging in everyday risks can severely impair adaptive decision making.) Thus, despite the widespread faith in expected utility, decision trees, and other rational approaches to decision making, adaptive risk taking is generally not characterized by a focus on such details, but, rather, on the "big picture" of what is important.

That is, adaptive decision making involves more than applying a rote formula, as suggested by fuzzy trace theory. Understanding functional significance (i.e., what the individual represents as important about options that involve risk) is a deep and highly contextual judgment. The concept of gist, which dates back to research on summarizing narratives, sheds some light on how people distill the substance of decisions (e.g., Clark & Clark, 1977). Although the representation of the gist of options—their meaning—seems to shape risk preferences, most neuroscience research employs tasks that fail to capture or even assess that meaning. Naturally, researchers who do not measure gist processing will not find it in the brain, omitting a major mode of real-world decision making.

The concept of self-control is also fraught with ambiguity in the current literature, but our review suggests some basic distinctions that may be helpful. As Casey et al. (2011) emphasized, responsiveness to enticing rewards represents a distinct vulnerability for impulsive individuals, and, presumably, for those who take risks (here, impulsivity is defined narrowly as failure to inhibit responses, but see Zuckerman, 1994). Response inhibition in the sense of restraint seems to be discriminable from reward sensitivity (i.e., temptation by valuation). The inability to engage in cognitive distraction or reappraisal of meaning because of low intelligence or poor coping skills is yet another source of vulnerability. The failure to learn the probabilities of events from experience or to detect conflict among decision strategies, and the absence of internal feeling cues, are additional risk factors for maladaptive decision making. How each of these factors operates to promote risk taking (alone or in combination)—and their neural circuitry—is poorly understood.

One impediment to progress in this area is the mistaken belief that laboratory risk-taking tasks that unconfound causal factors do not predict real-life risk taking. Many studies have refuted that misconception, and yet it persists. However, this does not imply that a narrow focus on college students of a certain age with little variation in culture or individual differences is adequate; representative samples of subjects are also needed. Rather than measure large numbers of people using poorly conceived tasks (and powerful statistics), however, progress in the neuroscience of risky decision making requires a greater focus on tasks motivated by process-oriented theory.

To some decision neuroscience researchers, theory harkens back to traditional expected utility models and simple Skinnerian behaviorism. Is risky decision making merely a matter of computing gains (rewards), losses, and probabilities (with perhaps a touch of Spence's notion of behavioral inhibition)? Certainly, at one level, such simple concepts successfully predict approach and avoidance behavior, including some aspects of risky decision making. However, behaving logically and trading off risk and reward do not seem to be sufficient for adaptive decision making. Children (by about 6 years of age), adolescents, and people with mild autism are less prone to classic judgment-and-decision-making biases, compared with neurodevelopmentally typical adults, but they nevertheless have deficits in real-world risky decision making (Reyna & Brainerd, 2011). Acknowledging "risk as feelings" is also not sufficient to predict or improve risky decision making to date (for a discussion of the shortcomings of this approach, see Sunstein, 2008). Instead, an integrative approach is needed that emphasizes prediction and hypothesis testing, an approach that incorporates motivational, emotional, and cognitive elements but goes beyond them in designing new tasks that capture the richness and relevance of risky decision making.

REFERENCES

American Psychiatric Association. (2000). *Diagnostic and Statistical Manual of Mental Disorders* (4th ed., text rev.). Washington, DC: Author.

Arnett, J. (1990a). Contraceptive use, sensation seeking, and adolescent egocentrism. *Journal of Youth and Adolescence, 19,* 171–180. doi:10.1007/BF01538720

Arnett, J. (1990b). Drunk driving, sensation seeking and egocentrism among adolescents. *Personality and Individual Differences, 11,* 541–546. doi:10.1016/0191-8869(90)90035-P

Arnett, J. (1992). Reckless behavior in adolescence: A developmental perspective. *Developmental Review, 12,* 339–373. doi:10.1016/0273-2297(92)90013-R

Basten, U., Biele, G., Heekeren, H. R., & Fiebach, C. J. (2010). How the brain integrates costs and benefits during decision making. *PNAS Proceedings of the National Academy of Sciences of the United States of America, 107,* 21767–21772. doi:10.1073/pnas.0908104107

Benartzi, S., & Thaler, R. H. (1995). Myopic loss aversion and the equity premium puzzle. *The Quarterly Journal of Economics, 110*(1), 73–92. doi:10.2307/2118511

Blais, A., & Weber, E. U. (2006). A domain-specific risk-taking (DOSPERT) scale for adult populations. *Judgment and Decision Making, 1,* 33–47. Retrieved from http://journal.sjdm.org/06005/jdm06005.htm

Bloom, D. (2010). Programs and policies to assist high school dropouts in the transition to adulthood. *The Future of Children, 20,* 89–108. doi:10.1353/foc.0.0039

Brainerd, C. J., Payne, D. G., Wright, R., & Reyna, V. F. (2003). Phantom recall. *Journal of Memory and Language, 48,* 445–467. doi:10.1016/S0749-596X(02)00501-6

Brainerd, C. J., Reyna, V. F., & Howe, M. L. (2009). Trichotomous processes in early memory development, aging, and neurocognitive impairment: A unified theory. *Psychological Review, 116,* 783–832. doi:10.1037/a0016963

Brainerd, C. J., Reyna, V. F., & Mojardin, A. H. (1999). Conjoint recognition. *Psychological Review, 106*, 160–179. doi:10.1037/0033-295X.106.1.160

Brown, J. W., & Braver, T. S. (2008). A computational model of risk, conflict, and individual difference effects in the anterior cingulated cortex. *Brain Research, 1202*, 99–108. doi:10.1016/j.brainres.2007.06.080

Bunge, S. A., Hazeltine, E., Scanlon, M. D., Rosen, A. C., & Gabrieli, J. D. (2002). Dissociable contributions of prefrontal and parietal cortices to response selection. *NeuroImage, 17*, 1562–1571. doi:10.1006/nimg.2002.1252

Burghy, C. A., Stodola, D. E., Ruttle, P. L., Molloy, E. K., Armstrong, J. M., Oler, J. A., . . . Birn, R. M. (2012). Developmental pathways to amygdala-prefrontal function and internalizing symptoms in adolescence. *Nature Neuroscience, 15*, 1736–1741. doi:10.1038/nn.3257

Cabeza, R. (2008). Role of parietal regions in episodic memory retrieval: The dual attentional processes hypothesis. *Neuropsychologia, 46*, 1813–1827. doi:10.1016/j.neuropsychologia.2008.03.019

Cabeza, R., Ciaramelli, E., Olson, I., & Moscovitch, M. (2008). The parietal cortex and episodic memory: An attentional account. *Nature Reviews Neuroscience, 9*, 613–625. doi:10.1038/nrn2459

Cai, X., & Padoa-Schioppa, C. (2012). Neuronal encoding of subjective value in dorsal and ventral anterior cingulate cortex. *The Journal of Neuroscience, 32*, 3791–3808. doi:10.1523/JNEUROSCI.3864-11.2012

Casey, B. J., Somerville, L. H., Gotlib, I. H., Ayduk, O., Franklin, N. T., Askren. M. K. . . . Shoda, Y. (2011). Behavioral and neural correlates of delay of gratification 40 years later. *Proceedings of the National Academy of Sciences of the United States of America, 108*, 14998–15003. doi:10.1073/pnas.1108561108

Centers for Disease Control and Prevention. (2012). *Web-Based Injury Statistics Query and Reporting System (WISQARS)*. National Center for Injury Prevention and Control, Centers for Disease Control and Prevention (producer). Retrieved from http://www.cdc.gov/injury/wisqars/fatal.html

Chib, V. S., Rangel, A., Shimojo, S., & O'Doherty, J. P. (2009). Evidence for a common representation of decision values for dissimilar goods in human ventromedial prefrontal cortex. *The Journal of Neuroscience, 29*, 12315–12320. doi:10.1523/JNEUROSCI.2575-09.2009

Chick, C. F., & Reyna, V. F. (2012). A fuzzy trace theory of adolescent risk taking: Beyond self-control and sensation seeking. In V. F. Reyna, S. Chapman, M. Dougherty, & J. Confrey (Eds.), *The adolescent brain: Learning, reasoning, and decision making* (pp. 379–428). Washington, DC: American Psychological Association. doi:10.1037/13493-013

Clark, H. H., & Clark, E. V. (1977). *Psychology and language: An introduction to psycholinguistics*. New York, NY: Harcourt Brace Jovanovich.

Clark, L., Bechara, A., Damasio, H., Aitken, M. R. F., Sahakian, B. J., & Robbins, T. W. (2008). Differential effects of insular and ventromedial prefrontal cortex lesions on risky decision-making. *Brain: A Journal of Neurology, 131*, 1311–1322. doi:10.1093/brain/awn066

Clithero, J. A., Carter, R. M., & Huettel, S. A. (2009). Local pattern classification differentiates processes of economic valuation. *NeuroImage, 45*, 1329–1338. doi:10.1016/j.neuroimage.2008.12.074

Craig, A. D., Chen, K., Bandy, D., & Reiman, E. (2000). Thermosensory activation of insular cortex. *Nature Neuroscience, 3*, 184–190. doi:10.1038/72131

Cunningham, W. A., & Brosch, T. (2012). Motivational salience: Amygdala tuning from traits, needs, values, and goals. *Current Directions in Psychological Science, 21*, 54–59. doi:10.1177/0963721411430832

Cunningham, W. A., Van Bavel, J. J., & Johnsen, I. R. (2008). Affective flexibility: Evaluative processing goals shape amygdala activity. *Psychological Science, 19*, 152–160. doi:10.1111/j.1467-9280.2008.02061.x

d'Acremont, M., Fornari, E., & Bossaerts, P. (2013). Activity in inferior parietal and medial prefrontal cortex signals the accumulation of evidence in a probability learning task. *PLoS Computational Biology*, 9, e1002895. doi:10.1371/journal.pcbi.1002895

Daselaar, S. M., Fleck, M. S., & Cabeza, R. E. (2006). Triple dissociation in the medial temporal lobes: Recollection, familiarity, and novelty. *Journal of Neurophysiology*, 96, 1902–1911. doi:10.1152/jn.01029.2005

Daw, N. D., O'Doherty, J. P., Dayan, P., Seymour, B., & Dolan, R. J. (2006). Cortical substrates for exploratory decisions in humans. *Nature, 441*, 876–879. doi:10.1038/nature04766

Delgado, M. R., Nystrom, L. E., Fissell, C., Noll, D. C., & Fiez, J. A. (2000). Tracking the hemodynamic responses to reward and punishment in the striatum. *Journal of Neurophysiology, 84*, 3072–3077.

Dennis, N. A., Bowman, C. R., & Vandekar, S. N. (2012). True and phantom recollection: An fMRI investigation of similar and distinct neural correlates and connectivity. *NeuroImage, 59*, 2982–2993. doi:10.1016/j.neuroimage.2011.09.079

De Martino, B., Camerer, C. F., & Adolphs, R. (2010). Amygdala damage eliminates monetary loss aversion. *Proceedings of the National Academy of Sciences of the United States of America, 107*, 3788–3792. doi:10.1073/pnas.0910230107

De Martino, B., Kumaran, D., Holt, B., & Dolan, R. J. (2009). The neurobiology of reference-dependent value computation. *The Journal of Neuroscience, 29*, 3833–3842. doi:10.1523/JNEUROSCI.4832-08.2009

De Martino, B., Kumaran, D., Seymour, B., & Dolan, R. J. (2006). Frames, biases, and rational decision-making in the human brain. *Science, 313*, 684–687. doi:10.1126/science.1128356

DeYoung, C. G. (2010). Impulsivity as a personality trait. In K. D. Vohs & R. F. Baumeister (Eds.), *Handbook of self-regulation: Research, theory, and applications* (2nd ed., pp. 485–502). New York, NY: Guilford Press.

Diana, R. A., Yonelinas, A. P., & Ranganath, C. (2007). Imaging recollection and familiarity in the medial temporal lobe: A three-component model. *Trends in Cognitive Sciences, 11*, 379–386. doi:10.1016/j.tics.2007.08.001

Eichenbaum, H., Sauvage, M., Fortin, N., Komorowski, R., & Lipton, P. (2012). Towards a functional organization of episodic memory in the medial temporal lobe. *Neuroscience and Biobehavioral Reviews, 36*, 1597–1608. doi:10.1016/j.neubiorev.2011.07.006

Eichenbaum, H., Yonelinas, A. P., & Ranganath, C. (2007). The medial temporal lobe and recognition memory. *Annual Review of Neuroscience, 30*, 123–152. doi:10.1146/annurev.neuro.30.051606.094328

Fecteau, S., Pascual-Leone, A., Zald, D. H., Liguori, P., Theoret, H., Boggio, P. S., & Fregni, F. (2007). Activation of prefrontal cortex by transcranial direct current stimulation reduces appetite for risk during ambiguous decision making. *The Journal of Neuroscience, 27*, 6212–6218. doi:10.1523/JNEUROSCI.0314-07.2007

FitzGerald, T. H., Seymour, B., & Dolan, R. J. (2009). The role of human orbitofrontal cortex in value comparison for incommensurable objects. *The Journal of Neuroscience, 29*, 8388–8395. doi:10.1523/JNEUROSCI.0717-09.2009

Fox, C. R., & Tannenbaum, D. (2011). The elusive search for stable risk preferences. *Frontiers in Psychology, 2*(298). doi:10.3389/fpsyg.2011.00298

Galvan, A. (2012). Risky behavior in adolescents: The role of the developing brain. In V. F. Reyna, S. B. Chapman, M. R. Dougherty, & J. Confrey (Eds.), *The adolescent brain: Learning, reasoning, and decision making* (pp. 267–289). Washington, DC: American Psychological Association.

Galvan, A., Hare, T., Voss, H., Glover, G., & Casey, B. J. (2007). Risk-taking and the adolescent brain: Who is at risk? *Developmental Science, 10*, F8–F14. doi:10.1111/j.1467-7687.2006.00579.x

Galvan, A., Hare, T. A., Parra, C. E., Penn, J., Voss, H., Glover, G., & Casey, B. J. (2006). Earlier development of the accumbens relative to orbitofrontal cortex might underlie risk-taking behavior in adolescents. *The Journal of Neuroscience, 26*, 6885–6892. doi:10.1523/JNEUROSCI.1062-06.2006

Gianotti, L. R., Knoch, D., Faber, P. L., Lehmann, D., Pascual-Marqui, R. D., Diezi, C., . . . Fehr, E. (2009). Tonic activity level in the right prefrontal cortex predicts individuals' risk taking. *Psychological Science, 20*(1), 33–38. doi:10.1111/j.1467-9280.2008.02260.x

Glimcher, P. W. (2011). Understanding dopamine and reinforcement learning: The dopamine reward prediction error hypothesis. *Proceedings of the National Academy of Sciences of the United States of America, 108*, 15647–15654. doi:10.1073/pnas.1014269108

Glimcher, P. W., Camerer, C. F., Fehr, E., & Poldrack, R. A. (Eds.). (2009). *Neuroeconomics: Decision making and the brain*. New York, NY: Academic Press.

Glimcher, P. W., Dorris, M. C., & Bayer, H. M. (2005). Physiological utility theory and the neuroeconomics of choice. *Games and Economic Behavior, 52*, 213–256. doi:10.1016/j.geb.2004.06.011

Hare, T. A., Camerer, C. F., & Rangel, A. (2009). Self-control in decision-making involves modulation of the vmPFC valuation system. *Science, 324*, 646–648. doi:10.1126/science.1168450

Hare, T. A., Schultz, W., Camerer, C. F., O'Doherty, J. P., & Rangel, A. (2011). Transformation of stimulus value signals into motor commands during simple choice. *Proceedings of the National Academy of Sciences of the United States of America, 108*, 18120–18125. doi:10.1073/pnas.1109322108

Hedgcock, W., Denburg, N., Levin, I. P., & Halfmann, K. (November, 2012). *Why older adults are impaired on some decision making tasks but not on others–Behavioral and neuroimaging evidence*. Paper presented at the Annual Meeting of the Society for Judgment and Decision Making, Minneapolis, MN.

Hochman, G., Yechiam, E., & Bechara, A. (2010). Recency gets larger as lesions move from anterior to posterior locations within the ventromedial prefrontal cortex. *Behavioural Brain Research, 213*, 27–34. doi:10.1016/j.bbr.2010.04.023

Hoyle, R. H., Fejfar, M. C., & Miller, J. D. (2000). Personality and sexual risk-taking: A quantitative review. *Journal of Personality*, 68, 1203–1231. doi:10.1111/1467-6494.00132

Huettel, S. A. (2006). Behavioral, but not reward, risk modulates activation of prefrontal, parietal, and insular cortices. *Cognitive, Affective & Behavioral Neuroscience*, 6, 141–151. doi:10.3758/CABN.6.2.141

Huettel, S. A. (2010). Ten challenges for decision neuroscience. *Frontiers in Decision Neuroscience*, 4(171). doi:10.3389/fnins.2010.00171

Huettel, S. A., Song, A. W., & McCarthy, G. W. (2009). *Functional magnetic resonance imaging* (2nd ed.). Sunderland, MA: Sinauer Associates Inc.

Huettel, S. A., Stowe, C. J., Gordon, E. M., Warner, B. T., & Platt, M. L. (2006). Neural signatures of economic preferences for risk and ambiguity. *Neuron, 49*, 765–775. doi:10.1016/j.neuron.2006.01.024

Hunt, L. T., Kolling, N., Soltani, A., Woolrich, M. W., Rushworth, M. F., & Behrens, T. E. (2012). Mechanisms underlying cortical activity during value-guided choice. *Nature Neuroscience, 15*, 470–476. doi:10.1038/nn.3017

Hutcherson, C. A., Plassmann, H., Gross, J. J., & Rangel, A. (2012). Cognitive regulation during decision-making shifts behavioral control between ventromedial and dorsolateral prefrontal value systems. *Journal of Neuroscience, 32*(39), 13543–13554.

Jessor, R. (1991). Risk behavior in adolescence: A psychosocial framework for understanding and action. *Journal of Adolescent Health, 12*, 597–605. doi:10.1016/1054-139X(91)90007-K

Kable, J. W., & Glimcher, P. W. (2007). The neural correlates of subjective value during intertemporal choice. *Nature Neuroscience, 10*, 1625–1633. doi:10.1038/nn2007

Kahneman, D., & Tversky, A. (Eds.). (2000). *Choices, values, and frames*. New York, NY: Cambridge University Press.

Kim, H., & Cabeza, R. (2007). Trusting our memories: Dissociating the neural correlates of confidence in veridical and illusory memories. *The Journal of Neuroscience, 27,* 12190–12197. doi:10.1523/JNEUROSCI.3408-07.2007

Kim, M. J., Gee, D. G., Loucks, R. A., Davis, F. C., & Whalen, P. J. (2011). Anxiety dissociates dorsal and ventral medial prefrontal cortex functional connectivity with the amygdala at rest. *Cerebral Cortex, 21,* 1667–1673. doi:10.1093/cercor/bhq237

Kim, M. J., Loucks, R. A., Neta, M., Davis, F. C., Oler, J. A., Mazzulla, E. C., & Whalen, P. J. (2010). Behind the mask: The influence of mask-type on amygdala response to fearful faces. *Social Cognitive and Affective Neuroscience, 5,* 363–368. doi:10.1093/scan/nsq014

Knoch, D., Gianotti, L. R., Pascual-Leone, A., Treyer, V., Regard, M., Hohmann, M., & Brugger, P. (2006). Disruption of right prefrontal cortex by low-frequency repetitive transcranial magnetic stimulation induces risk-taking behavior. *The Journal of Neuroscience, 26,* 6469–6472. doi:10.1523/JNEUROSCI.0804-06.2006

Knutson, B., Fong, G. W., Bennett, S. M., Adams, C. M., & Hommer, D. (2003). A region of mesial prefrontal cortex tracks monetarily rewarding outcomes: Characterization with rapid event-related fMRI. *NeuroImage, 18,* 263–272. doi:10.1016/S1053-8119(02)00057-5

Kühberger, A., & Tanner, C. (2010). Risky choice framing: Task versions and a comparison of prospect theory and fuzzy-trace theory. *Journal of Behavioral Decision Making, 23,* 314–329. doi:10.1002/bdm.656

Kuhnen, C. M., & Knutson, B. (2005). The neural basis of financial risk taking. *Neuron, 47,* 763–770. doi:10.1016/j.neuron.2005.08.008

Lejuez, C. W., Aklin, W. M., Zvolensky, M. J., & Pedulla, C. M. (2003). Evaluation of the balloon analogue risk task (BART) as a predictor of adolescent real-world risk-taking behaviours. *Journal of Adolescence, 26,* 475–479. doi:10.1016/S0140-1971(03)00036-8

Levy, D. J., & Glimcher, P. W. (2011). Comparing apples and oranges: Using reward-specific and reward-general subjective value representation in the brain. *The Journal of Neuroscience, 31,* 14693–14707. doi:10.1523/JNEUROSCI.2218-11.2011

Levy, D. J., & Glimcher, P. W. (2012). The root of all value: A neural common currency for choice. *Current Opinion in Neurobiology, 22,* 1027–1038. doi:10.1016/j.conb.2012.06.001

Levy, I., Snell, J., Nelson, A. J., Rustichini, A., & Glimcher, P. W. (2010). Neural representation of subjective value under risk and ambiguity. *Journal of Neurophysiology, 103,* 1036–1047. doi:10.1152/jn.00853.2009

Mills, B. A., Reyna, V. F., & Estrada, S. M. (2008). Explaining contradictory relations between risk perception and risk taking. *Psychological Science, 19*(5), 429–433. doi:10.1111/j.1467-9280.2008.02104.x

Mohr, P. N., Biele, G., & Heerkeren, H. R. (2010). Neural processing of risk. *Journal of Neuroscience, 30,* 6613–6619. doi:10.1523/JNEUROSCI.0003-10.2010

Montague, P. R., & Berns, G. S. (2002). Neural economics and biological substrates of valuation. *Neuron, 36*, 265–284. doi:10.1016/S0896-6273(02)00974-1

Murray, E. A. (2007). The amygdala, reward, and emotion. *Trends in Cognitive Sciences, 11*, 489–497. doi:10.1016/j.tics.2007.08.013

Ochsner, K. N., & Gross, J. J. (2008). Cognitive emotion regulation: Insights from social cognitive and affective neuroscience. *Current Directions in Psychological Science, 17*, 153–158. doi:10.1111/j.1467-8721.2008.00566.x

Parker, A., & Fischhoff, B. (2005). Decision-making competence: External validation through an individual-differences approach. *Journal of Behavioral Decision Making, 18*, 1–27. doi:10.1002/bdm.481

Peters, J., & Buchel, C. (2009). Overlapping and distinct neural systems code for subjective value during intertemporal and risky decision making. *The Journal of Neuroscience, 29*, 15727–15734. doi:10.1523/JNEUROSCI.3489-09.2009

Phillips, M. L., Drevets, W. C., Rauch, S. L., & Lane, R. (2003). Neurobiology of emotion perception II: Implications for major psychiatric disorders. *Biological Psychiatry, 54*, 515–528. doi:10.1016/S0006-3223(03)00171-9

Plassmann, H., O'Doherty, J., & Rangel, A. (2007). Orbitofrontal cortex encodes willingness to pay in everyday economic transactions. *The Journal of Neuroscience, 27*, 9984–9988. doi:10.1523/JNEUROSCI.2131-07.2007

Plassmann, H., O'Doherty, J. P., & Rangel, A. (2010). Appetitive and aversive goal values are encoded in the medial orbitofrontal cortex at the time of decision making. *The Journal of Neuroscience, 30*, 10799–10808. doi:10.1523/JNEUROSCI.0788-10.2010

Platt, M. L., & Huettel, S. A. (2008). Risky business: The neuroeconomics of decision making under uncertainty. *Nature Neuroscience, 11*, 398–403. doi:10.1038/nn2062

Pleskac, T. J. (2008). Decision making and learning while taking sequential risks. *Journal of Experimental Psychology: Learning, Memory, and Cognition, 34*, 167–185. doi:10.1037/0278-7393.34.1.167

Pochon, J. B., Riis, J., Sanfey, A. G., Nystrom, L. E., & Cohen, J. D. (2008). Functional imaging of decision conflict. *The Journal of Neuroscience, 28*, 3468–3473. doi:10.1523/JNEUROSCI.4195-07.2008

Poldrack, R. A. (2006). Can cognitive processes be inferred from neuroimaging data? *Trends in Cognitive Sciences, 10*, 59–63. doi:10.1016/j.tics.2005.12.004

Poldrack, R. A., Kittur, A., Kalar, D., Miller, E., Seppa, C., Gil, Y., . . . Bilder, R. M. (2011). The cognitive atlas: Towards a knowledge foundation for cognitive neuroscience. *Frontiers in Neuroinformatics, 5*(17). doi:10.3389/fninf.2011.00017

Porcelli, A. J., & Delgado, M. R. (2009). Neural systems of reward processing in humans. In J. C. Dreher & L. Tremblay (Eds.), *Handbook of reward and decision making* (pp. 165–184). Oxford, England: Academic Press. doi:10.1016/B978-0-12-374620-7.00007-8

Prévost, C., Pessiglione, M., Météreau, E., Cléry-Melin, M.L., & Dreher, J.C. (2010). Separate valuation subsystems for delay and effort decision costs. *The Journal of Neuroscience, 30,* 14080–14090. doi:10.1523/JNEUROSCI.2752-10.2010

Raichle, M. E., & Snyder, A. Z. (2007). A default mode of brain function: A brief history of an evolving idea. *NeuroImage, 37,* 1083–1090, discussion 1097–1099. doi:10.1016/j.neuroimage.2007.02.041

Reyna, V. F. (1995). Interference effects in memory and reasoning: A fuzzy-trace theory analysis. In F. N. Dempster & C. J. Brainerd (Eds.), *Interference and inhibition in cognition* (pp. 29–59). San Diego, CA: Academic Press. doi:10.1016/B978-012208930-5/50003-9

Reyna, V. F. (2008). Theories of medical decision making and health: An evidence-based approach. *Medical Decision Making, 28*(6), 829–833. doi:10.1177/0272989X08327069

Reyna, V. F. (2012). A new intuitionism: Meaning, memory, and development in fuzzy-trace theory. *Judgment and Decision Making, 7,* 332–359.

Reyna, V. F. (2013). Intuition, reasoning, and development: A fuzzy-trace theory approach. In P. Barrouillet & C. Gauffroy (Eds.), *The development of thinking and reasoning* (pp. 193–220). Hove, England: Psychology Press.

Reyna, V. F., & Adam, M. B. (2003). Fuzzy-trace theory, risk communication, and product labeling in sexually transmitted diseases. *Risk Analysis, 23,* 325–342. doi:10.1111/1539-6924.00332

Reyna, V. F., & Brainerd, C. J. (1991). Fuzzy-trace theory and framing effects in choice: Gist extraction, truncation, and conversion. *Journal of Behavioral Decision Making, 4,* 249–262. doi:10.1002/bdm.3960040403

Reyna, V. F., & Brainerd, C. J. (1994). The origins of probability judgment: A review of data and theories. In G. Wright & P. Ayton (Eds.), *Subjective probability* (pp. 239–272). New York, NY: Wiley.

Reyna, V. F., & Brainerd, C. J. (1995). Fuzzy-trace theory: An interim synthesis. *Learning and Individual Differences, 7*(1), 1–75. doi:10.1016/1041-6080(95)90031-4

Reyna, V. F., & Brainerd, C. J. (2011). Dual processes in decision making and developmental neuroscience: A fuzzy-trace model. *Developmental Review, 31,* 180–206. doi:10.1016/j.dr.2011.07.004

Reyna, V. F., Chapman, S., Dougherty, M., & Confrey, J. (Eds.). (2012). *The adolescent brain: Learning, reasoning, and decision making.* Washington, DC: American Psychological Association. doi:10.1037/13493-000

Reyna, V. F., & Ellis, S. C. (1994). Fuzzy-trace theory and framing effects in children's risky decision making. *Psychological Science, 5,* 275–279. doi:10.1111/j.1467-9280.1994.tb00625.x

Reyna, V. F., Estrada, S. M., DeMarinis, J. A., Myers, R. M., Stanisz, J. M., & Mills, B. A. (2011). Neurobiological and memory models of risky decision making in adolescents versus young adults. *Journal of Experimental Psychology: Learning, Memory, and Cognition, 37,* 1125–1142. doi:10.1037/a0023943

Reyna, V. F., & Farley, F. (2006). Risk and rationality in adolescent decision-making: Implications for theory, practice, and public policy. *Psychological Science in the Public Interest, 7*(1), 1–44. doi:10.1111/j.1529-1006.2006.00026.x

Reyna, V. F., & Lloyd, F. J. (2006). Physician decision-making and cardiac risk: Effects of knowledge, risk perception, risk tolerance, and fuzzy processing. *Journal of Experimental Psychology: Applied, 12,* 179–195. doi:10.1037/1076-898X.12.3.179

Reyna, V. F., & Mills, B. A. (2007). Converging evidence supports fuzzy-trace theory's nested sets hypothesis (but not the frequency hypothesis). *Behavioral and Brain Sciences, 30,* 278–280. doi:10.1017/S0140525X07001872

Reyna, V. F., & Rivers, S. E. (2008). Current theories of risk and rational decision making. *Developmental Review, 28,* 1–11. doi:10.1016/j.dr.2008.01.002

Rick, S. I., Cryder, C. E., & Loewenstein, G. (2008). Tightwads and spendthrifts. *Journal of Consumer Research, 34,* 767–782. doi:10.1086/523285

Roiser, J. P., De Martino, B., Tan, G. C. Y., Kumaran, D., Seymour, B., Wood, N. W., & Dolan, R. J. (2009). A genetically mediated bias in decision making driven by failure of amygdala control. *The Journal of Neuroscience, 29,* 5985–5991. doi:10.1523/JNEUROSCI.0407-09.2009

Rushworth, M. F., Kolling, N., Sallet, J., & Mars, R. B. (2012). Valuation and decision-making in frontal cortex: One or many serial or parallel systems? *Current Opinion in Neurobiology, 22,* 946–955. doi:10.1016/j.conb.2012.04.011

Rushworth, M. F., Noonan, M. P., Boorman, E. D., Walton, M. E., & Behrens, T. E. (2011). Frontal cortex and reward-guided learning and decision-making. *Neuron, 70,* 1054–1069. doi:10.1016/j.neuron.2011.05.014

Schonberg, T., Craig, F. R., Mumford, J. A., Congdon, E., Trepel, C., & Poldrack, R. A. (2012). Decreasing ventromedial prefrontal cortex activity during sequential risk-taking: An fMRI investigation of the balloon analog risk task. *Frontiers in Decision Neuroscience,* 6(80). doi:10.3389/fnins.2012.00080

Schonberg, T., Fox, C. R., & Poldrack, R. A. (2011). Mind the gap: Bridging economic and naturalistic risk-taking with cognitive neuroscience. *Trends in Cognitive Sciences, 15*(1), 11–19. doi:10.1016/j.tics.2010.10.002

Shannon, B. J., Raichle, M. E., Snyder, A. Z., Fair, D. A., Mills, K. L., Zhang, D., . . . Kiehl, K. A. (2011). Premotor functional connectivity predicts impulsivity in juvenile offenders. *Proceedings of the National Academy of Sciences of the United States of America, 108,* 11241–11245. doi:10.1073/pnas.1108241108

Singer, M., & Remillard, G. (2008). Veridical and false memory for text: A multiprocess analysis. *Journal of Memory and Language, 59,* 18–35. doi:10.1016/j.jml.2008.01.005

Slotnick, S. D., & Schacter, D. L. (2004). A sensory signature that distinguishes true from false memories. *Nature Neuroscience, 7,* 664–672. doi:10.1038/nn1252

Smith, D. V., Hayden, B. Y., Truong, T. K., Song, A. W., Platt, M. L., & Huettel, S. A. (2010). Distinct value signals in anterior and posterior ventromedial prefrontal cortex. *The Journal of Neuroscience, 30*, 2490–2495. doi:10.1523/JNEUROSCI.3319-09.2010

Spaniol, J., Davidson, P. S., Kim, A. S., Han, H., Moscovitch, M., & Grady, C. L. (2009). Event-related fMRI studies of episodic encoding and retrieval: Meta-analyses using activation likelihood estimation. *Neuropsychologia, 47*, 1765–1779. doi:10.1016/j.neuropsychologia.2009.02.028

Spreng, R. N. (2012). The fallacy of a "task-negative" network. *Frontiers in Psychology, 3*(145). doi:10.3389/fpsyg.2012.00145

Steinberg, L., Cauffman, E., Woolard, J., Graham, S., & Banich, M. (2009). Are adolescents less mature than adults? Minors' access to abortion, the juvenile death penalty, and the alleged APA "flip-flop." *American Psychologist, 64*, 583–594. doi:10.1037/a0014763

Stout, J. C., Rock, S. L., Campbell, M. C., Busemeyer, J. R., & Finn, P. R. (2005). Psychological processes underlying risky decisions in drug abusers. *Psychology of Addictive Behaviors, 19*, 148–157. doi:10.1037/0893-164X.19.2.148

Sunstein, C. R. (2008). Adolescent risk-taking and social meaning: A commentary. *Developmental Review, 28*, 145–152. doi:10.1016/j.dr.2007.11.003

Taren, A. A., Venkatraman, V., & Huettel, S. A. (2011). A parallel functional topography between medial and lateral prefrontal cortex: Evidence and implications for cognitive control. *The Journal of Neuroscience, 31*, 5026–5031. doi:10.1523/JNEUROSCI.5762-10.2011

Tom, S. M., Fox, C. R., Trepel, C., & Poldrack, R. A. (2007). The neural basis of loss aversion in decision-making under risk. *Science, 315*, 515–518. doi:10.1126/science.1134239

Tversky, A., & Kahneman, D. (1986). Rational choice and the framing of decisions. *The Journal of Business, 59*, S251–S278. doi:10.1086/296365

Van Duijvenvoorde, A. C. K., Jansen, B. R. J., Bredman, J., & Huizenga, H. M. (2012). Age-related changes in decision-making: Comparing informed and noninformed situations. *Developmental Psychology, 48*, 192–203. doi:10.1037/a0025601

Venkatraman, V., & Huettel, S. A. (2012). Strategic control in decision making under uncertainty. *European Journal of Neuroscience, 35*, 1075–1082. doi:10.1111/j.1460-9568.2012.08009.x

Venkatraman, V., Payne, J. W., Bettman, J. R., Luce, M. F., & Huettel, S. A. (2009). Separate neural mechanisms underlie choices and strategic preferences in risky decision making. *Neuron, 62*, 593–602. doi:10.1016/j.neuron.2009.04.007

von Neumann, J., & Morgenstern, O. (1944). *Theory of games and economic behavior*. Princeton, NJ: Princeton University Press.

von Winterfeldt, D., & Edwards, W. (1986). *Decision analysis and behavioral research*. Cambridge, England: Cambridge University Press.

Wagner, A. D., Shannon, B., Kahn, I., & Buckner, R. (2005). Parietal lobe contributions to episodic memory retrieval. *Trends in Cognitive Sciences, 9*, 445–453. doi:10.1016/j.tics.2005.07.001

Weber, E. U., Blais, A.-R., & Betz, N. (2002). A domain-specific risk-attitude scale: Measuring risk perceptions and risk behaviors. *Journal of Behavioral Decision Making, 15*, 263–290. doi:10.1002/bdm.414

Weber, E. U., & Johnson, E. J. (2009). Mindful judgment and decision making. *Annual Review of Psychology, 60*, 53–85. doi:10.1146/annurev.psych.60.110707.163633

Weller, J. A., Levin, I. P., Shiv, B., & Bechara, A. (2007). Neural correlates of adaptive decision making for risky gains and losses. *Psychological Science, 18*, 958–964. doi:10.1111/j.1467-9280.2007.02009.x

Willemsen, M. C., Böckenholt, U., & Johnson, E. (2011). Choice by value encoding and value construction: Processes of loss aversion. *Journal of Experimental Psychology: General, 140*, 303–324. doi:10.1037/a0023493

Winecoff, A., Clithero, J. A., Carter, R. M., Bergman, S. R., Wang, L., & Huettel, S. A. (2013). Ventromedial prefrontal cortex encodes emotional value. *Journal of Neuroscience, 33*(27), 11032–11039

World Health Organization. (2010). *International statistical classification of diseases and related health problems* (10th ed.). Geneva, Switzerland: Author.

Wunderlich, K., Rangel, A., & O'Doherty, J. P. (2010). Economic choices can be made using only stimulus values. *Proceedings of the National Academy of Sciences of the United States of America, 107*, 15005–15010. doi:10.1073/pnas.1002258107

Yechiam, E., Barron, G., & Erev, I. (2005). The role of personal experience in contributing to different patterns of response to rare terrorist attacks. *Journal of Conflict Resolution, 49*, 430–439. doi:10.1177/0022002704270847

Yechiam, E., & Telpaz, A. (2013). Losses induce consistency in risk taking even without loss aversion. *Journal of Behavioral Decision Making, 26*, 31–40. doi:10.1002/bdm.758

Yonelinas, A. P., Otten, L. J., Shaw, K. N., & Rugg, M. D. (2005). Separating the brain regions involved in recollection and familiarity in recognition memory. *The Journal of Neuroscience, 25*, 3002–3008. doi:10.1523/JNEUROSCI.5295-04.2005

Zhang, X., & Hirsch, J. (2013). The temporal derivative of expected utility: A neural mechanism for dynamic decision-making. *NeuroImage, 65*, 223–230. doi:10.1016/j.neuroimage.2012.08.063

Zuckerman, M. (1994). *Behavioral expressions and biosocial bases of sensation seeking.* New York, NY: Cambridge University Press.

2

BEHAVIORAL AND NEUROSCIENCE METHODS FOR STUDYING NEUROECONOMIC PROCESSES: WHAT WE CAN LEARN FROM FRAMING EFFECTS

IRWIN P. LEVIN, TODD McELROY, GARY J. GAETH, WILLIAM HEDGCOCK, AND NATALIE L. DENBURG

In this chapter, we illustrate how framing effects can be used to examine the complementary contributions of behavioral and neuroscience research in understanding neuroeconomic decision processes, particularly those involving risk. Framing effects are ubiquitous in everyday life, yet they can be studied under controlled conditions with simple manipulations (e.g., describing a medical treatment as either having a 50% success rate or a 50% failure rate). Objectively equivalent information presented in different frames has been shown to lead to substantially different preference ratings that are accompanied by different brain activation patterns. An array of multidisciplinary tools across a growing body of literature shows that framing effects play a fundamental role in decision making. In this chapter, we explore this recent research using different framing paradigms (attribute and risky-choice framing) in conjunction with recently developed neuroeconomic risky-choice tasks such as the Iowa Gambling Task and the "cups" task, which differentially tap into affective and cognitive systems. Studies include brain scanning, eye tracking, circadian

http://dx.doi.org/10.1037/14322-003
The Neuroscience of Risky Decision Making, by V. F. Reyna and V. Zayas (Editors)

rhythms, and life-span developmental techniques. We discuss results in terms of current dual-process theories of decision making. Evidence is converging to allow us to better answer the basic question of "Why (and when) do you and I make different decisions?"

Decision making is a complex process that is affected by many factors, and sometimes the inputs are conflicting. For example, in economic decisions the most desirable outcome may be the one that involves the most risk. Human decision makers are characterized by a correspondingly complex, intricately related system that is bound as much by its basic physiological underpinnings as it is by its dependency on willful thought. Every psychological and biological process operates in conjunction with other processes. Decision making, like any other task, functions within this synergistic environment and is reliant on both affect and cognition. We focus on framing effects in decision making in this chapter because evidence is accumulating at both the behavioral and the neural levels that framing effects represent an appropriate setting for examining the individual and complementary roles of affect and cognition in neuroeconomic decision making. Framing effects are ubiquitous in everyday life and thus have been a popular topic for the laboratory. We find that frames affect judgments about gambles, consumer goods and services, medical procedures, and political candidates. We concentrate on valence framing effects, which are particularly interesting because they represent different responses to objectively equivalent information by simply varying whether the information is expressed in positive or negative terms.

The history of studying framing effects is long and is often traced to Tversky and Kahneman's (1981) seminal paper on the Asian disease problem. New research tools have allowed us to go beyond the early demonstration of biased responding, that is, departure from normative principles, to examine in more detail when and why framing effects occur. This in turn provides deeper insight into basic decision-making processes, especially the ability to separate cognitive and affective or emotional systems; the separate impact of these two systems is at the core of our chapter.

INTRODUCTION

Evidence is accumulating that common decision-making biases such as framing effects can be more thoroughly understood at the neural level, particularly through the activation of affective systems in the brain (De Martino, Kumaran, Seymour, & Dolan, 2006; Huettel, Stowe, Gordon, Warner, & Platt, 2006; Kuhnen & Knutson, 2005; Sanfey, Rilling, Aronson, Nystrom, & Cohen, 2003; Tom, Fox, Trepel, & Poldrack, 2007; Weller, Levin, Shiv, & Bechara, 2007). Neuroscientific research suggests that because of the evolutionary importance of avoiding negative consequences, the mere presence of uncertainty induces a primary "fear" response elicited by the amygdala, which has been associated specifically with fear processing and avoidance of negative consequences (LeDoux, 2000; Phelps, 2006; Trepel, Fox, & Poldrak, 2005). This fear response activates the ventromedial prefrontal cortex (vmPFC) whose function is to mediate decision making and to allow for more careful deliberative processes by linking together working memory and emotional systems (Damasio, 1994). Structures such as the insular cortex, which are independent of the amygdala, are also likely to impact decision making under uncertainty by providing complementary systems for dealing with potential losses (Kuhnen & Knutson, 2005; Weller, Levin, Shiv, & Bechara, 2009). This account parallels the proposed dual System 1/System 2 approach of decision making (Kahneman, 2003, 2011), which represents an interaction between emotional intuitive processing and more deliberative processing of choice options.

The idea that humans process information in either an automatic fashion that is fast or a thoughtful manner that is more deliberative traces its roots to William James and has been applied in many areas of psychology that directly relate to decision making (e.g., Epstein, Lipson, Holstein, & Huh, 1992; Gilbert, 1991; Reyna & Brainerd, 1991; Shiffrin & Schneider, 1977; Sloman, 1996; Stanovich & West, 2000). More recently, Kahneman and Frederick (2002; see also Kahneman, 2003, 2011) adapted a two-system approach that mirrors much of the prior contribution by Stanovich and West (2000) and creates a new vision for the two-process model. In this approach an automatic System 1 operates without attention or control processes using basic intuitive associations and emotional intensity and in the end supplies us with quick preferences that can guide decision making. In contrast to System 1, System 2 is deliberative and thoughtful, and its hallmark is that it requires effort. According to the dual-process approach, much of our decision making is driven by System 1, which allows for choices to be made with cognitive ease and factors such as emotional intensity to become the guiding principles for choice preference. However, if the situation sufficiently motivates us and cognitive resources are available, then the more thoughtful System 2 is employed, and more elaborative, effortful, and time-consuming processing occurs. In System 2 processing, attention is directed to the task, alternatives are generated from memory, thoughtful (e.g., mathematical) comparisons are made, and alternatives may then be weighed in a deliberative fashion.

System 1 is relatively automatic as well as holistic, leads to an automatic contextualization of problems, and brings potential solutions to consideration relatively quickly. System 2 involves a controlled and analytic processing style that serves to decontextualize and depersonalize problems. From this route, people will normally rely on individual elements of the task and their logical consistencies. Stanovich and West (2000) further argue that intellect can predispose people to this route of processing, such that people with higher levels of analytic intelligence will be more likely to rely on System 2 processing.

Across many different approaches we see that cognition and emotion play complementary roles, with the emotionally laden System 1 quickly pulling us toward an alternative and the cognitively heavy System 2 having the potential for overriding the initial impulse. The significance of avoiding losses leads to the belief that the mere framing of equivalent outcomes in terms of gains or losses could influence the activation of these different systems. In a recent review, Levin et al. (2012) did in fact show that different neural systems appear to be activated in dealing with potential gains and potential losses, especially when neural activation was assessed at the crucial prechoice stage when positively or negatively framed options were being considered.

A distinction has been made in the literature between *reflection effects*, a term referring to tasks involving literal gains and losses (e.g., gambling tasks), and *framing effects*, a term referring to equivalent outcomes expressed in terms of gains or losses (Levin, Schneider, & Gaeth, 1998). Because of the apparent commonality of processes involved, we will not make this distinction here.

In this chapter, we discuss framing effect differences across tasks and individuals and what they tell us about why decisions differ both between and within groups. We stress the complementarity of behavioral and biological/neurological measures, and we describe studies in which age-related deficits in cognitive and emotional functioning sometimes lead to impaired decisions and sometimes to unimpaired decisions. We are aided in this pursuit by subtle but important distinctions between different framing manipulations.

We include both recently published data and current unpublished data that highlight the role of framing in illuminating decision processes. Specifically, we will show the following:

- Different types of framing manipulations evoke different levels of emotional reliance.
- These differences are revealed both in behavioral measures and biological/neurological indicators.
- Normal metabolic and biological fluctuations related to circadian rhythms affect decision making and are revealed by different levels of framing effects at different times of the day.
- Naturally occurring hemispheric laterality differences are revealed by handedness impact framing effects.
- Gaze duration as revealed by eye-tracking techniques provides further insight into attentional processes underlying framing effects.

- The most basic of all biological processes, aging, results in changes in the balance between emotional and cognitive processes that can lead to impaired performance on some tasks but improved performance on other tasks in the form of resistance to some forms of framing.

We then integrate these various findings to better evaluate theories of framing effects and their more widespread application to understanding basic decision processes.

BACKGROUND: FRAMING EFFECTS

Based on confusions in the literature at the time as to why framing effects differed across studies and investigators, we suggested that "all frames are not created equal" (Levin et al., 1998; see also Kühberger, 1998 and Levin, Gaeth, Schreiber, & Lauriola, 2002) and laid out a scheme for classifying framing studies in terms of their operational definitions, typical findings, and possible explanations. In this chapter, we focus on two types of framing effects, risky-choice framing and attribute framing, selected because of their potential for separating the relative roles of System 1 and System 2 processing in decision making.

Risky-choice framing, as exemplified by the Asian disease problem, requires a choice between a risky and a riskless option of equal expected value, where outcomes are alternatively expressed in positive terms (e.g., lives saved by a medical procedure) or negative terms (lives lost). In the classic example, respondents are offered a treatment choice for dealing with a disease that is expected to kill 600 persons. For half the respondents (the positive frame condition) the choice is between an option that offers a sure saving of 200 lives and an option that offers a 1/3 chance of saving all 600 lives and a 2/3 chance of saving no lives. For the other half (the negative frame condition) the objectively identical choice is between an option that offers a sure loss of 400 lives and an option that offers a 1/3 chance of losing no lives and a 2/3 chance of losing all 600 lives. The most common result is that subjects are more apt to make the risky choice (selecting the option that offers a 1/3 possibility of no lives lost) in the negative condition but choose the riskless option (a sure saving of 1/3 of the lives) in the positive condition. Later work revealed a fourfold pattern of risk aversion for potential gains and risk seeking for potential losses of high probability, as in the Asian disease problem, but the opposite for losses of low probability (Tversky & Kahneman, 1992). These results are explained in terms of separate value functions for gains and losses and nonlinear weighting of probabilities in Kahneman and Tversky's (1979) prospect theory.

Attribute framing, as exemplified by the percentage lean versus percentage fat labeling of ground beef (Levin & Gaeth, 1988), is a simpler form of framing because it involves only the alternative labeling of a single attribute of an object or event and does not require comparisons based on the element of risk. The typical finding is more favorable evaluations when alternatives are labeled in positive terms (percentage lean, success rate) rather than negative terms (percentage fat, failure rate). These results were explained in terms of associative networks primed by positive or negative labels (Levin, 1987).

Levin and Gaeth (1988) found that even after consuming an identical sample of ground beef, those who were told that it was 75% lean ground beef gave higher ratings of healthiness and quality than did those who were told that they were tasting 25% fat ground beef. Later, Levin et al. (2002) found that economic decisions were also affected, with participants willing to spend more for a package of ground beef with the percentage lean label. In an extension of this research, Braun, Gaeth, and Levin (1997) investigated attribute framing effects in a realistic environment where the label was embedded in an actual product package. Following a taste test, 80% fat-free chocolate was given higher ratings than 20% fat chocolate, especially by female consumers for whom the framed attribute was particularly salient.

APPLIED ATTRIBUTE FRAMING

Much of the research on attribute framing effects has emerged from controlled conditions carried out in the laboratory; however, a number of studies have demonstrated the relevance for applied decision making. For example, using practicing physicians, researchers showed that when the option of surgery was expressed in terms of "survival rate" as opposed to "mortality rate," significantly more surgeons selected surgery in the survival condition (McNeil, Pauker, Sox, & Tversky, 1982).

Also in the domain of health, Jasper, Goel, Einarson, Gallo, and Koren (2001) examined the effects of attribute framing on pregnant women's perceptions of fetal risk and their subsequent intentions to use a particular drug during pregnancy. Half the women received positively framed information (97%–99% chance of having a normal child) and half received the negative version (1%–3% chance of having a malformed child). Participants in the negative condition had a significantly higher perception of risk and were significantly less likely to contemplate taking the drug.

In a study of real consumers, Diamond and Sanyal (1990) showed that consumers were more likely to redeem coupons when the value was framed as a gain than when it was framed as a "reduced loss." Because this was a situation in which a gain (product plus free item) was compared with a loss (two paid products) and a gain (discount), consumers avoided the coupon expressed as having a loss and preferred coupons expressed as a gain. In fact, research has shown that attribute framing plays a profoundly influential role in many important economic decisions, such as fairness in health care decisions (Gamliel & Peer, 2010) and allocation of resources (Gamliel & Peer, 2006).

Recently, in a study involving life annuities, a team of researchers looked at how framing the question of life expectancy affects consumers' subsequent estimate of their expected life span and concomitant economic decisions (Payne, Sagara, Shu, Appelt, & Johnson, 2012). The positive frame asks people to provide probabilities of living to a certain age or older; the negative frame asks people to provide probabilities of dying by a certain age or younger. These two answers should be complements, but Payne et al. (2012) found that estimated probabilities differed significantly in the two conditions. People in the live-to frame reported that they have a 55% chance of being alive at age 85, whereas people in the die-by frame reported that they have a 68% chance of being dead at age 85. Overall, estimated mean life expectancies, across three studies and over 2,300 respondents, were between 7.29 and 9.17 years longer when solicited in the live-to frame.

Importantly, Payne et al. (2012) showed that frame-induced life expectancies predicted economic behavioral intentions. Differences in life expectancies were predictive of stated preferences for life annuities, a product that provides insurance against outliving one's savings. On a process level, the authors showed that the attribute framing effect on judgments was partially mediated by the relative number of thoughts in favor of being alive at that age. This is consistent with Levin's (1987) associative model of attribute framing effects.

Sparked largely by the work of Stanovich and West (Stanovich, 1999; Stanovich & West, 1998a, 1998b; see also Levin, 1999), there has been a growing movement to extend aggregate-level analysis of behavioral decision making to focus on individual differences in rational thought. For example, although we talk about "typical" findings in studies of risky choice and attribute framing, there are systematic variations in the magnitude and existence of these effects as a function of specific task and situational characteristics and their interaction with individual difference factors (Lauriola & Levin, 2001; Levin et al., 2002; Mahoney, Buboltz, Levin, Doverspike, & Svyantek, 2011; McElroy & Seta, 2003; Peters & Levin, 2008; Simon, Fagley, & Halleran, 2004; Smith & Levin, 1996). We rely heavily on such systematic sources of variance when presenting and interpreting the data provided in this chapter.

Before proceeding, we will briefly describe how we think the distinction between risky-choice framing and attribute framing is important for our purposes. Based on its simpler form and our associative model of its effects, attribute framing seems particularly amenable to System 1 processing. Specifically, attribute framing problems are comparatively simple and can be processed with relative ease. And because System 1 is the default processing style for cognitively easy tasks, it seems likely that System 1 processing will dominate for most individuals.

Conversely, because risky-choice framing has the added element of processing numeric risk information and comparing risky and riskless options, both elements associated with System 2, we presume that System 2 processing is more likely to occur in risky-choice framing. To preview what comes later, we use this distinction to better understand why some individuals show biased responses on a risky-choice framing task but not on an attribute framing task and why different brain mechanisms are involved.

Because we are interested in the process by which framing guides choice and how the emotional component of this process differs across types of framing, for some of the more recent studies we constructed slightly modified versions of the standard risky-choice framing and attribute framing tasks in which the response scale is equated across tasks. This serves to remove any confound between the deliberation of choice options and the mechanical process of response elicitation, which becomes particularly important in brain imaging studies. As illustrated below, a 4-point preference scale is used for each. The positive framing conditions are shown.

Example of Risky-Choice Framing

Because of changes in tax laws, you may get back as much as $1,200 in income tax. Your accountant has been exploring two ways to take advantage of this situation:

- If Plan A is adopted, you will get back $400 of the possible $1,200.
- If Plan B is adopted, you have a 33% chance of getting back all of the $1,200, and a 67% chance of getting back no money.
- Which option do you prefer?
- Strongly Prefer A Weakly Prefer A
Strongly Prefer B Weakly Prefer B

Example of Attribute Framing

As R&D manager, two project teams have come to you requesting additional funds for a project you instituted several months ago. You can only fund one team.

- Team A is proposing a project that has historically been successful in 24 of the last 50 attempts. It will cost $100,000.

- Team B is proposing a project that has historically been successful in 20 of the last 50 attempts. It will cost $65,000.
- Which option do you prefer?
- Strongly Prefer A   Weakly Prefer A
  Strongly Prefer B   Weakly Prefer B

Note that in the attribute framing example, Team A has a better record but higher cost than Team B. Across conditions, only success versus failure rate is manipulated; cost does not change. Thus, based on the associative model of attribute framing effects (Levin, 1987), positive framing is expected to lead to greater preference for A, because focusing on successes will make Team A seem especially attractive compared with Team B, even with the higher cost. In contrast, by focusing on failures in the negative condition, Team A will seem less attractive and not worth the extra cost, which will lead to greater preference for B.

EMOTION SUPPRESSION

One way to examine the differential role of affect or emotion in decision tasks is to manipulate the extent of emotional processing through instructional variations, including emotion suppression. Gross and Levenson (1993) defined *emotion suppression* as the conscious inhibition of emotional expressive behavior while emotionally aroused. In their study, participants who watched a disgust-eliciting film and were subject to emotion suppression instructions showed decreased somatic activity and decreased heart rate compared with controls. Using this manipulation, we provide preliminary data on the comparative role of emotion in the two types of framing tasks.

A 2 (instructions) × 2 (frame type: risk/attribute) × 2 (valence: positive/negative) × 10 (domains) design was employed where the first factor was manipulated between subjects and the rest within. Within-subject manipulation of frame type and valence allows for each type of framing effect to be measured and compared at the level of the individual respondent. *Domain* refers to the varied content areas of the problems (financial, medical, recreational, etc.) included to increase generality.

The baseline condition instructed participants to indicate their preference using the 4-point scale described earlier. The emotion control condition was identical except for the additional instruction to adopt a "detached and unemotional attitude." Risky-choice framing resulted in the usual finding of significantly greater risk taking in the negative framing condition than in the positive condition, both in the baseline condition and in the suppression condition. By contrast, attribute framing resulted in the typical finding of lower evaluations for negatively framed stimuli only in the baseline condition but not in the suppression condition. The same participants who exhibited risky-choice framing effects in the emotion suppression condition were resistant to attribute framing effects.

Given that resistance to framing is seen as a component of decision-making competence (Bruine de Bruin, Parker, & Fischhoff, 2007; Parker & Fischhoff, 2005; Weller, Levin, Rose, & Bossard, 2012), our results indicate that in the case of attribute framing, suppression of emotions is associated with reducing or eliminating biased decision making. Because attribute framing was more affected by emotion suppression than risky-choice framing, the results are consistent with the hypothesis that attribute framing is more influenced by emotional (System 1) processes than risky-choice framing, and in that sense, the sources of the two types of framing differ at a basic level.

Apart from task and individual characteristics that promote deliberative versus intuitive processing during choice, there is evidence that the same person performing the same task may vary in processing choices simply due to natural biological processes that vary across times of the day. Again, framing effects shed light on such processes.

BRAIN METABOLIC LEVELS INFLUENCE PROCESSING OF RISKY-CHOICE FRAMING TASKS

The body's metabolic activity influences all aspects of physiological and psychological functioning. Factors that affect metabolic activity should either enhance or inhibit System 2–type processing. This change in cognitive processing should, in turn, provide clues about the extent to which deliberative System 2 processing is involved in risky choice and attribute framing. To explore this, we focus on two main contributors to metabolic activity: circadian rhythms and glucose. Both of these factors have recently drawn the interest of decision researchers, largely because of their effects on cognitive processing.

We live in an environment that is filled with many externally regulated changes, but the most profound is the day–night cycle. Not surprisingly, our bodies have developed a host of biological fluctuations that accompany variations in the diurnal cycle, all geared toward giving us specific temporal advantages. On any normal day, our internal biological clock cycles through changes in a variety of physiological functions that include corporal temperature, hormones, heart rate, and blood pressure. And the list is not limited to biological functions; cognitive abilities also vary with the circadian cycle. These circadian variations occur on a roughly 24-hour cycle and appear to be controlled by an area deep within our brain, the suprachiasmatic nucleus (SCN), which acts as a circadian oscillator.

Although a great deal of evidence supports the SCN as the major player in circadian rhythm, perhaps the most convincing evidence for its central role was put forth by Ralph, Foster, Davis, and Menaker (1990) when they grafted the SCN of a mutant strain of hamster with very short circadian cycles onto hamsters with a nonfunctioning SCN. Ralph et al. found that the recipient hamster always took on the circadian cycle of the mutant donor, even though it was different from their previous cycles. Thus, it appears that the SCN is the controller of circadian cycles.

Given the important biological functions that are regulated by the circadian rhythm cycle, it seems evident that diurnal cycles will have important influences on many aspects of human behavior, including decision making. Studies investigating this topic have shown that circadian mismatched participants (e.g., morning type in the evening) rely more on judgmental heuristics, which lead to greater stereotyping (Bodenhausen, 1990), and they have lower levels of strategic reasoning when making decisions (Dickinson & McElroy, 2010, 2012). Both findings suggest attenuation in deliberative thought.

McElroy and Dickinson (2010) investigated how changes in deliberative thought, observed across the circadian cycle, influenced risky-choice and attribute framing. To achieve this, they used online survey software and randomly assigned participants to specific time slots across the full 24-hour cycle. Overall, these findings showed that risky-choice framing effects were significantly stronger during circadian off-times than during circadian on-times and the effect was most pronounced in the losses condition where risk-taking was especially high during off times. These changes in framing effects were interpreted through a dual-process approach wherein more automatic processing is hypothesized to occur during circadian off-times and more thoughtful, deliberative processing is hypothesized to occur during on-times. Importantly, circadian variation had no effect on attribute framing.

In tune with circadian rhythm, a variety of metabolic and physiological processes operate in conjunction with SCN oscillation. One of the key metabolic factors that varies is glucose. The SCN has been shown to regulate daily cycles in blood glucose levels to create an interactive circadian arousal system that runs in parallel with the glucose fuel source (e.g., La Fleur, 2003). The key benefactor of glucose utilization is the brain—it accounts for roughly 25% of the body's total glucose utilization.

Researchers have begun to focus on how glucose levels may influence decision making. For example, Masicampo and Baumeister (2008) used an attraction task wherein participants are attracted to an option because it is similar to a decoy that is not desirable. When choosing between two apartments based on their size and distance from school, the introduction of a third option (the decoy), which is inferior to the others on both attributes, can nevertheless affect the choice between the two most viable options. They found that glucose-deficient participants were more likely to make less optimal choices (rely on the decoy) than glucose-enriched participants. In another investigation, McMahon and Scheel (2010) looked at probability learning and found that participants relied more on simple probability rules when they were glucose deprived, and as a result, mimicked the percentage of occurrence for each event (a less advantageous strategy) rather than choosing the event of greater likelihood. Further research by Wang and Dvorak (2010) showed that glucose enrichment reduced the rate of future discounting, suggesting a better ability to regulate expected rewards. Thus, these findings seem to indicate that glucose deprivation impedes a decision maker's ability to ignore irrelevant information, apply more complex rules, and thoughtfully consider future rewards. This seems to suggest that glucose acts as circadian fuel either to inhibit or to encourage more thoughtful processing of decisions.

These circadian rhythm and glucose findings provide further evidence that processing differences have pronounced effects on risky-choice framing. It is well established that cognitive processing is constrained by the cognitive resources currently available (Hasher & Zacks, 1988). Behavioral research has shown that during circadian off-times cognitive resources are depleted (e.g., Schmidt, Collette, Cajochen, & Peigneux, 2007). Furthermore, neurological evidence indicates that during circadian off-times cognitive resources are constrained because of reduced frontal lobe functioning (e.g., Manly, Lewis, Robertson, Watson, & Datta, 2002). Together, both behavioral and neurological evidence suggest that circadian off-times decrease glucose levels and inhibit cognitive resources. Consequently, deliberative, effortful processing should be impeded during circadian off-times and advanced during on-times. This parallels circadian effects on risky-choice framing wherein framing effects are strongest during off-times and weakest during on-times. However, circadian rhythm had no effect on attribute framing. Taken together, these findings suggest that deliberative processing is a central component in risky-choice framing but plays little or no role in attribute framing, thus solidifying the distinction between risky-choice and attribute framing as representing different balances of cognitive and affective processing.

HANDEDNESS AND THE HEMISPHERES: CONNECTIONS AND PROCESSING STYLES

Another important link between processing styles and biological processes is handedness as an observable element of right brain/left brain functions. There has been a great deal of research investigating how handedness differences represent underlying anatomical differences in the brain. A growing body of research has been focusing on how these differences may affect decision making (e.g., Christman, Jasper, Sontam, & Cooil, 2007; Jasper, Barry, & Christman, 2008; Jasper & Christman, 2005). At the heart of this literature lies the belief that mixed-handed people have greater interaction between the left and right hemispheres and consequently greater access to right-hemisphere processing than "strong-handers" (those with a dominant hand). Research based on this premise has shown that this access leads "mixed-handers" to demonstrate more risk propensity and stronger informational framing effects (Jasper, Fournier, & Christman, 2013).

How processing differences associated with the respective hemispheres may influence risky-choice framing has also been a topic of research. Historically, hemispheric research suggests that the left hemisphere processes information in an analytic fashion, whereas the right hemisphere tends to process information in a more holistic style (e.g., Ornstein, 1972). The outcome of these respective processing styles is that left hemisphere processing is reliant on numerically derived information and the right hemisphere is especially sensitive to context cues.

McElroy and Seta (2004) manipulated hemispheric activation to capitalize on the different hemispheric processing styles and test their effects on a traditional risky-choice framing task. Their findings revealed that the respective hemispheric processing styles had significant effects on risky-choice framing, with pronounced framing effects under holistic processing and no framing effects when analytic processing was induced. Thus, both manipulated hemispheric activation and naturally occurring differences provide converging evidence of the role of processing style on risky-choice framing effects.

HOW PHYSIOLOGICAL MEASURES CAN COMPLEMENT BEHAVIORAL MEASURES IN TESTING THEORIES OF DECISION MAKING

The following examples also illustrate how the use of framing tasks in conjunction with physiological/biological indicators can help us understand and refine our theories about decision processes. Traced back to the early work of Kahneman and Tversky (1979), prospect theory represents a psychophysical approach to describing rational choice; yet at its core, the approach maintains a theoretical basis that is consistent with traditional approaches to decision making. The traditional approach assumes that decision makers mathematically combine quantitative information by transposing numerical amounts and probabilities into some quantitative value or utility that is then compared and contrasted across alternatives. This assumption has its foundation in some of the earliest beginnings of rational decision making (Bernoulli, 1738/1954) and during its formative stages (e.g., Edwards, 1954).

The more recent fuzzy trace theory (Reyna, 2012; Reyna & Brainerd, 2011), like earlier dual process theories, involves two complementary styles that can lead decision makers to different choice preferences. However, fuzzy trace theory differs from prospect theory and other decision-making theories first and foremost because under most decision-making conditions it does not take a quantitative transformation approach. Rather, fuzzy trace theory is a dual process, memory-based theory in which one memory system involves precise, verbatim representations of information and extracts a level of detail critical for more analytic comparisons. The other memory system extracts only vague "fuzzy" impressions but is the source of meaning and captures generalized "gist" appeal that directs an intuitive inclination toward an alternative. These two memory systems operate in parallel fashion, each individually extracting representations from a target stimulus and then encoding and storing the information independently. The end result for decision making is that these functionally independent memory systems often lead people to different choice preferences.

According to fuzzy trace theory, adults normally process in as fuzzy and impressionistic a way as is reasonable, and consequently they normally make decisions using only vague representations that capture the gist of the task's information. Thus, in gist processing, numeric information is extracted in a very simplified form and precise quantities are often neglected. For example, 33% might be extracted as "some," 67% as "most," and 0% as "none." As a consequence of this processing style, alternatives are perceived in an ordinal gist and individuals are directed by a sense of "intuition" toward the alternative with the greatest extracted value. Applying this to framing effects, in the positive framing condition of the Asian disease problem, saving some lives is more attractive than taking a chance that no lives will be saved, and in the negative condition, losing some lives is less attractive than having a chance of losing no lives. Likewise, in the ground beef attribute framing problem, "fat" is less desirable than "lean."

Recently, a good deal of research has set out to test fuzzy trace theory with prospect theory and other utility models. A means for testing these theories has emerged that involves the importance of presenting "0" (null) information to the decision maker. Because prospect theory and other standard utility models rely on a numerical transformation of the information, the presence or absence of the zero complement (e.g., 2/3 chance of saving no lives) should be irrelevant because the quantitative value of the alternative (1/3 chance of saving all 600) does not change with its presence. However, in fuzzy trace theory, null information is vital in gist processing as it represents a basic categorical distinction that the decision maker will use for comparison.

For example, in gist processing the alternative "1/3 chance of saving all 600 lives and a 2/3 chance of saving no lives" should be encoded as "some people saved and none saved," which creates a strikingly different representation than when the zero complement is removed resulting in "some saved." Kühberger and Tanner (2010) tested this theoretical assumption by manipulating whether participants had access to the zero complement. Kühberger and Tanner found that framing effects were present when the zero complement was presented but were not observed when the zero complement was removed, and thus supported fuzzy trace theory assumptions.

In a recent study, McElroy, Dickinson, Corbin, and Beck (2013) used eye-tracking technology during a risky-choice task to test the more quantitative processing approach of prospect theory and the memory-based processing of fuzzy trace theory. Eye-tracking technology allows comparative analysis of discrete eye movements and can measure gaze duration, thus allowing researchers to operationalize "processing" by associating inward cognitive processing with observational differences in eye gaze duration. McElroy et al. hypothesized that because of prospect theory's traditional decision-making approach, numerical transformation of the quantitative information determines value, and no difference in gaze duration should be observed between those who demonstrate a risky-choice framing effect and those who do not. Conversely, because zero-complement information is so important in gist processing, they predicted from fuzzy trace theory that gaze duration of the zero complement (i.e., the amount of time the pupil rests on the null information) should be greater for those who demonstrate risky-choice framing effects.

McElroy et al.'s (2013) findings were consistent with fuzzy trace theory in the losses condition where participants who demonstrated framing effects had significantly longer gaze duration for the zero complement. However, in the gains condition no significant differences were observed, suggesting that the gains condition may lack sufficient intensity. This is consistent with the special role of loss aversion (Weller et al., 2009). Thus, in this example eye-tracking technology is used to corroborate behavioral data and show how physiological techniques and behavioral data can complement one another. Furthermore, it shows how processing differences underlie risky-choice framing effects.

DECISION MAKING IN OLDER ADULTS

For the closing sections of this chapter, we turn to a basic biological process—aging—and its relation to decision making in framing and other neuroeconomic tasks. Studies of the life-span trajectory of brain functions provide insight into age-related differences in decision making, which, in turn, are associated with changes in the brain. Much of this research has focused on the early preadulthood ages when incomplete maturation of some brain regions leads to decision-making deficits. For example, functional maturation of the prefrontal cortex has been shown to be protracted compared with the development of subcortical reward-processing structures, and this limits top-down control processes in the processing of fear and reward signals (Casey, Giedd, & Thomas, 2000; Crone & van der Molen, 2004; Galvan et al., 2006; Hare & Casey, 2005). The result is often inappropriate risk taking at the younger ages. These findings suggest a neurobiological basis for age-related differences in decision making.

At the other end of the spectrum, there is growing support for the frontal lobe hypothesis of aging (Brown & Park, 2003; Pardo et al., 2007; Resnick, Pham, Kraut, Zonderman, & Davatzikos, 2003; West, 1996, 2000) whereby age-related structural declines in the prefrontal cortex, particularly the orbitofrontal and lateral prefrontal cortices, lead to declines in executive functioning tasks in the elderly that are mediated by frontal lobe functioning (West, Murphy, Armillo, Craik, & Stuss, 2002). However, results are not always clear-cut as to when older adults do and do not exhibit decision deficits.

Some researchers have found that older adults were less sensitive to risk level than younger adults (Deakin, Aitken, Robbins, & Shahakian, 2004; Denburg, Tranel, & Bechara, 2005; Weller, Levin, & Denburg, 2011), but other researchers have found that older adults performed as well as younger adults on risky decision-making tasks (Kovalchik, Camerer, Grether, Plott, & Allman, 2005; Wood, Busemeyer, Kolings, Cox, & Davis, 2005). Bruine de Bruin, Parker, and Fischhoff (2012) explained some of these mixed results by showing that some decision-making skills decline with age while others remain unchanged or improve. One theme of the current chapter is that the net effect of this age-related mixture of skill levels depends on task demands.

In studying age-related differences in decision making, Weller et al. (2011) used a relatively new task, the cups task (Levin & Hart, 2003), designed to mimic the risky-choice framing task but with actual gains and losses. Analogous to the separate gain- and loss-framed versions of the risky-choice framing task, the cups task includes separate trials involving risky gains and risky losses. Because of its economic consequences and its potential usefulness in scanner research, the cups task is ideally suited for neuroeconomic research.

Gain trials require the choice between an option that offers a sure gain of one quarter and another option that offers a designated probability of winning multiple quarters or no quarters, where probability information is conveyed simply by the number of cups from which to choose. This property allows the task to be administered to all age groups. Loss trials require the choice between a sure loss of one quarter and a designated probability of losing multiple quarters or no quarters.

On each trial an array of two, three, or five cups is shown on each side of a computer screen. One array is identified as the certain or riskless side where one quarter would be gained (lost) for whichever cup was selected. The other array is designated as the risky side where the selection of one cup would lead to a designated number of quarters gained (lost) and the other cups would lead to no gain (loss). Participants select one cup from either the riskless or the risky side. By manipulating the number of cups from which to choose and the possible outcome magnitude, some trials represent "risk advantageous" choices because the expected value of a risky choice is more favorable than the sure gain or loss (e.g., one out of three chances of winning five quarters vs. winning one quarter for sure, or one out of five chances of losing three quarters vs. losing one quarter for sure). Conversely, other trials are "risk disadvantageous" because the expected value of a risky choice is less favorable than the sure gain or loss (e.g., one out of five chances of winning three quarters, or one out of three chances of losing five quarters).

These design features allow for comparisons across age groups of overall risk taking to achieve gains or avoid losses and of the tendency to make risk-advantageous or -disadvantageous choices for risky gains and losses. Overall level of risk taking to achieve gains was shown to decrease steadily across the life span, while risk seeking to avoid a loss was remarkably constant across age levels, a result attributed to the pervasiveness of loss aversion (Weller et al., 2011). All but the youngest groups showed the classic risky-choice framing effect of more risk taking to avoid a loss than to achieve a gain of the same magnitude. More interestingly, age-related differences were found in the tendency to make risk-advantageous/disadvantageous choices. The difference in the number of risk-advantageous and risk-disadvantageous choices increased from childhood through young and middle adulthood but decreased for those 65 years and older. This demonstrates that the sensitivity to risk-relevant information decreases in older adults in a manner consistent with the frontal lobe hypothesis.

FRAMING EFFECTS FOR "IMPAIRED" AND "UNIMPAIRED" OLDER DECISION MAKERS

The goal of this line of research is to identify when older adults do and do not display impaired decision making and to identify the neurological correlates. Earlier we showed that emotion suppression was associated with reduced attribute framing effects. Another task in which emotional involvement plays a key role is the Iowa Gambling Task (IGT; Bechara, 2007; Bechara, Damasio, Tranel, & Damasio, 1997). Because of its wide use with brain-damaged patients and in scanner research, the IGT has perhaps become the prototypical "neuroscience" task. Successful performance on the most widely used version of this task requires the avoidance of choices providing immediate reward but larger subsequent losses. In a recent study using this task, Bauer et al. (2013) found age-related deficits in performance consistent with the notion that decisions by older persons are disproportionately influenced by prospects of receiving rewards, irrespective of the degree of punishment.

Participants are asked to select cards from four different decks, each with its own distribution of gains and losses. No information about differences between decks is given ahead of time, and participants have to learn from repeated trials which are the two "good" decks and which are the two "bad" decks. Repeated sampling from the two good decks will lead to greater gains than losses in the long run, whereas sampling from the bad decks, while offering initial gains, will lead to greater losses than gains in the long run. Bechara, Damasio, Damasio, & Anderson (1994) and Bechara et al. (1997) showed that patients with lesions to the vmPFC were unable to learn in this task because the activation of brain mechanisms that signal potential loss based on prior experiences was dampened.

In a current preliminary study of IGT impairment and framing effects in older decision makers (Hedgcock, Denburg, Levin, & Halfmann, 2012), adults over age 65 were administered both the IGT and the framing problems. They were classified as "unimpaired" ($n = 16$) if they selected significantly more cards from the good decks than from the bad decks or as "impaired" ($n = 16$) if they selected significantly more cards from the bad decks than the good decks. ("Unimpaired" older adults are indistinguishable from healthy young adults on the IGT.) Functional magnetic resonance imaging (fMRI) activation patterns were examined as a function of IGT score and type of framing effect. The difference between brain activation for the positive and negative versions of each type of framing manipulation was correlated with IGT score. This allowed us to determine which parts of the brain were most sensitive to individual differences in performing the two types of framing problems.

For attribute framing difference scores, IGT scores correlated with activity in cortical midline structures including the vmPFC, the dorsomedial prefrontal cortex, and the anterior cingulate cortex. Of particular interest, the vmPFC has been implicated in processing emotional stimuli (Damasio, 1994; Northoff & Bermpohl, 2004). (See, however, Huettel's 2010 cautionary note that some brain regions can be labeled as making cognitive or emotional contributions in different contexts.) Perhaps even more important, these areas have been implicated in age-related declines. Pardo et al. (2007) found that the largest declines in brain activity with normal aging were localized in a medial network including the anterior cingulate/medial prefrontal cortex. The only area associated with risky-choice framing in the present study was the parietal cortex.

These results provide evidence, backed by earlier reports in this chapter, that attribute framing and risky-choice framing are different in the extent to which they evoke emotional processing. Furthermore, this work shows that different levels of emotional processing can help or hurt rational decision making depending on task demands. Finally, they help explain why the aging process can simultaneously hurt performance on some tasks but improve performance on others as structural changes in the brain influence response to cues that are sometimes relevant and sometimes not.

SUMMARY, CONCLUSIONS, AND FUTURE RESEARCH

In this chapter, we focused on framing effects to help readers understand neuroeconomic processes for several reasons:

- framing effects represent a well-known decision bias with important real-world consequences
- framing effects have a long history of basic research in behavioral decision making and a shorter, but growing, history of research in decision neuroscience and neuroeconomics
- framing effects are not an isolated phenomenon but are tied to broader principles such as loss aversion or risk aversion
- the simplicity of tasks that demonstrate framing effects allows for use with populations ranging from young children to the elderly and persons with known decision impairments
- they can easily be studied using technologically current methods such as brain scanning or eye tracking as well as in the traditional laboratory or online setting.

New features illustrated in the applications sampled here include the identification of distinct types of framing effects with a different balance of cognitive processing and emotional involvement. This then allows the different paradigms to be used to address issues of broader scope, such as age-related changes in the balance of skills that lead to impaired decision making on some tasks but not on others. Another important feature is that with proper experimental design features, framing effects can be studied not just in the aggregate but at the level of the individual decision maker. This allowed us, for example, to show which areas of the brain are differentially activated as a function of the size of the framing effect displayed by different decision makers.

The evidence provided about the concordance of biological and behavioral factors associated with the circadian rhythm cycle came from the use of a risky-choice framing task administered at different points in the cycle. Susceptibility to risky-choice framing effects was significantly greater during circadian off-times than during circadian on-times and this was related to the actions of an area deep in the brain, the SCN, which governs glucose level and metabolic activity, a physiological correlate of effort. Equally insightful was the revelation that circadian cycle had no impact on attribute framing, a finding supporting our hypothesis of different processes for attribute and risky-choice framing.

Related findings were that eye-fixation patterns were predictive of the presence versus absence of risky-choice framing effects and that right-hemispheric versus left-hemispheric processing was also related to risky-choice framing effects, each result being indicative of variations in cognitive processing. The important point for the present purposes is that these demonstrations of the relation between brain functions and behavior using a framing paradigm serve as a tool for understanding such relations. McElroy et al. (2013) were able to use their measure of gaze duration to assess the dual processing assumptions of fuzzy trace theory.

In a similar vein, the emotion suppression study revealed that the two types of framing manipulations—attribute framing and risky-choice framing—do in fact call into play fundamentally different forms of decision making. Attribute framing appears to involve a purer form of emotionally driven choice, similar to System 1 processing, whereas risky-choice framing involves more deliberative analysis, similar to System 2 processing. This was confirmed in an fMRI study in which attribute framing was more closely linked to activation of brain areas associated with the emotional system than was risky-choice framing. These results then provide impetus for using this imbalance to target specific populations, in this case the older decision maker, whose decision making in different domains is likely affected by varying levels of specific functions. The fMRI study with older adults not only affirmed the relation between types of framing and differential activation of brain systems but also showed that those systems exhibiting age-related declines can sometimes lead to impaired performance, such as on the IGT where learning from past errors is key, but can sometimes lead to improved performance, such as resistance to the emotional lure of attribute framing.

The illustrations focusing on framing effects in this chapter provide only a thin slice of the fascinating phenomena revealed in a systematic study of the neuroscience of human judgment and decision making. One suggestion we have for future researchers is to not consider framing effects as a unified concept but to specify how they are operationalized in ways that can account for different results in different studies. It is our hope that the key features illustrated here will serve future researchers investigating other phenomena that separate normatively rational behavior from the reality of the human experience. Among these features are the use of brain imaging, eye-tracking, and other biological measures to complement traditional behavioral measures;

inclusion of both variables manipulated in the laboratory and individual difference factors that account for why you and I make different decisions, particularly as these individual differences interact with task demands; and, finally, strategic selection of participant populations with distinctive characteristics to provide tests of theories as well as applications of those theories.

REFERENCES

Bauer, A. S., Timpe, J. C., Edmonds, E. C., Bechara, A., Tranel, D., & Denburg, N. L. (2013). Myopia for the future or hyposensitivity to reward? Age-related changes in decision making on the Iowa Gambling Task. *Emotion, 13*(1), 19–24. doi:10.1037/a0029970

Bechara, A. (2007). *Iowa Gambling Task (IGT) professional manual.* Lutz, FL: Psychological Assessment Resources.

Bechara, A., Damasio, A. R., Damasio, H., & Anderson, S. W. (1994). Insensitivity to future consequences following damage to human prefrontal cortex. *Cognition, 50,* 7–15. doi:10.1016/0010-0277(94)90018-3

Bechara, A., Damasio, H., Tranel, D., & Damasio, A. R. (1997). Deciding advantageously before knowing the advantageous strategy. *Science, 275,* 1293–1295. doi:10.1126/science.275.5304.1293

Bernoulli, D. (1954). Exposition of a new theory on the measurement of risk. *Econometrica, 22,* 23–36. (Original work published 1738)

Bodenhausen, G. Y. (1990). Stereotypes as judgmental heuristics: Evidence of circadian variations in discrimination. *Psychological Science, 1,* 319–322. doi:10.1111/j.1467-9280.1990.tb00226.x

Braun, K. A., Gaeth, G. J., & Levin, I. P. (1997). Framing effects with differential impact: The role of attribute salience. In M. Brucks & D. J. Mac Innis (Eds.), *Advances in consumer research, Vol. 24* (pp. 405–411). Provo, UT: Association for Consumer Research.

Brown, S. C., & Park, D. C. (2003). Theoretical models of cognitive aging and implications for translational research. *The Gerontologist, 43,* 57–67. doi:10.1093/geront/43.suppl_1.57

Bruine de Bruin, W., Parker, A. M., & Fischhoff, B. (2007). Individual differences in adult decision-making competence. *Journal of Personality and Social Psychology, 92,* 938–956. doi:10.1037/0022-3514.92.5.938

Bruine de Bruin, W., Parker, A. M., & Fischhoff, B. (2012). Explaining adult age differences in decision-making competence. *Journal of Behavioral Decision Making, 25,* 352–360. doi:10.1002/bdm.712

Casey, B. J., Giedd, J. N., & Thomas, K. M. (2000). Structural and functional brain development and its relation to cognitive development. *Biological Psychology, 54,* 241–257. doi:10.1016/S0301-0511(00)00058-2

Christman, S. D., Jasper, J. D., Sontam, V., & Cooil, B. (2007). Individual differences in risk perception versus risk taking: Handedness and interhemispheric interaction. *Brain and Cognition, 63*, 51–58. doi:10.1016/j.bandc.2006.08.001

Crone, E. A., & van der Molen, M. W. (2004). Developmental changes in real life decision making: Performance on a gambling task previously shown to depend on the ventromedial prefrontal cortex. *Developmental Neuropsychology, 25*, 251–279. doi:10.1207/s15326942dn2503_2

Damasio, A. R. (1994). *Descartes' error: Emotion, reason, and the human brain*. New York, NY: Putnam.

Deakin, J., Aitken, M., Robbins, T., & Sahakian, B. J. (2004). Risk taking during decision-making in normal volunteers changes with age. *Journal of the International Neuropsychological Society, 10*, 590–598. doi:10.1017/S1355617704104104

De Martino, B., Kumaran, D., Seymour, B., & Dolan, R. J. (2006). Frames, biases, and rational decision-making in the human brain. *Science, 313*, 684–687. doi:10.1126/science.1128356

Denburg, N. L., Tranel, D., & Bechara, A. (2005). The ability to decide advantageously declines in some normal older persons. *Neuropsychologia, 43*, 1099–1106. doi:10.1016/j.neuropsychologia.2004.09.012

Diamond, W. D., & Sanyal, A. (1990). The effect of frame on the choice of supermarket coupons. *Advances in Consumer Research. Association for Consumer Research (U.S.), 17*, 488–493.

Dickinson, D. L., & McElroy, T. (2010). Rationality around the clock: Sleep and time-of-day effects on guessing game responses. *Economic Letter, 108*, 245–248.

Dickinson, D. L., & McElroy, T. (2012). Circadian effects on strategic reasoning. *Experimental Economics, 15*, 444–459. doi:10.1007/s10683-011-9307-3

Edwards, W. (1954). The theory of decision making. *Psychological Bulletin, 51*, 380–417. doi:10.1037/h0053870

Epstein, S., Lipson, A., Holstein, C., & Huh, E. (1992). Irrational reactions to negative outcomes: Evidence for two conceptual systems. *Journal of Personality and Social Psychology, 62*, 328–339. doi:10.1037/0022-3514.62.2.328

Galvan, A., Hare, T. A., Parra, C. E., Penn, J., Voss, H., Glover, G., & Casey, B. J. (2006). Earlier development of the accumbens relative to orbitofrontal cortex might underlie risk taking behavior in adolescents. *The Journal of Neuroscience, 26*, 6885–6892. doi:10.1523/JNEUROSCI.1062-06.2006

Gamliel, E., & Peer, E. (2006). Positive versus negative framing affects justice judgments. *Social Justice Research, 19*, 307–322. doi:10.1007/s11211-006-0009-5

Gamliel, E., & Peer, E. (2010). Attribute framing affects the perceived fairness of allocation principles. *Judgment and Decision Making, 5*, 11–20.

Gilbert, D. T. (1991). How mental systems believe. *American Psychologist, 46*, 107–119. doi:10.1037/0003-066X.46.2.107

Gross, J. J., & Levenson, R. W. (1993). Emotion suppression: Physiology, self-report, and expressive behavior. *Journal of Personality and Social Psychology, 64*, 970–986. doi:10.1037/0022-3514.64.6.970

Hare, T. A., & Casey, B. J. (2005). The neurobiology and development of cognitive and affective control. *Cognition, Brain, & Behavior, 3*, 273–286.

Hasher, L., & Zacks, R. T. (1988). Working memory, comprehension, and aging: A review and a new view. *Psychology of Learning and Motivation, 22*, 193–225. doi:10.1016/S0079-7421(08)60041-9

Hedgcock, W., Denburg, N., Levin, I. P., & Halfmann, K. (2012, November). *Why older adults are impaired on some decision making tasks but not on others—Behavioral and neuroimaging evidence*. Paper presented at the Annual Meeting of the Society for Judgment and Decision Making, Minneapolis, MN.

Huettel, S. A. (2010). Ten challenges for decision neuroscience. *Frontiers in Decision Neuroscience, 4*(171), 1–7. doi:10.3389/fnins.2010.00171

Huettel, S. A., Stowe, C. J., Gordon, E. M., Warner, B. T., & Platt, M. L. (2006). Neural signatures of economic preferences for risk and ambiguity. *Neuron, 49*, 765–775. doi:10.1016/j.neuron.2006.01.024

Jasper, J., & Christman, S. (2005). A neuropsychological dimension for anchoring effects. *Journal of Behavioral Decision Making, 18*, 343–369. doi:10.1002/bdm.511

Jasper, J. D., Barry, K., & Christman, S. D. (2008). Individual differences in counterfactual production. *Personality and Individual Differences, 45*, 488–492. doi:10.1016/j.paid.2008.05.026

Jasper, J. D., Fournier, C., & Christman, S.D. (2013). Handedness differences in information framing. Manuscript under review.

Jasper, J. D., Goel, R., Einarson, A., Gallo, M., & Koren, G. (2001). Effects of framing on teratogenic risk perception in pregnant women. *The Lancet, 358*, 1237–1238. doi:10.1016/S0140-6736(01)06353-X

Kahneman, D. (2003). Perspective on judgment and choice: Mapping bounded rationality. *American Psychologist, 58*, 697–720. doi:10.1037/0003-066X.58.9.697

Kahneman, D. (2011). *Thinking, fast and slow*. New York, NY: Farrer, Straus and Giroux.

Kahneman, D., & Frederick, S. (2002). Representativeness revisited: Attribute substitution in intuitive judgment. In T. Gilovich, D. Griffin, & D. Kahneman (Eds.), *Heuristics & biases: The psychology of intuitive judgment* (pp.548–558). New York, NY: Cambridge University Press. doi:10.1017/CBO9780511808098.004

Kahneman, D., & Tversky, A. (1979). Prospect theory–Analysis of decision under risk. *Econometrica, 47*, 263–291. doi:10.2307/1914185

Kovalchik, S., Camerer, C. F., Grether, D. M., Plott, C. R., & Allman, J. M. (2005). Aging and decision making: A comparison between neurologically healthy elderly and young individuals. *Journal of Economic Behavior & Organization, 58*, 79–94. doi:10.1016/j.jebo.2003.12.001

Kühberger, A. (1998). The influence of framing on risky decisions: A meta-analysis. *Organizational Behavior and Human Decision Processes, 75*, 23–55. doi:10.1006/obhd.1998.2781

Kühberger, A., & Tanner, C. (2010). Risky choice framing: Task versions and a comparison of prospect theory and fuzzy-trace theory. *Journal of Behavioral Decision Making, 23*, 314–329. doi:10.1002/bdm.656

Kuhnen, C. M., & Knutson, B. (2005). The neural basis of financial risk taking. *Neuron, 47*, 763–770. doi:10.1016/j.neuron.2005.08.008

La Fleur, S. E. (2003). Daily rhythms in glucose metabolism. Suprachiasmatic nucleus output to peripheral tissue. *Journal of Neuroendocrinology, 15*, 315–322. doi:10.1046/j.1365-2826.2003.01019.x

Lauriola, M., & Levin, I. P. (2001). Personality traits and risky decision making in a controlled experimental task: An exploratory study. *Personality and Individual Differences, 31*, 215–226. doi:10.1016/S0191-8869(00)00130-6

LeDoux, J. E. (2000). Emotion circuits in the brain. *Annual Review of Neuroscience, 2*, 155–184. doi:10.1146/annurev.neuro.23.1.155

Levin, I. P. (1987). Associative effects of information framing. *Bulletin of the Psychonomic Society, 25*, 85–86.

Levin, I. P. (1999). *Why do you and I make difference decisions? Tracking individual differences in decision making*. Los Angeles, CA: Presidential Address for Society for Judgment and Decision Making. doi:10.1037/e683312011-044

Levin, I. P., & Gaeth, G. J. (1988). How consumers are affected by the framing of attribute information before and after consuming the product. *Journal of Consumer Research, 15*, 374–378. doi:10.1086/209174

Levin, I. P., Gaeth, G. J., Schreiber, J., & Lauriola, M. (2002). A new look at framing effects: Distribution of effect sizes, individual differences, and independence of types of effects. *Organizational Behavior and Human Decision Processes, 88*, 411–429. doi:10.1006/obhd.2001.2983

Levin, I. P., Gui, X., Weller, J. A., Reimann, M., Lauriola, M., & Bechara, A. (2012). A neuropsychological approach to understanding risk-taking for potential gains and losses. *Frontiers in Decision Neuroscience, 6*(15). doi:10.3389/fnins.2012.00015

Levin, I. P., & Hart, S. S. (2003). Risk preferences in young children: Early evidence of individual differences in reaction to potential gains and losses. *Journal of Behavioral Decision Making, 16*, 397–413. doi:10.1002/bdm.453

Levin, I. P., Schneider, S. L., & Gaeth, G. J. (1998). All frames are not created equal: A typology and critical analysis of framing effects. *Organizational Behavior and Human Decision Processes, 76*, 149–188. doi:10.1006/obhd.1998.2804

Mahoney, K. T., Buboltz, W., Levin, I. P., Doverspike, D., & Svyantek, D. J. (2011). Individual differences in a within-subjects risky-choice framing study. *Personality and Individual Differences, 51*, 248–257. doi:10.1016/j.paid.2010.03.035

Manly, T., Lewis, G. H., Robertson, I. H., Watson, P. C., & Datta, A. K. (2002). Coffee in the cornflakes: Time of day as a modulator of executive response control. *Neuropsychologia, 40*, 1–6. doi:10.1016/S0028-3932(01)00086-0

Masicampo, E. J., & Baumeister, R. F. (2008). Toward a physiology of dual-process reasoning and judgment: Lemonade, willpower, and expensive rule-based analysis. *Psychological Science, 19*, 255–260. doi:10.1111/j.1467-9280.2008.02077.x

McElroy, T., Dickinson, C., Corbin, J., & Beck, H. (2013). Tracking risky decisions: Comparing fuzzy-trace theory and prospect theory through eye-tracking. Manuscript submitted for publication.

McElroy, T., & Dickinson, D. L. (2010). Thoughtful days and valenced nights: How much will you think about the problem? *Judgment and Decision Making, 5*, 516–523.

McElroy, T., & Seta, J. (2003). Framing effect: An analytic-holistic perspective. *Journal of Experimental Social Psychology, 39*, 610–617. doi:10.1016/S0022-1031(03)00036-2

McElroy, T., & Seta, J. (2004). On the other hand am I rational? Hemispheric activation and the framing effect. *Brain and Cognition, 55*, 572–580. doi:10.1016/j.bandc.2004.04.002

McMahon, A. J., & Scheel, M. H. (2010). Glucose promotes controlled processing: Matching, maximizing, and root beer. *Judgment and Decision Making, 5*, 450–457.

McNeil, B. J., Pauker, S. G., Sox, H. C., & Tversky, A. (1982). On the elicitation of preferences for alternative therapies. *The New England Journal of Medicine, 306*, 1259–1262. doi:10.1056/NEJM198205273062103

Northoff, G., & Bermpohl, F. (2004). Cortical midline structures and the self. *Trends in Cognitive Sciences, 8*, 102–107. doi:10.1016/j.tics.2004.01.004

Ornstein, R. E. (1972). *The psychology of consciousness*. San Francisco, CA: Freeman.

Pardo, J. V., Lee, J. T., Sheikh, S. A., Surerus-Johnson, C., Shah, H., Munch, K. R., . . . Dysken, M. W. (2007). Where the brain grows old: Decline in anterior cingulate and medial prefrontal function with normal aging. *NeuroImage, 35*, 1231–1237. doi:10.1016/j.neuroimage.2006.12.044

Parker, A. M., & Fischhoff, B. (2005). Decision-making competence: External validation through an individual-differences approach. *Journal of Behavioral Decision Making, 18*, 1–27. doi:10.1002/bdm.481

Payne, J. W., Sagara, N., Shu, S. B., Appelt, K. C., & Johnson, E. J. (2012). Life expectancy as a constructed belief: Evidence of a live-to or die-by framing effect. Columbia Business School Research Paper No. 12-10l. doi:10.2139/ssrn.1987618

Peters, E., & Levin, I. P. (2008). Dissecting the risky-choice framing effect: Numeracy as an individual difference factor in weighting risky and riskless options. *Judgment and Decision Making, 3*, 435–448.

Phelps, E. A. (2006). Emotion and cognition: Insights from studies of the human amygdala. *Annual Review of Psychology, 57*, 27–53. doi:10.1146/annurev.psych.56.091103.070234

Ralph, M. R., Foster, R. G., Davis, F. C., & Menaker, M. (1990). Transplanted suprachiasmatic nucleus determines circadian period. *Science*, *247*, 975–978. doi:10.1126/science.2305266

Resnick, S. M., Pham, D. L., Kraut, M. A., Zonderman, A. B., & Davatzikos, C. (2003). Longitudinal magnetic resonance imaging studies of older adults: A shrinking brain. *The Journal of Neuroscience*, *23*, 3295–3301.

Reyna, V. F. (2012). A new intuitionism: Meaning, memory, and development in fuzzy-trace theory. *Judgment and Decision Making*, *7*, 332–359.

Reyna, V. F., & Brainerd, C. J. (1991). Fuzzy-trace theory and framing effects in choice: Gist extraction, truncation, and conversion. *Journal of Behavioral Decision Making*, *4*, 249–262. doi:10.1002/bdm.3960040403

Reyna, V. F., & Brainerd, C. J. (2011). Dual processes in decision making and developmental neuroscience: A fuzzy-trace model. *Developmental Review*, *31*, 180–206.

Sanfey, A. G., Rilling, J. K., Aronson, J. A., Nystrom, L. E., & Cohen, J. D. (2003). The neural basis of economic decision-making in the Ultimatum Game. *Science*, *300*, 1755–1758. doi:10.1126/science.1082976

Schmidt, C., Collette, F., Cajochen, C., & Peigneux, P. (2007). A time to think: Circadian rhythms in human cognition. *Cognitive Neuropsychology*, *24*, 755–789. doi:10.1080/02643290701754158

Shiffrin, R. M., & Schneider, W. (1977). Controlled and automatic information processing: II. Perceptual learning, automatic attending, and a general theory. *Psychological Review*, *84*, 127–190. doi:10.1037/0033-295X.84.2.127

Simon, A. F., Fagley, N. S., & Halleran, J. G. (2004). Decision framing: Moderating effects of individual differences and cognitive processing. *Journal of Behavioral Decision Making*, *17*, 77–93. doi:10.1002/bdm.463

Sloman, S. A. (1996). The empirical case for two systems of reasoning. *Psychological Bulletin*, *119*, 3–22. doi:10.1037/0033-2909.119.1.3

Smith, S. M., & Levin, I. P. (1996). Need for cognition and choice framing effects. *Journal of Behavioral Decision Making*, *9*, 283–290. doi:10.1002/(SICI)1099-0771(199612)9:4<283::AID-BDM241>3.0.CO;2-7

Stanovich, K. E. (1999). *Who is rational? Studies of individual differences in reasoning*. Mahwah, NJ: Erlbaum.

Stanovich, K. E., & West, R. F. (1998a). Cognitive ability and variation in selection task performance. *Thinking & Reasoning*, *4*, 193–230. doi:10.1080/135467898394139

Stanovich, K. E., & West, R. F. (1998b). Individual differences in rational thought. *Journal of Experimental Psychology: General*, *127*, 161–188. doi:10.1037/0096-3445.127.2.161

Stanovich, K. E., & West, R. F. (2000). Individual differences in reasoning: Implications for the rationality debate? *Behavioral and Brain Sciences*, *23*, 645–665. doi:10.1017/S0140525X00003435

Tom, S. M., Fox, C. R., Trepel, C., & Poldrack, R. A. (2007). The neural basis of loss aversion in decision-making under risk. *Science, 315*, 515–518. doi:10.1126/science.1134239

Trepel, C., Fox, C. R., & Poldrack, R. A. (2005). Prospect theory on the brain? Toward a cognitive neuroscience of decisions under risk. *Cognitive Brain Research, 23*, 34–50. doi:10.1016/j.cogbrainres.2005.01.016

Tversky, A., & Kahneman, D. (1981). The framing of decisions and the psychology of choice. *Science, 211*, 453–458. doi:10.1126/science.7455683

Tversky, A., & Kahneman, D. (1992). Advances in prospect theory: Cumulative representation of uncertainty. *Journal of Risk and Uncertainty, 5*, 297–323. doi:10.1007/BF00122574

Wang, X. T., & Dvorak, R. D. (2010). Sweet future: Fluctuating blood glucose levels affect future discounting. *Psychological Science, 21*, 183–188. doi:10.1177/0956797609358096

Weller, J. A., Levin, I. P., & Denburg, N. L. (2011). Trajectory of risky decision making for potential gains and losses from ages 5 to 85. *Journal of Behavioral Decision Making, 24*, 331–344. doi:10.1002/bdm.690

Weller, J. A., Levin, I. P., Rose, J., & Bossard, E. (2012). Assessment of decision-making competence in preadolescence. *Journal of Behavioral Decision Making, 25*, 414–426. doi:10.1002/bdm.744

Weller, J. A., Levin, I. P., Shiv, B., & Bechara, A. (2007). Neural correlates of adaptive decision making in risky gains and losses. *Psychological Science, 18*, 958–964. doi:10.1111/j.1467-9280.2007.02009.x

Weller, J. A., Levin, I. P., Shiv, B., & Bechara, A. (2009). The effects of insula damage on decision-making for risky gains and losses. *Social Neuroscience, 4*, 347–358. doi:10.1080/17470910902934400

West, R. (2000). In defense of the frontal lobe hypothesis of cognitive aging. *Journal of the International Neuropsychological Society, 6*, 727–729. doi:10.1017/S1355617700666109

West, R., Murphy, K. J., Armillo, M. L., Craik, F. I. M., & Stuss, D. (2002). Lapses of intention and performance variability reveal age-related increases in fluctuations of executive control. *Brain and Cognition, 49*, 402–419. doi:10.1006/brcg.2001.1507

West, R. L. (1996). An application of prefrontal cortex function theory to cognitive aging. *Psychological Bulletin, 120*, 272–292. doi:10.1037/0033-2909.120.2.272

Wood, S., Busemeyer, J., Kolings, A., Cox, C. R., & Davis, H. (2005). Older adults as adaptive decision makers: Evidence from the Iowa Gambling Task. *Psychology and Aging, 20*, 220–225. doi:10.1037/0882-7974.20.2.220

II

NEURODEVELOPMENT

3

RISKS, REWARDS, AND THE DEVELOPING BRAIN IN CHILDHOOD AND ADOLESCENCE

BARBARA R. BRAAMS, LINDA VAN LEIJENHORST, AND EVELINE A. CRONE

Childhood and adolescence are a time of changes in the physical, cognitive, and social–emotional domains. Behaviorally, one of the prominent features of adolescence is an increase in risk taking. In this chapter, we review current theories and research to explain risk-taking behavior from a neural perspective. After a general introduction, we lay out behavioral findings focusing on risk taking, then describe current models of adolescent brain development that provide possible explanations for the observed risk taking. Next, we describe neuroimaging research and how the findings map to the models. Finally, we propose new directions for future research.

Adolescence, defined as the transition phase between childhood and adulthood, is a time of many physical, cognitive, and social–emotional changes. It is a natural time of exploring, thrill seeking, and eventually setting long-term goals and aspirations (Dahl, 2004; Steinberg, 2008b). The first phase of adolescence (also defined as early to middle adolescence) starts with the onset

http://dx.doi.org/10.1037/14322-004
The Neuroscience of Risky Decision Making, by V. F. Reyna and V. Zayas (Editors)

of pubertal maturation around the age of 10 to 11 years (but approximately 1.5 years earlier for girls than for boys) and lasts until approximately ages 15 to 16 (Shirtcliff, Dahl, & Pollak, 2009). At the onset of puberty, a dramatic increase in the secretion of adrenal androgens, gonadal steroids, and growth hormone causes many changes in physical appearance (e.g., facial and physical changes) and in brain regions with high receptor density for gonadal hormones such as testosterone and estradiol (Scherf, Berman, & Dahl, 2012). Following pubertal maturation (Op de Macks et al., 2011), the second phase of adolescence (also defined as middle to late adolescence) lasts from approximately ages 15–16 to 21–22 years, during which adolescents gradually reach independence from parents and obtain mature social goals (Steinberg, 2008b; Steinberg & Morris, 2001).

WHY DO ADOLESCENTS TAKE RISKS?

One of the most prominent findings in observational studies (i.e., correlational studies) is that adolescents take more risks than children or adults (Beyth-Marom & Fischhoff, 1997; Boyer, 2006). *Risks* are defined as engagement in behaviors that are associated with potentially negative outcomes. For example, adolescents are more likely to have casual sexual partners, engage in binge drinking, and get into car accidents, and they seem to act without thinking about the long-term consequences of their actions (Eaton et al., 2008; Steinberg, 2008b). In a striking juxtaposition, although adolescents are physically in the best condition of their lives, mortality rates go up by 200% to 300% compared with children (Dahl, 2004). This mortality is primarily due to preventable causes, such as getting involved in accidents; driving under the influence; and engaging in high-risk behaviors under pressure from peers or when with friends, such as driving with friends encourages reckless driving (presumably to show off and impress peers, but the mechanisms are not fully understood; see Steinberg, 2008b).

Yet, as we describe in the next section of this chapter, the behavior observed in the laboratory does not always support the observation of increased risk taking in adolescents' daily lives. Given this, it is perhaps not surprising that programs that teach adolescents to engage in less risky behaviors or teach them the consequences of their actions have doubtful efficacy in the reduction of risk taking (but see Fischhoff, Bruine de Bruin, Parker, Millstein, & Halpern-Felsher, 2010).

We propose that the deficits in risky decision making observed during adolescence are most likely related not only to cognitive immaturities but also to a combination of cognitive, emotional, and social factors (Crone & Dahl, 2012; Steinberg, 2008b). Understanding these factors is of great importance in eventually changing behavior and preventing adverse consequences of risk taking in the future. There is a great need for an integrative approach focusing on contextual influences on behavior, brain maturation, hormonal investigation, and genetic susceptibility to understand this crucial phase in life.

In the present chapter, we argue for such an integrative approach. We start by reviewing the empirical evidence, both from daily, naturalistic settings and controlled laboratory settings, regarding whether adolescents show greater risky behaviors. We next show that approaching the problem from a cognitive neuroscience perspective is a promising way to advance understanding of when adolescents take risks, why they take risks, and who is at risk. We then focus specifically on the neural responses to rewards, covering both reward anticipation and reward processing. These processes seem to show differential developmental trajectories in terms of neural activity, illuminating that brain imaging informs risk-taking understanding in a way that has additive value above behavioral observations only. Finally, we lay out future directions and conclude with a new working model for studying the dynamics of adolescent risk taking.

EVIDENCE FOR INCREASES IN RISK TAKING IN ADOLESCENCE

The ability to identify and avoid immediate and long-term undesirable consequences of actions and avoid excessive risk is one of the key aspects of mature decision making, and its development has been studied by developmental psychologists and developmental cognitive neuroscientists using various approaches. Developmental neuroscience research is influenced most by studies using a cognitive perspective, which tries to explain risk-taking behavior in adolescence by examining the development of decision-making skills. In these studies, risk-taking behavior is defined as the consequence of immature decision-making abilities. Although the epidemiological support for a peak in risky behavior in adolescence (Dahl, 2004; Eaton et al., 2008; Steinberg, 2008a) seems clear, it has been difficult to capture in laboratory research, which poses a challenge for neuroscience studies that take place in a laboratory context.

In most cognitive theories of decision making, decisions are seen as the result of an evaluative process in which both the value of an outcome and the probability with which it will be attained are considered. These concepts are described in terms of the expected value (EV) of choice alternatives. The EV is defined as the multiplication of the value of a possible outcome and the likelihood that that outcome will be obtained. Mature, rational decisions should favor the choice options with the higher EV, and decisions can be defined as risky if these rules are not followed. Adolescents' risky behavior suggests that the evaluative process underlying decisions is immature in this developmental period, and the curvilinear pattern with a peak in risky behavior specific to adolescence suggests that decision-making skills do not improve linearly with development.

However, numerous behavioral experimental studies have found linear patterns of change with development. That is, in several studies children's decisions were more risky than were adolescents' and adults' decisions. Similarly, the ability to take the long-term consequences of choices into account improves from childhood until late adolescence. In addition, several studies suggest that key components of decision making are relatively mature in adolescence. For example, in our lab we used the cake gambling task, in which the demands on learning and working memory are minimized by making outcome values and associated probabilities explicit (van Leijenhorst, Westenberg, & Crone, 2008). Decision-making behavior did not differ from age 8 to 30 on this task, which suggests that from late childhood on, participants are able to take both reward and probability information into account when making decisions. Other developmental studies have shown that children as young as 4 years already show these kinds of decision-making skills (Anderson, 1991, 1996; Schlottmann, 2001; Schlottmann & Anderson, 1994). This suggests that decision-making skills improve with age but that the foundation is laid relatively early in childhood. These findings lead to the question of why the developmental trajectory of risky behaviors as identified in epidemiological work is curvilinear, whereas the developmental trajectory as identified with many lab-based measures suggests that adolescents' decision making is relatively mature and comparable with those of adults. How can adolescent-specific risk-taking behaviors be understood using laboratory tasks?

One approach has been to connect laboratory-based findings to real-life risk taking or personality constructs linked to real-life risk taking by assessing both in the same participants. In the previously mentioned study by van Leijenhorst et al. (2008), decision making did not differ between age groups. Yet, there were consistent differences within groups; participants scoring high on a self-report measure of sensation seeking, which is associated with a vulnerability for problematic behaviors (e.g., Horvath & Zuckerman, 1993), showed more risky behavior in the experiment. Similarly, a recent study by Reyna et al. (2011) found individual differences; a laboratory measure of (gist-based) reasoning and reward sensitivity (e.g., sensation seeking) was found to independently predict real-life risky sexual behavior in adolescent participants. These findings support the ecological validity of theory-driven laboratory-based measures that assess causal mechanisms underlying risky decision making.

A second direction of research that assists in resolving the apparent discrepancy between the epidemiological findings and the lab-based findings has been to develop lab-based measures of adolescents' decision-making skills that more closely mimic the complex context in which decisions are made outside of the laboratory. One aspect of context that is gaining attention is whether the choice context is affective ("hot") or neutral ("cool"; Metcalfe & Mischel, 1999). Recent studies have taken this dual process (hot vs. cool) approach to studying adolescents' decision-making skills and have found interesting results. For example, Figner, Mackinlay, Wilkening, and Weber (2009) examined the effects of choice context on differences in risk-taking behavior between adolescents age 13 to 16 years and adults in terms of risk preferences and the amount of information that is taken into account when decisions are made. This study used two versions of a card gambling paradigm. One version was emotionally arousing and the other was emotionally neutral. The arousing version was hypothesized to make more demands on cognitive resources and as a consequence would result in an immature and risky decision strategy. In contrast, the neutral version was hypothesized to result in a deliberative, reasoning-based strategy. Indeed, adolescents were found to take more risks and base their decisions on less information in the emotionally arousing condition compared with the neutral condition, in which their performance was similar to that of adults. Comparable results were found by van Duijvenvoorde, Jansen, Visser, and Huizenga (2010), who contrasted 13- to 15-year-olds' behavior in an affective decision-making task, the hungry donkey task, a child-adapted version of the Iowa gambling task (Crone & van der Molen, 2004) in which participants receive reward and loss feedback on each trial, to a neutral decision-making task, the gambling machine task, in which no performance feedback is given. The two tasks involve a similar comparison of choice dimensions and require equally complex reasoning capacities. Adolescents made suboptimal EV decisions in the affective compared with the neutral task. The authors explain this in terms of the complexity of the reasoning that adolescents used, which was reduced in the affective context in which adolescents focused on only one of three relevant choice dimensions. Finally, Burnett, Bault, Coricelli, and Blakemore (2010) examined risk preferences in 9- to 35-year-old males using a paired gambles task in which choice alternatives differed in the degree of risk involved. While the ability to make optimal decisions in terms of EV showed a linear increase with age, the number of risky gambles peaked around age 14. The findings from these studies suggest that an affective or hot context more closely mimics the complex context in which decisions are made outside of the laboratory and that adolescents are particularly influenced by reward and loss information.

Taken together, a body of research supports the ecological validity of lab-based measures of risk taking. This work has shown increases in decision-making abilities with development, and importantly, individual differences in performance on these lab-based measures of decision-making ability are related to individual differences in risk-taking behavior outside the lab. Moreover, a second line of research that has focused on decision making in affective contexts has shown the curvilinear trend that is characteristic of the development trajectory of risk taking identified in epidemiological work. Collectively, these results suggest that the difference between adolescents and adults in decision making is relatively weak or absent when assessed with neutral tasks, consistent with the idea that decision-making skills in neutral contexts are relatively intact in adolescence. However, individuals do vary in reasoning abilities, and these neutral tasks appear to capture such within-group individual differences. The latter findings indicate that age differences are more likely to be observed in hot, affectively charged decision-making situations. These results highlight the need for a more integrative approach, which takes cognitive, emotional, and social context factors into account, as well as the need for a more mechanistic understanding of risk taking in adolescence. A better understanding of the mechanisms underlying decision making and their change with development can help explain the interactions of the development of cognitive abilities and contextual factors, which will help understand risky behavior in adolescence. A promising approach in this regard is to study components of risk taking (e.g., reward sensitivity, inhibition) from a cognitive neuroscience perspective, an approach to which we turn in the next section.

NEUROBIOLOGICAL MODELS OF ADOLESCENT RISK TAKING: PROMISES AND CHALLENGES

From a neuroscientific perspective, several partly overlapping and partly complementary theoretical models have been proposed about how trajectories of brain maturation may explain behavioral changes in adolescence. Even though the models have broader goals than solely understanding risk taking in adolescence, they provide intriguing hypotheses with respect to the question of why adolescence may be a vulnerable period for risk taking.

The model that is probably most explicit in hypothesizing about risk taking in adolescence is the dual processing model postulated by Somerville, Jones, and Casey (2010). According to this model, there is an imbalance between the development of subcortical brain regions, such as the ventral striatum and the amygdala, which are thought to precede the development of the prefrontal cortex. Among the subcortical areas, the ventral striatum is involved with reward processing and decision making based on incentives (Delgado, 2007), whereas the amygdala is involved with processing highly salient and motivational emotional stimuli (Cunningham, Arbuckle, Jahn, Mowrer, & Abduljalil, 2010), such as potential threats and emotional states of others. Also, the role of the amygdala in fear and anxiety has been well established (LeDoux, 2007). The prefrontal cortex is involved with tasks such as planning, inhibition, and cognitive control more generally (Miller & Cohen, 2001). The interplay between a not fully developed prefrontal cortex, which is therefore not fully capable of executing control-related functions, and further developed emotional areas such as the amygdala and the ventral striatum causes an imbalance resulting in a primarily emotion-driven approach to rewards and risks in middle adolescence.

A comparable model is the triadic model proposed by Ernst and colleagues (Ernst, Pine, & Hardin, 2006; Ernst & Fudge, 2009). The triadic model is based on the interplay between three systems. The first is the approach system, tailored to rewards; the second the avoidance system, tailored to prevent harm; and the last is the regulatory system. The neural correlates underlying these systems are the ventral striatum, the amygdala, and the prefrontal cortex, respectively. These three systems interact with each other and, when balanced, work together in a beneficial way facilitating learning and harm avoidance. However, during adolescence the balance often tips toward the approach system, resulting in reward-driven behavior. The model is comparable to the Somerville et al. (2010) dual processing model, although it differs with respect to the assumptions about speed of maturation. Where the dual processing approach predicts that the subcortical areas develop earlier than the prefrontal areas, the triadic model does not make assumptions about earlier or later maturation. Instead, this model suggests that there is a fragile balance, which may result in tipping to approach or avoidance more easily in adolescence.

Finally, the third model that is relevant for our discussion is the social information processing model proposed by Nelson, Leibenluft, McClure, and Pine (2005). During adolescence, social reorientation takes place. This model provides a broad explanation for changes in social processing (social perception, social emotion, and social cognition) in adolescence but also makes predictions about brain regions involved in risk taking. The social information processing network distinguishes three nodes: a detection node, an affective node, and a cognitive-regulation node (Nelson et al., 2005). Although different information is being processed in the different nodes, they are connected and influence each other. In this model, the amygdala and ventral striatum are considered to be part of the affective node, and the prefrontal cortex is part of the cognitive-regulatory node, mirroring the earlier described models. The detection node is involved in basic processing of social stimuli and includes the fusiform face area, superior temporal sulcus, and anterior temporal cortex. The social information processing model differs from the earlier described models in that the developmental pattern seen in risk taking is ascribed to hormonally induced changes in the affective node. Specifically, Nelson et al. (2005) propose that activation in the ventral striatum is elevated due to the rise in gonadal hormones at the onset of puberty, which causes a fragile balance with the slowly developing prefrontal cortex. Therefore, this model does not necessarily predict that the structural development of the ventral striatum precedes structural development of the prefrontal cortex but instead that the ventral striatum is more sensitive to specific pubertal changes and therefore becomes more active (see also Steinberg et al., 2008, for a similar dual processing hypothesis based on behavioral empirical evidence).

Together, these models provide excellent starting points for a more in-depth analysis of neural patterns related to risk taking in adolescence, and as we will see below, they each have received empirical support. Yet, as we will also see in the next section, the models are not very specific with respect to the subprocesses that are involved in risk taking and how the striatum and prefrontal cortex are expected to respond to risks versus rewards.

PUTTING THE MODELS TO THE TEST: HOW DOES BRAIN IMAGING INFORM RISK-TAKING RESEARCH IN ADOLESCENCE?

The empirical studies available to date have mostly used functional magnetic resonance imaging (fMRI), a safe and noninvasive technique that allows for the study of neural activation during specific phases of a task. These studies have focused on two task-related processes that are important for risk-taking investigation: reward anticipation and responses to receiving a reward.

In such neuroimaging studies, responses to anticipated and received rewards are usually investigated using tasks in which participants can receive an outcome that is favorable to them. Outcomes can be points, money, or primary rewards such as juice (Delgado, 2007). A consistent finding in these studies is involvement of the ventral striatum/nucleus accumbens in response to receipt of rewards. In addition, the amygdala, anterior cingulate cortex, dorsolateral prefrontal cortex, ventromedial prefrontal cortex, and orbitofrontal cortex are found to be active, although these findings are not consistent across studies and possibly depend on specific task demands. Here we will focus on the developmental pattern in the ventral striatum specifically, as this region is most consistently activated in response to reward anticipation and reward processing.

Ventral Striatum Responses to Reward

In reward studies both under- and overrecruitment of the ventral striatum have been reported in adolescents compared with children and adults.

The most prominent finding is an overrecruitment of the ventral striatum in response to reward receipt for adolescents. These results have been found with different tasks and in a wide age range that included participants between 7 and 40 years of age, which strengthened the credibility of the results. Four of these studies used tasks that involved a passive or active aspect of gambling. With passive gambling, we refer to paradigms in which the participant cannot influence the outcome, whereas an active task means that the participant can choose to take a risk or not. Two studies with passive gambling tasks support the hypothesis of overrecruitment of the ventral striatum to reward in adolescence. Van Leijenhorst, Zanolie, et al. (2010) used a task in which participants are shown a slot machine that they can start with a button press. The slots can fill with three types of fruit. They win only when all three slots show the same fruit. Winning was associated with increased activation in the ventral striatum, and more so for middle adolescents. Similarly, Galvan et al. (2006) used a delayed response two-choice task. In this task, participants are presented with a cue, after which they need to respond by indicating the location of the cue when prompted. Correct responses within the time interval set for the response are rewarded. Each cue is paired with a distinct reward amount. Again, winning was associated with increased activation in the ventral striatum, and more so for middle adolescents.

Tasks with an active aspect of gambling, such as the wheel of fortune task (Ernst et al., 2005) and the cake gambling task (van Leijenhorst, Gunther Moor, et al., 2010), similarly show greater activation of the ventral striatum in response to reward receipt. In the wheel of fortune task, participants are shown a circle divided into two colors. Only trials were analyzed in which both colors covered 50% of the circle in this case, but divisions and therefore probabilities of winning can differ. Participants choose one of the colors, and if the computer randomly picks the same color, they win. The cake gambling task is a slightly modified version of the wheel of fortune task. To make the task more suitable for children, the wheel is explained as a cake with different flavors. Participants can choose which flavor they would like to bet on, and if the computer picks the same flavor, they win. Participants can choose between a low-risk gamble with a 66% chance of winning 1 euro and a high-risk gamble with a 33% chance of winning 2, 4, 6, or 8 euros. In these tasks, winning was associated with increased activation in the ventral striatum, and more so in middle adolescence. This pattern of elevated ventral striatum response in middle adolescence was further confirmed in other paradigms that have used reward conditions, such as a temporal discounting task (Christakou, Brammer, & Rubia, 2011) and an antisaccade task (Geier, Terwilliger, Teslovich, Velanova, & Luna, 2010; Padmanabhan, Geier, Ordaz, Teslovich, & Luna, 2011). Smith, Halari, Giampetro, Brammer, and Rubia (2011) used a sustained attention task in which adolescents showed elevated ventral striatum responses to rewarded trials compared with adults, but not compared with the youngest group. The results from this set of studies seem to provide consistent evidence for enhanced activation in the ventral striatum in middle adolescence.

However, in work focusing on the *anticipation* of rewards, the results have in some studies been opposite to the pattern described above. Two studies have found *underrecruitment* of the striatum in middle adolescence. Both of these studies used the monetary incentive delay (MID) task (Bjork et al., 2004; Bjork, Smith, Chen, & Hommer, 2010). In the MID task, participants can win (or avoid losing) different amounts of money by pressing a button within a short interval after a target is presented. Failure to press within the response interval results in omission of gain (or loss), whereas pressing the button within the response interval results in winning (or avoidance of loss). Participants win in 66% of the trials. Individual response intervals are determined on the basis of a response time task, assessed before the start of the MID task. The MID task has two distinguished phases, separated in time to allow for fMRI analyses for both phases. As such, it has been specifically designed to enable testing for differences in brain activation during anticipation, as well as receipt, of a reward. Both studies (Bjork et al., 2004, 2010) found underrecruitment of the right ventral striatum for adolescents, compared with an adult group, during gain versus nongain anticipation. Activation during reward receipt, in contrast, did not yield any significant differences between the groups. The MID task allows for the possibility that groups engage in differential strategies. For example, whether the participant will receive the outcome is dependent on behavior, pressing a button as fast as possible, and there is a 66% reward scheme. For some participants, this may lead to greater certainty about the anticipated reward (knowing that they can influence the outcome by behavior), whereas for others, this may make the task more uncertain (learning that the reward is only given on 66% of the trials). Whether and how these tasks differ should be an avenue for future research, but it is clear that intriguing shifts in response patterns may occur depending on how the task is framed (Bjork, Lynne-Landsman, Sirocco, & Boyce, 2012).

Based on the studies described above, two general phases can be distinguished—the anticipation of reward and the receipt of the reward (feedback although others have also distinguished between other phases, such as cue-related response and anticipation of outcome, see Geier et al., 2010). The apparent inconsistency of results might stem from confounding the anticipation of reward and receipt of reward. Taken together, and consistent with the dual processing model (Somerville et al., 2010) as well as the triadic model (Ernst & Fudge, 2009), the studies presented show that the ventral striatum is most likely differentially involved in adolescents, and most studies point toward enhanced activity, at least for reward receipt (see Color Plate 1 for a meta-analysis; Christakou et al., 2011; Ernst et al., 2005; Galvan et al., 2006; van Leijenhorst, Gunther Moor, et al., 2010; van Leijenhorst, Zanolie, et al., 2010). No studies found an underrecruitment of the ventral striatum during reward receipt. However, during anticipation, findings are more mixed. Studies find overrecruitment (Galvan et al., 2006; van Leijenhorst, Gunther Moor, et al., 2010) as well as underrecruitment (Bjork et al., 2004, 2010). Although the models proposed by Somerville et al. (2010) and Ernst et al. (2006) provide a framework by which some of the results can be explained, there may be other factors mediating the effects. Since adolescents go through major changes in hormonal levels as well as in the social domain, this leads to the hypothesis that emotional and social contextual factors may influence these developmental sensitivities, as proposed by the social information processing model (Nelson et al., 2005).

Peers and Pubertal Hormones

The social influences on neural correlates of risk taking have hardly been studied, even though it is well known that peers strongly influence the behavior of adolescents. As already pointed out by the social information processing model (Nelson et al., 2005), adolescence is a time when peers become very important (Dahl, 2004). Also, much risk-taking behavior takes place in groups (Steinberg, 2004). Adolescents can assess risks and can reason logically when they are asked about risks or consequences (Boyer, 2006). When adolescents are asked to perform a task in the lab, they are usually alone or in the presence of an experimenter, not among their peers. The risk-taking behavior that is observed in a natural setting may therefore not be captured in the standard laboratory environment.

One intriguing new fMRI study investigated risk taking in a setting with peers for three age groups: adolescents, ages 14 to 18; young adults ages 19 to 22, and adults ages 24 to 29. In this study by Chein, Albert, O'Brien, Uckert, and Steinberg (2011; see also Gardner & Steinberg, 2005), participants were asked to play a game in which they were driving a simulated car. Their goal was to drive from A to B as fast as possible. On the way, they encountered several crossings. On some of these crossings a stoplight turned orange just when they approached. On each crossing they could decide to (continue to) go and take a risk, or stop. When they decided to take a risk, this could result in a crash, setting them back further than deciding to wait would have. In one condition, participants were told that they were performing this task alone and that no one would see what they did. In the other condition, however, their peers were physically present and watching them. All groups showed elevated risk-taking in the peer-present condition, but adolescents took even more risks than young adults and adults. Intriguingly, adolescents also showed elevated ventral striatum responses in the peer-present condition compared with the other age groups (see Color Plate 2).

Peers are assumed to have a large influence on the behavior of adolescents in real life. One mediating factor, which may provide a mechanistic explanation for peer sensitivity, is the role of specific pubertal hormones. These hormones may not only trigger reproductive development but also influence social behaviors and interest in peers, such as sensation seeking, seeking of social status, fear of social rejection, and a drive toward social acceptance (Dahl, 2004; Nelson et al., 2005). Preliminary evidence for this assumed role of pubertal hormones in adolescent decision making and reward processing comes from two studies, which investigated the role of testosterone on reward processing and risk anticipation (Hermans et al., 2010; van Honk et al., 2004).

The influence of testosterone on risk taking has been studied mainly through the measurement of naturally fluctuating hormone levels, but recently, exciting new advances in testosterone research have focused on the administration of testosterone in healthy (mostly female) adult participants. Administering small doses of testosterone resulted in increased risk taking on the Iowa gambling task (van Honk et al., 2004). In addition, administration of the same dose of testosterone in females results in enhanced activation in the nucleus accumbens during reward anticipation in the MID task (Hermans, et al., 2010). It is well known that in puberty the increase in testosterone is orders of magnitude larger than the increase due to administration of testosterone in the examples described above. Therefore, an intriguing question is whether hormone level increases are predictive of neural responses to risk and reward in pubertal adolescents.

Two studies used this approach. Op de Macks et al. (2011) found that boys and girls with higher natural testosterone levels also showed higher ventral striatum responses to reward receipt, thereby confirming prior studies that showed that testosterone administration in adults also leads to enhanced ventral striatal responses to reward (Hermans et al., 2010; see Color Plate 3). However, as described before, responses to reward anticipation and reward receipt may rely on different mechanisms. This is highlighted in a study by Forbes et al. (2010) in which testosterone levels correlated positively with striatum responses in boys during anticipation but correlated negatively with striatum responses to reward receipt in both boys and girls. Taken together, these findings shed light on the link between social influence, hormones, and decision making as described in the social information processing model (Nelson et al., 2005). However, future research is necessary to unravel these apparently inconsistent findings and integrate different approached to understand the interaction between peer sensitivity and pubertal hormones.

FUTURE DIRECTIONS

Major changes take place in the body and brain of adolescents. An increase in risk-taking behavior is evident in daily life. Findings from the laboratory show that greater risk taking among adolescents, compared with other age groups, is only evident under specific contextually arousing conditions (high rewards, peer presence; Burnett et al., 2010; Figner et al., 2009; Gardner & Steinberg, 2005; van Duijvenvoorde et al., 2010). Brain research investigating the underlying neural correlates of risk-taking behavior in adolescence has revealed partly consistent (elevated neural response to reward outcome) and partly inconsistent results (reduced and elevated neural responses to reward anticipation). To understand risk taking more fully, future researchers should continue to disentangle neural responses to anticipation and receipt of reward and to focus on sensitivities to social and emotional contexts (see also Reyna & Farley, 2006; Rivers, Reyna, & Mills, 2008). We propose that the new advances in brain imaging research, integrated with different approaches, take us to another level of explanation of neural responses to risks and rewards in adolescence. Three of these advances are highlighted here.

First, very few studies until now have investigated testosterone levels and the influence on risk taking and reward processing. Bodily changes during puberty are primarily driven by hormonal changes, and therefore the influence of hormones is an important area to explore in future work. Testosterone administration studies in adult women show a relationship between nucleus accumbens activity as well as increased risk taking (Hermans et al., 2010; van Honk et al., 2004). Individual measures of hormone levels as assessed by, for instance, morning saliva samples provide valuable information above and beyond the effects of puberty (Op de Macks et al., 2011). Reliably investigating individual differences calls for large sample sizes, preferably spread over a wide age range. Participants who have not yet reached puberty, as well as midpubertal and postpubertal participants, should be included in order to unravel puberty effects independent of age changes (Quevedo, Benning, Gunnar, & Dahl, 2009). To track the developmental pattern, a longitudinal design would be optimal in the investigation of the combined influence of early or late puberty onset and how this interacts with social environmental influences.

Second, it is well known that most risk-taking behavior takes place when adolescents are in the presence of peers, yet social factors influencing neural responses to risks and rewards have hardly been studied. Only one study investigated the effects of peer presence on brain activity (Chein et al., 2011). Especially for adolescents, the presence of peers was found to have a significantly elevating effect on striatum responses. Due to the confined space and limitations provided by the MRI scanner, it is challenging to manipulate peer presence within an MRI setting. Two possibilities, other than directly manipulating actual peer presence, are to investigate the influence of social stimuli on risk taking and the relationship between real-life risk taking and neural responses. Social stimuli could, for instance, be status within the peer group or the influence of emotional faces on risk taking (Casey et al., 2011).

Similar to the approach described earlier in behavioral research, real-life risk taking could be measured by the use of illicit substances, such as alcohol or marijuana, or engagement in sexual behavior. Yet another possibility would be to investigate attitudes toward risk taking, for instance, how likely someone thinks it is that a certain risk will yield a positive outcome. For example, Galvan, Hare, Voss, Glover, and Casey (2007) reported a significant positive correlation between the self-reported likelihood of engaging in risky behavior and nucleus accumbens reactivity in response to winning. Similar correlations can possibly be found between social relations in real life (e.g., resistance to peer influence) and neural responses to risks and rewards in the laboratory (see also Paus, Keshavan, & Giedd, 2008, for a similar approach), which provide us with more information about the underlying mechanism of risk taking at the neural level and disentangles who is at risk of showing exaggerated risk taking in real life.

Third, integrating different theoretical approaches as described in the literature so far, such as affective and social neuroscience, can help unravel risk-taking behavior. For example, besides numerous behavioral models, only the neuroscientific model by Nelson et al. (2005) explicitly takes social information processing into account, but the model is not yet specific with respect to how developmental and individual differences in theory of mind or resistance to peer influence may interact with individual tendencies toward risk taking. Recently, Blakemore and colleagues (Blakemore, 2008; Burnett, Thompson, Bird, & Blakemore, 2011) have demonstrated that adolescence is characterized by large changes in the brain networks important for mentalizing about intentions of others. Especially regions in the social brain network, such as the medial prefrontal cortex, precuneus, temporal parietal junction, and insula, were shown to develop both functionally and structurally during adolescence (Blakemore, 2008; Gogtay et al., 2004). Thus, it is of great importance to examine neural responses to rewards not in isolation, but in an integrative approach with interaction between affective neuroscience (neural responses to risks and rewards) and social neuroscience (ability to take perspective, understand intentions, and resist peer influence).

The approach for the future is therefore to study risk taking and neural structure and function in relation to pubertal development, sensitivity versus resistance to peer influences, and mentalizing about intentions of others. Ultimately, we would like to be able to assess individual differences to enable identification of adolescents who are most likely to exhibit excessive risk-taking behavior. This knowledge has far-reaching implications for policy questions and for developing interventions that are specific for adolescents who need them, focusing on developmentally specific sensitivities.

REFERENCES

Anderson, N. H. (1991). Probability development. In N. H. Anderson (Ed.), *Contributions to information integration theory: Vol. III. Developmental* (pp. 83–108). Hillsdale, NJ: Erlbaum.

Anderson, N. H. (1996). *A functional theory of cognition*. Mahway, NJ: Erlbaum.

Beyth-Marom, R., & Fischhoff, B. (1997). Adolescents' decisions about risks: A cognitive perspective. In J. Schulenberg & J. L. Maggs (Eds.), *Health risks and developmental transitions in adolescence* (pp. 110–135). New York, NY: Cambridge University Press.

Bjork, J. M., Knutson, B., Fong, G. W., Caggiano, D. M., Bennett, S. M., & Hommer, D. W. (2004). Incentive-elicited brain activation in adolescents: Similarities and differences from young adults. *The Journal of Neuroscience, 24*, 1793–1802. doi:10.1523/JNEUROSCI.4862-03.2004

Bjork, J. M., Lynne-Landsman, S. D., Sirocco, K., & Boyce, C. A. (2012). Brain maturation and risky behavior: The promise and the challenges of neuroimaging-based accounts. *Child Development Perspectives*, 6, 385–391. doi:10.1111/cdep.12001

Bjork, J. M., Smith, A. R., Chen, G., & Hommer, D. W. (2010). Adolescents, adults and rewards: Comparing motivational neurocircuitry recruitment using fMRI. *PLoS ONE, 5*(7), e11440. doi:10.1371/journal.pone.0011440

Blakemore, S. J. (2008). The social brain in adolescence. *Nature Reviews Neuroscience*, 9, 267–277. doi:10.1038/nrn2353

Boyer, T. W. (2006). The development of risk-taking: A multi-perspective review. *Developmental Review, 26*, 291–345. doi:10.1016/j.dr.2006.05.002

Burnett, S., Bault, N., Coricelli, G., & Blakemore, S. J. (2010). Adolescents' heightened risk-seeking in a probabilistic gambling task. *Cognitive Development, 25*, 183–196. doi:10.1016/j.cogdev.2009.11.003

Burnett, S., Thompson, S., Bird, G., & Blakemore, S. J. (2011). Pubertal development of the understanding of social emotions: Implications for education. *Learning and Individual Differences, 21*, 681–689. doi:10.1016/j.lindif.2010.05.007

Casey, B. J., Somerville, L. H., Gotlib, I. H., Ayduk, O., Franklin, N. T., Askren, M. K., . . . Shoda, Y. (2011). Behavioral and neural correlates of delay of gratification 40 years later. *Proceedings of the National Academy of Sciences of the United States of America, 108*, 14998–15003. doi:10.1073/pnas.1108561108

Chein, J., Albert, D., O'Brien, L., Uckert, K., & Steinberg, L. (2011). Peers increase adolescent risk taking by enhancing activity in the brain's reward circuitry. *Developmental Science, 14*, F1–F10. doi:10.1111/j.1467-7687.2010.01035.x

Christakou, A., Brammer, M., & Rubia, K. (2011). Maturation of limbic corticostriatal activation and connectivity associated with developmental changes in temporal discounting. *NeuroImage, 54*, 1344–1354. doi:10.1016/j.neuroimage.2010.08.067

Crone, E. A., & Dahl, R. E. (2012). Understanding adolescence as a period of social-affective engagement and goal flexibility. *Nature Reviews Neuroscience, 13*, 636–650. doi:10.1038/nrn3313

Crone, E. A., & van der Molen, M. W. (2004). Developmental changes in real life decision making: Performance on a gambling task previously shown to depend on the ventromedial prefrontal cortex. *Developmental Neuropsychology, 25*, 251–279. doi:10.1207/s15326942dn2503_2

Cunningham, W. A., Arbuckle, N. L., Jahn, A., Mowrer, S. M., & Abduljalil, A. M. (2010). Aspects of neuroticism and the amygdala: Chronic tuning from motivational styles. *Neuropsychologia, 48*, 3399–3404. doi:10.1016/j.neuropsychologia.2010.06.026

Dahl, R. E. (2004). Adolescent brain development: A period of vulnerabilities and opportunities. *Annals of the New York Academy of Sciences, 1021*, 1–22. doi:10.1196/annals.1308.001

Delgado, M. R. (2007). Reward-related responses in the human striatum. *Annals of the New York Academy of Sciences, 1104*, 70–88. doi:10.1196/annals.1390.002

Eaton, D. K., Kann, L., Kinchen, S., Shanklin, S., Ross, J., Hawkins, J., . . . Wechsler, H. (2008). Youth risk behavior surveillance—United States, 2007. *MMWR. Surveillance summaries: Morbidity and mortality weekly report. CDC Surveillance summaries, 57*(4), 1–131. Available at http://www.cdc.gov/mmwr/preview/mmwrhtml/ss5704a1.htm

Ernst, M., & Fudge, J. L. (2009). A developmental neurobiological model of motivated behavior: Anatomy, connectivity and ontogeny of the triadic nodes. *Neuroscience and Biobehavioral Reviews, 33*, 367–382. doi:10.1016/j.neubiorev.2008.10.009

Ernst, M., Nelson, E. E., Jazbec, S., McClure, E. B., Monk, C. S., Leibenluft, E., . . . Pine, D. S. (2005). Amygdala and nucleus accumbens in responses to receipt and omission of gains in adults and adolescents. *NeuroImage, 25*, 1279–1291. doi:10.1016/j.neuroimage.2004.12.038

Ernst, M., Pine, D. S., & Hardin, M. (2006). Triadic model of the neurobiology of motivated behavior in adolescence. *Psychological Medicine, 36*, 299–312. doi:10.1017/S0033291705005891

Figner, B., Mackinlay, R. J., Wilkening, F., & Weber, E. U. (2009). Affective and deliberative processes in risky choice: Age differences in risk taking in the Columbia Card Task. *Journal of Experimental Psychology: Learning, Memory, and Cognition, 35*, 709–730. doi:10.1037/a0014983

Fischhoff, B., Bruine de Bruin, W., Parker, A. M., Millstein, S. G., & Halpern-Felsher, B. L. (2010). Adolescents' perceived risk of dying. *Journal of Adolescent Health, 46*, 265–269. doi:10.1016/j.jadohealth.2009.06.026

Forbes, E. E., Ryan, N. D., Phillips, M. L., Manuck, S. B., Worthman, C. M., Moyles, D. L., . . . Dahl, R. E. (2010). Healthy adolescents' neural response to reward: Associations with puberty, positive affect, and depressive symptoms. *Journal of the American Academy of Child and Adolescent Psychiatry, 49*, 162–172. Retrieved from http://www.ncbi.nlm.nih.gov/pmc/articles/PMC2837556/

Galvan, A., Hare, T., Voss, H., Glover, G., & Casey, B. J. (2007). Risk-taking and the adolescent brain: Who is at risk? *Developmental Science, 10*, F8–F14. doi:10.1111/j.1467-7687.2006.00579.x

Galvan, A., Hare, T. A., Parra, C. E., Penn, J., Voss, H., Glover, G., & Casey, B. J. (2006). Earlier development of the accumbens relative to orbitofrontal cortex might underlie risk-taking behavior in adolescents. *The Journal of Neuroscience, 26*, 6885–6892. doi:10.1523/JNEUROSCI.1062-06.2006

Gardner, M., & Steinberg, L. (2005). Peer influence on risk taking, risk preference, and risky decision making in adolescence and adulthood: An experimental study. *Developmental Psychology, 41*, 625–635. doi:10.1037/0012-1649.41.4.625

Geier, C. F., Terwilliger, R., Teslovich, T., Velanova, K., & Luna, B. (2010). Immaturities in reward processing and its influence on inhibitory control in adolescence. *Cerebral Cortex, 20*, 1613–1629. doi:10.1093/cercor/bhp225

Gogtay, N., Giedd, J. N., Lusk, L., Hayashi, K. M., Greenstein, D., Vaituzis, A. C., . . . Thompson, P. M. (2004). Dynamic mapping of human cortical development during childhood through early adulthood. *Proceedings of the National Academy of Sciences of the United States of America, 101*, 8174–8179. doi:10.1073/pnas.0402680101

Hermans, E. J., Bos, P. A., Ossewaarde, L., Ramsey, N. F., Fernandez, G., & van Honk, J. (2010). Effects of exogenous testosterone on the ventral striatal BOLD response during reward anticipation in healthy women. *NeuroImage, 52*(1), 277–283. doi:10.1016/j.neuroimage.2010.04.019

Horvath, P., & Zuckerman, M. (1993). Sensation seeking, risk appraisal, and risky behavior. *Personality and Individual Differences, 14*(1), 41–52. doi:10.1016/0191-8869(93)90173-Z

LeDoux, J. (2007). The amygdala. *Current Biology, 17*, R868–R874.

Metcalfe, J., & Mischel, W. (1999). A hot/cool-system analysis of delay of gratification: Dynamics of willpower. *Psychological Review, 106*(1), 3–19. doi:10.1037/0033-295X.106.1.3

Miller, E. K., & Cohen, J. D. (2001). An integrative theory of prefrontal cortex function. *Annual Review of Neuroscience, 24*, 167–202. doi:10.1146/annurev.neuro.24.1.167

Nelson, E. E., Leibenluft, E., McClure, E. B., & Pine, D. S. (2005). The social reorientation of adolescence: A neuroscience perspective on the process and its relation to psychopathology. *Psychological Medicine, 35*, 163–174. doi:10.1017/S0033291704003915

Op de Macks, Z. A., Gunther Moor, B., Overgaauw, S., Guroglu, B., Dahl, R. E., & Crone, E. A. (2011). Testosterone levels correspond with increased ventral striatum activation in response to monetary rewards in adolescents. *Developmental Cognitive Neuroscience, 1*, 506–516. doi:10.1016/j.dcn.2011.06.003

Padmanabhan, A., Geier, C. F., Ordaz, S. J., Teslovich, T., & Luna, B. (2011). Developmental changes in brain function underlying the influence of reward processing on inhibitory control. *Developmental Cognitive Neuroscience, 1*, 517–529. doi:10.1016/j.dcn.2011.06.004

Paus, T., Keshavan, M., & Giedd, J. N. (2008). Why do many psychiatric disorders emerge during adolescence? *Nature Reviews Neuroscience, 9*, 947–957. doi:10.1038/nrn2513

Quevedo, K. M., Benning, S. D., Gunnar, M. R., & Dahl, R. E. (2009). The onset of puberty: Effects on the psychophysiology of defensive and appetitive motivation. *Development and Psychopathology, 21*(1), 27–45. doi:10.1017/S0954579409000030

Reyna, V. F., Estrada, S. M., DeMarinis, J. A., Myers, R. M., Stanisz, J. M., & Mills, B. A. (2011). Neurobiological and memory models of risky decision making in adolescents versus young adults. *Journal of Experimental Psychology, 37*, 1125–1142. doi:10.1037/a0023943

Reyna, V. F., & Farley, F. (2006). Risk and rationality in adolescent decision making: Implications for theory, practice, and public policy. *Psychological Science in the Public Interest, 7*(1), 1–44. doi:10.1111/j.1529-1006.2006.00026.x

Rivers, S. E., Reyna, V. F., & Mills, B. (2008). Risk taking under the influence: A fuzzy-trace theory of emotion in adolescence. *Developmental Review, 28*(1), 107–144. doi:10.1016/j.dr.2007.11.002

Scherf, K. S., Berman, M., & Dahl, R. E. (2012). Facing changes and changing faces in adolescence: A new model for investigating adolescent-specific interactions between pubertal, brain, and behavioral development. *Developmental Cognitive Neuroscience, 2*, 199–219. doi:10.1016/j.dcn.2011.07.016

Schlottmann, A. (2001). Children's probability intuitions: Understanding the expected value of complex gambles. *Child Development, 72*, 103–122. doi:10.1111/1467-8624.00268

Schlottmann, A., & Anderson, N. H. (1994). Children's judgments of expected value. *Developmental Psychology, 30*, 56–66. doi:10.1037/0012-1649.30.1.56

Shirtcliff, E. A., Dahl, R. E., & Pollak, S. D. (2009). Pubertal development: Correspondence between hormonal and physical development. *Child Development, 80*, 327–337. doi:10.1111/j.1467-8624.2009.01263.x

Smith, A. B., Halari, R., Giampetro, V., Brammer, M., & Rubia, K. (2011). Developmental effects of reward on sustained attention networks. *NeuroImage, 56*, 1693–1704. doi:10.1016/j.neuroimage.2011.01.072

Somerville, L. H., Jones, R. M., & Casey, B. J. (2010). A time of change: Behavioral and neural correlates of adolescent sensitivity to appetitive and aversive environmental cues. *Brain and Cognition, 72*(1), 124–133. doi:10.1016/j.bandc.2009.07.003

Steinberg, L. (2004). Risk taking in adolescence: What changes, and why? *Annals of the New York Academy of Sciences, 1021*, 51–58. doi:10.1196/annals.1308.005

Steinberg, L. (2008a). *Adolescence*. New York, NY: McGraw-Hill.

Steinberg, L. (2008b). A social neuroscience perspective on adolescent risk-taking. *Developmental Review, 28*(1), 78–106. doi:10.1016/j.dr.2007.08.002

Steinberg, L., Albert, D., Cauffman, E., Banich, M., Graham, S., & Woolard, J. (2008). Age differences in sensation seeking and impulsivity as indexed by behavior and self-report: Evidence for a dual systems model. *Developmental Psychology, 44*, 1764–1778. doi:10.1037/a0012955

Steinberg, L., & Morris, A. S. (2001). Adolescent development. *Annual Review of Psychology, 52*, 83–110. doi:10.1146/annurev.psych.52.1.83

van Duijvenvoorde, A. C. K., Jansen, B. R. J., Visser, I., & Huizenga, H. M. (2010). Affective and cognitive decision-making in adolescents. *Developmental Neuropsychology, 35*, 539–554. doi:10.1080/87565641.2010.494749

van Honk, J., Schutter, D. J., Hermans, E. J., Putman, P., Tuiten, A., & Koppeschaar, H. (2004). Testosterone shifts the balance between sensitivity for punishment and reward in healthy young women. *Psychoneuroendocrinology, 29*, 937–943. doi:10.1016/j.psyneuen.2003.08.007

van Leijenhorst, L., Gunther Moor, B., Op de Macks, Z. A., Rombouts, S. A., Westenberg, P. M., & Crone, E. A. (2010). Adolescent risky decision-making: Neurocognitive development of reward and control regions. *NeuroImage, 51*(1), 345–355. doi:10.1016/j.neuroimage.2010.02.038

van Leijenhorst, L., Westenberg, P. M., & Crone, E. A. (2008). A developmental study of risky decisions on the cake gambling task: Age and gender analyses of probability estimation and reward evaluation. *Developmental Neuropsychology, 33*, 179–196. doi:10.1080/87565640701884287

van Leijenhorst, L., Zanolie, K., Van Meel, C. S., Westenberg, P. M., Rombouts, S. A., & Crone, E. A. (2010). What motivates the adolescent? Brain regions mediating reward sensitivity across adolescence. *Cerebral Cortex, 20*(1), 61–69. doi:10.1093/cercor/bhp078

4

THE ADOLESCENT SENSATION-SEEKING PERIOD: DEVELOPMENT OF REWARD PROCESSING AND ITS EFFECTS ON COGNITIVE CONTROL

BEATRIZ LUNA, AARTHI PADMANABHAN, AND CHARLES GEIER

In this chapter, we review existing animal models and human literature on the adolescent brain in the context of risk-taking behaviors. Specific changes in brain structure and neurochemistry as well as a review of the functional neuroimaging literature reflecting the development of cognitive control and incentive processing will be discussed. We extend previous reviews (e.g., Geier & Luna, 2009; Wahlstrom, White, & Luciana, 2010) by proposing that relative immaturities in the adolescent brain, specific to networks supporting motivated behaviors, may underlie increases in sensation-seeking behaviors in adolescence. Finally, the implications for juvenile law and education are discussed. Which aspects can and cannot be informed by this research are carefully delineated, especially with regard to ecological validity.

Adolescence is typically demarcated by the onset of puberty, early in the second decade of life in humans, and the acquisition of adult psychosocial roles (approximately early 20s). This period is widely recognized across cultures and species as demonstrating a peak in sensation seeking—the propensity

http://dx.doi.org/10.1037/14322-005
The Neuroscience of Risky Decision Making, by V. F. Reyna and V. Zayas (Editors)

to approach novel and varied experiences (Spear, 2010). Sensation seeking during adolescence is increasingly theorized to be an adaptive mechanism leading to the acquisition of skills that can be implemented independently of adult supervision supporting lifelong survival (although there are, to our knowledge, no studies that have tested this directly). Increased sensation seeking can also lead to risk taking (engaging in behaviors with a high perceived reward value but known potential negative consequences), which can undermine survival. Increased risk taking during adolescence plays a primary role in increased mortality rates relative to childhood (Heron, 2012). As discussed below, the unique neurobiological changes that occur during this time may play a crucial role in supporting a rise in sensation seeking and risk taking. On the one hand, brain systems supporting executive function are reaching adult levels during adolescence, supporting their ability to make goal-directed decisions in a manner similar to that of adults. However, important limitations in the ability to engage these executive processes in a controlled and flexible manner may enhance their vulnerability to errors in executive function, such as failing to suppress an automatic response. Neurobiological changes, in conjunction with still-maturing executive processes, affect motivated behaviors (behaviors that are influenced by reward and punishment) and increase adolescent sensitivity to reward incentives. Taken together, the maturation of executive control of behavior, coupled with immaturities in assessing rewards and punishment, may lead to a system that is optimally tuned for exploration and sensation seeking.

ADOLESCENT RISK TAKING

Adolescence is well recognized to be a period of peak risk taking (Steinberg et al., 2008), which can undermine survival. Accidental deaths and unintended injuries peak during the adolescent period (see Figure 4.1) due in great part to risky and reckless behaviors, including substance abuse, criminal behavior, and unprotected sex (Chambers, Taylor, & Pentenza, 2003). The decision-making process involved in risk taking is affected by many component processes and includes the following: the ability to assess the value of a potential reward relative to potential consequences, arousal processes in response to potential rewards, and the planning of behaviors that increase the probability of obtaining the reward. Investigating the maturational integrity of brain processes that support components that affect the risk-taking decision-making process can inform us with regard to the nature of an adolescent predisposition for engaging in risk taking.

To better conceptualize this multiprocess perspective on decision making, it is useful to more carefully consider what goes into a "risky" decision.

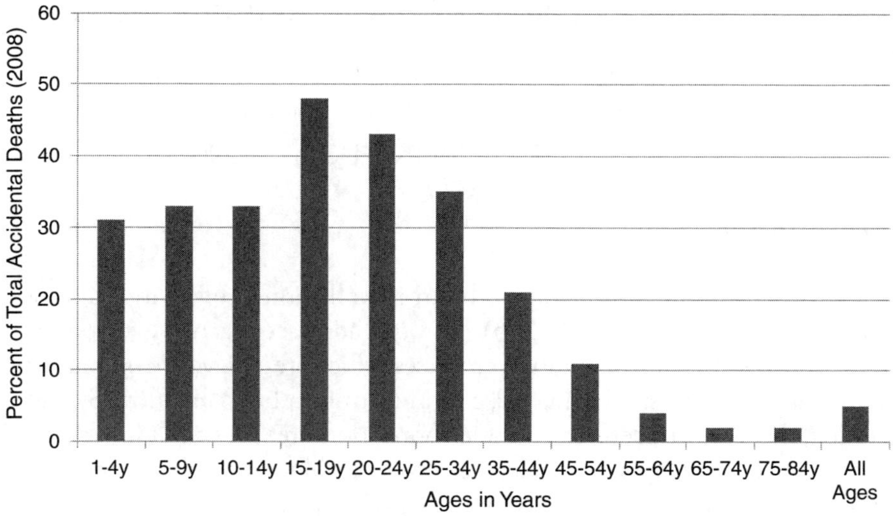

Figure 4.1. Percentage of total accidental deaths by age. From "Deaths: Leading Causes for 2008," by M. Heron, 2012, *National Vital Statistics Reports, 60,* 17–19. In the public domain.

For example, envision a scenario in which an adolescent is faced with the choice to share his or her friend's lit cigarette. The adolescent faces at least two distinct behavioral choices here: take a drag or refuse. Initially, the adolescent must first assess and generate representations of the benefits and costs of each action, supported in large measure by reward system processing. For example, "If I take a puff, my friend will think I'm cool [social reward], but I might get sick and get in trouble" versus "If I don't take a puff, I won't get sick, but I might lose 'face' [social punishment]." The costs and benefits of each action must then be evaluated against each other, supported in part by executive processes (i.e., working memory) and processing of potential rewarding outcomes. Next, behavioral action toward one option is planned and executed while action toward the alternative is inhibited. Finally, the reward/loss outcome associated with the behavioral choice is noted and stored to help guide future choices.

Although there are important environmental factors, such as social demands and learned responses, that influence decision making, the mechanisms that support the basic aspects of reward processing and goal-directed behaviors are supported by brain processes that are still immature in adolescence. As we discuss next, the adolescent brain systems that coordinate and integrate reward and cognitive processes may be distinct from those of adults, biasing toward impulsive behaviors driven by a greater influence of reward anticipation. Hence, adolescents may have the ability to assess risk, but the value of rewards may have a larger impact on the behaviors that are ultimately engaged.

BRAIN MATURATION IN ADOLESCENCE

Brain Structure

The gross morphology of the brain is well formed even in childhood (Caviness, Kennedy, & Bates, 1996). Through adolescence, however, progressive and regressive brain maturation processes, which are believed to optimize the brain to its environmental demands, continue to affect brain function. Synaptic pruning, the loss of underused synaptic connections, reaches adult levels in the visual cortex and temporal language regions in childhood, while the prefrontal cortex (PFC) reaches adult levels in middle adolescence (Huttenlocher, 1990; Huttenlocher & Dabholkar, 1997). Magnetic resonance imaging (MRI) studies of gray matter thickness indicate that gray matter specialization proceeds in an inverted U fashion with increased thickening into adolescence and thinning proceeding into adulthood (Giedd et al., 1999; Gogtay et al., 2004; see also Chapter 3, this volume).

Importantly, the regions in PFC and basal ganglia, which support executive function and reward processing, show continued thinning through adolescence (Gogtay et al., 2004; Sowell, Thompson, Holmes, Jernigan, & Toga, 1999). Pruning of excess synaptic connections in the PFC, which contributes to gray matter thinning, provides more streamlined and direct computations (decreasing signal-to-noise), which can enhance more complex information processing, such as working memory and the ability to voluntarily inhibit responses (Fuster, 2002). As a result, the adolescent period is characterized by a generalized streamlining of localized circuitry including the addition of specialized inputs (see Neurochemical Maturation below) supporting more complex, integrated function.

In addition to gray matter remodeling, processes influencing white matter integrity continue to develop through adolescence. The myelin sheath surrounding axons continues to thicken across the brain through myelination, speeding neuronal transmission and enhancing neuronal connectivity, which contributes to the establishment of specialized neural networks. Histological studies indicate earlier myelination in the visual cortex, with frontal, temporal, and parietal myelination continuing through adolescence and early adulthood (Yakovlev & Lecours, 1967). Diffusion tensor imaging studies indicate that white matter integrity in pathways such as the cingulum, the superior longitudinal fasciculus, and uncinate fasciculus continues to mature through childhood and adolescence and even into early adulthood

(Asato, Terwilliger, Woo, & Luna, 2010; Eluvathingal, Hasan, Kramer, Fletcher, & Ewing-Cobbs, 2007; Lebel, Walker, Leemans, Phillips, & Beaulieu, 2008; Giorgio et al., 2008). These increases in white matter integrity support speeding of neuronal transmission of cortico-cortical and cortico-subcortical integration. Effective cortico-subcortical connectivity is essential for top-down modulation of behavior where executive cognitive systems can exert control over more reflexive/impulsive systems (Hwang, Velanova, & Luna, 2010). Taken together, these results indicate that the structural maturation of the adolescent prefrontal system is newly online while white matter pathways are beginning to strengthen. These milestones may support the ability of adolescents to have access to executive processes as adults, but their reliable implementation may still be suboptimal, possibly undermining the engagement of this system when there are competing processes such as those of the reward system, which also have a unique status in adolescence, as discussed below.

Neurochemical Maturation

Underlying behavioral and systems-level maturation, a number of changes occur at a more micro level over childhood and adolescence, including an overexpression of receptors for serotonin, dopamine, adrenergic, and endocannabinoids (Lidow & Rakic, 1992); a peak in the density of interneurons with a subsequent decline into adulthood (Anderson, Classey, Conde, Lund, & Lewis, 1995; Erickson & Lewis, 2002; Lewis, 1997); an increase in levels of the inhibitory neurotransmitter gamma-aminobutyric acid (GABA; Hedner, Iverson, & Lundberg, 1984), and a change in the expression of glutamate activating receptors in the PFC. These changes are believed to refine neuronal signaling and connectivity, which enhance efficient cellular signaling into adulthood.

The reward system is highly dependent on the function of the neurotransmitter dopamine (DA). Lesion, single-cell recording, neuroimaging, electrical self-stimulation, and drug studies have collectively demonstrated that DA neurons respond to reward prediction, expected reward value, salience, punishment, and valence (for reviews, see Cools, 2008; Schultz et al., 2008; Wise, 2004). DA, which primarily modulates fast-acting synapses (i.e., glutamate and GABA), extensively innervates brain circuitry and modulates a strong reciprocal relationship between the striatum and the PFC (Cools, 2008). The prevalence and function of DA as well as its influence on modulating neuronal processes demonstrate protracted change over adolescence, which we briefly summarize below (for more extensive reviews, see Chambers et al., 2003; Spear, 2000; Wahlstrom, Collins, White, & Luciana, 2010; Wahlstrom, White, & Luciana, 2010).

In nonhuman primates, there is evidence of pubertal "peaks" in DA neuron activity in the midbrain (McCutcheon, White, & Marinelli, 2009), increased DA tissue concentration in the PFC in adolescence (Goldman-Rakic & Brown, 1982), a peak in DA tone in the striatum (Andersen, Thompson, Krenzel, & Teicher, 2002), and a peak in activity in D1-expressing neurons (Brenhouse, Sonntag, & Andersen, 2008). Postmortem human studies demonstrate that DA innervations to the PFC peak in adolescence (Benes, Taylor, & Cunningham, 2000; Lambe, Krimer, & Goldman-Rakic, 2000; Rosenberg & Lewis, 1994, 1995), with the largest increase in PFC cortical layer III, where neural processing supporting cognitive behaviors (i.e., working memory) has been characterized (Lewis, Melchitzky, & Burgos, 2002). The major DA receptors (D1 and D2) show increased density in the PFC and the striatum in adolescence, with peaks in late childhood and subsequent declines through adolescence (Andersen et al., 2002; Lidow & Rakic, 1992; Montague, Lawler, Mailman, & Gilmore, 1999; Seeman et al., 1987). The changes in D1- and D2-receptor function in the PFC serve to balance excitatory and inhibitory responses in the brain, fine-tuning neuronal responses and supporting more efficient processing in the PFC (Tseng & O'Donnell, 2005). The striatum has relatively more D2 receptors than the PFC, while the opposite is the case for D1 receptors. It is not yet clear how changes in the density of the DA receptors would specifically underlie adolescent behavior. The peak in DA signaling in the midbrain in adolescence has also been corroborated by evidence that adolescent animals exhibit increased reinforcing effects of stimulant drugs (Adriani, Chiarotti, & Laviola, 1998; Adriani & Laviola, 2000; Badanich, Adler, & Kirstein, 2006; Laviola, Adriani, Terranova, & Gerra, 1999; Mathews & McCormick, 2007) and demonstrate increased sensitivity to neuroleptics that are DA receptor antagonists (Spear & Brake, 1983; Spear, Shalaby, & Brick, 1980).

Overall, changes in maturational rates in D1 and D2 receptors, metabolite function, and midbrain DA neuron function may underlie changes seen in motivated behaviors in adolescence as well as confer risk for addiction and other pathologies related to DA function that emerge in adolescence. Tonic levels of DA are elevated in adolescence, which may result in inefficient regulation of phasic signaling in response to rewards (for review, see Luciana, Wahlstrom, Porter, & Collins, 2012). Taken together, this literature indicates an overall peak in DA availability, which may enhance reward reactivity in adolescence, coupled with a short-acting response bias toward immediate rewards and resulting in overexcitation to perceived reward incentives and enhanced sensation seeking (Chambers et al., 2003). In addition to reward assessment, risk taking involves engaging in an action that results in reward receipt. Next, we discuss the state of the cognitive executive system in adolescence.

Crucial to decision making is the ability to engage systems that support immediate goal-directed responses (vs. reflexive responses or habits) to interact optimally with the environment. Motivation is a key component, which can be guided by a potential reward with high perceived value. Executive control of behavior is available early in development, as demonstrated in tasks that assess the ability to update goal-driven responses (Diamond & Goldman-Rakic, 1989; Johnson, 1995). However, executive control becomes increasingly flexible and stable with age as prefrontal networks become more readily engaged, as evident in working memory tasks and tasks where rules are unexpectedly changed (Bjorklund & Harnishfeger, 1995; Hwang & Luna, 2011; Luciana & Nelson, 1998).

Developmental functional MRI (fMRI) studies of working memory, where subjects' performance is guided by information retained online, show that prefrontal systems play a primary role (Goldman-Rakic, 1987) and the core processes to engage working memory are available starting in childhood (Nelson et al., 2000; Thomas et al., 1999). When more complex computations are required by the experimental task (i.e., manipulating information held in working memory), developmental differences are often more apparent. These increases in cognitive abilities from early childhood to adolescence include increases in the ability to engage optimally the prefrontal systems in generating an accurate response and to suppress distracters (Ciesielski, Lesnik, Savoy, Grant, & Ahlfors, 2006; Crone, Wendelken, Donohue, van Leijenhorst, & Bunge, 2006; Geier, Garver, Terwilliger, & Luna, 2009; Klingberg, Forssberg, & Westerberg, 2002; Olesen, Macoveanu, Tegner, & Klingberg, 2007; Scherf, Sweeney, & Luna, 2006), suggesting that refinements in executive function are relatively late maturing. The fMRI studies on the development of inhibitory control, that is, the ability to suppress reflexive goal-incompatible responses, also demonstrate immaturities that persist through adolescence in engaging optimal brain circuitries. Immaturities are reflected in both increases and decreases in engaging the PFC as well as the concomitant cortical and subcortical regions (Bunge, Dudukovic, Thomason, Vaidya, & Gabrieli, 2002; Crone et al., 2006; Luna et al., 2001; Rubia et al., 2006).

Although the main circuitry supporting cognitive control is online by adolescence, specific processes underlying the ability to effectively engage cognitive control continue to show limitations. The anterior cingulate cortex, which is robustly engaged in adults when inhibitory control errors are committed, is not reliably engaged in adolescence, contributing to limitations in error monitoring and performance monitoring (Velanova, Wheeler, & Luna, 2008; see Color Plate 4a). In addition, the circuitry, including prefrontal and posterior cortical regions (e.g., inferior parietal sulcus), that supports the ability to sustain attention is also engaged to a lesser degree in adolescence than in adulthood and limits the ability for adolescents to establish a controlled cognitive state and reach adult rates of correct performance (Velanova, Wheeler, & Luna, 2009; see Color Plate 4b). These limitations may be due to immaturities in functional connectivity of top-down control processes that support the ability to exert executive control (Hwang et al., 2010; Stevens, Kiehl, Pearlson, & Calhoun, 2007; see Color Plate 4c).

Prior research has suggested that from childhood to adolescence the reliance on posterior parietal systems shifts to prefrontally guided circuitry (Hwang et al., 2010; Luna et al., 2001). By adolescence, the foundational architecture of a prefrontally guided circuitry is evident. From adolescence to adulthood there are increases in the number and strength of prefrontally guided connections supporting a ready system to control responses in adulthood (Hwang, Hallquist, & Luna, 2012; see Color Plate 4d). These developmental advances in readily recruiting integrated networks are likely supported by age-related weakening of short-range functional connections that give way to long-distance connections in adulthood (Fair et al., 2007). Effective executive control is supported by the ability of prefrontal executive regions to readily integrate attention and sensory information in order to exert control over subcortical regions to execute goal-directed behavior.

Taken together, these studies provide evidence that by adolescence the brain systems supporting cognitive control are indeed available, supporting the ability to plan and execute decisions. However, ready access to networks that support controlled use of cognitive processes continues to strengthen through adulthood, undermining the ability to sustain activity and monitor performance. As such, on the one hand, access to prefrontal networks may provide adolescents with the ability to start making complex executive decisions without assistance from adults as had been needed in childhood and to engage in new experiences. On the other hand, limitations in the flexible, reliable, and prompt engagement of optimal executive networks can increase the occurrence of failures of exerting executive control in favor of more impulsive responses. As described below, adolescents may have a greater demand on inhibitory control as motivation may play a larger role in affecting behavior and further undermining the effective engagement of cognitive control. Hence, although the ability to mathematically assess risk has been shown to be available in adolescence (Reyna & Brainerd, 2011), the ability to readily integrate this information in situations with competing processes, such as in adolescent risk taking, may be limited.

NEUROIMAGING EVIDENCE OF UNIQUE REWARD PROCESSING IN ADOLESCENCE

Extensive work in animal models (Apicella, Ljungberg, Scarnati, & Schultz, 1991; Hikosaka, Nakumura, & Nakahara, 2006; Roesch & Olson, 2003, 2004; Schultz, 2000; Wise, 2002) and with human adults using functional neuroimaging (Breiter, Aharon, Kahneman, Dale, & Shizgal, 2001; Delgado, Locke, Stenger, & Fiez, 2003; Delgado, Nystrom, Fissell, Noll, & Fiez, 2000; Elliott, Newman, Longe, & Deakin, 2003; Knutson, Westdorp, Kaiser, & Hommer, 2000; McClure, York, & Montague, 2004; O'Doherty, 2004; Thut et al., 1997;) have carefully delineated reward-related neurocircuitry, providing the essential groundwork for developmental investigations. Indeed, a growing number of developmental neuroimaging studies have focused on characterizing developmental differences in how incentives (rewards, losses) are processed during adolescence (for reviews, see Geier & Luna, 2009; Somerville & Casey, 2010). Studies consistently have demonstrated central roles for the ventral striatum (VS) and orbitofrontal cortex (OFC) in multiple aspects of reward processing; as such, these regions will be the primary focus below.

The VS, including the nucleus accumbens, is rich in DA receptors and has extensive connections throughout cortical and subcortical structures (Chikama, McFarland, Amaral, & Haber, 1997; Di Martino et al., 2008; Fudge, Kinishio, Walsh, Richard, & Haber, 2002; Haber, Kunishio, Mizobuchi, & Lynd-Balta, 1995; Selemon & Goldman-Rakic, 1985). This key node in the reward circuitry is involved in various aspects of motivated behaviors, including the detection of incentives, the processing of value, and reward prediction (Knutson & Cooper, 2005). The OFC, a functionally heterogeneous and complex prefrontal executive region, has important connections to the basal ganglia (Fuster, 1989; Rushworth, Noonan, Boorman, Walton, & Behrens, 2011), positioning it to support varied functions related to the executive assessment of rewards, including representations of subjective preference, valence and value estimation, and, importantly, the regulation of planned behavior associated with incentives (Bechara, Damasio, Damasio, & Anderson, 1994; Hare, O'Doherty, Camerer, Schultz, & Rangel, 2008; Kringelbach, 2005). Interestingly, the VS and OFC may be recruited differentially during the adolescent period, with adolescent behavior being relatively more driven by stimulus or bottom-up (e.g., stronger VS influence) than planned or regulated (e.g., a weaker OFC influence) processes, relative to adults. Below, we review evidence for both immature recruitment of the VS and decreased engagement of the OFC during reward processing.

Increased engagement of the VS in adolescence has been found across different task contexts, including those in which subjects had to guess which response would generate a monetary reward (e.g., Ernst et al., 2005), when monetary incentives were dependent on simple working memory responses (e.g., Galvan et al., 2006), during passive viewing of different reward probabilities (van Leijenhorst, Gunther Moor, et al., 2010), and when reward was dependent on cognitive control performance (Geier, Terwilliger, Teslovich, Velanova, & Luna, 2010; Padmanabhan, Geier, Ordaz, Teslovich, & Luna, 2011; van Leijenhorst, Gunther Moor, et al., 2010; see Figure 4.2). However, when participants are prompted by an abstract cue associated with rewards to make a quick button press to earn the reward (using the monetary incentive delay task), adolescents show decreased VS activity compared to adults during initial stages of reward processing (Bjork et al., 2004; Bjork, Smith, Chen, & Hommer, 2010). These results may be due in part to the use of an

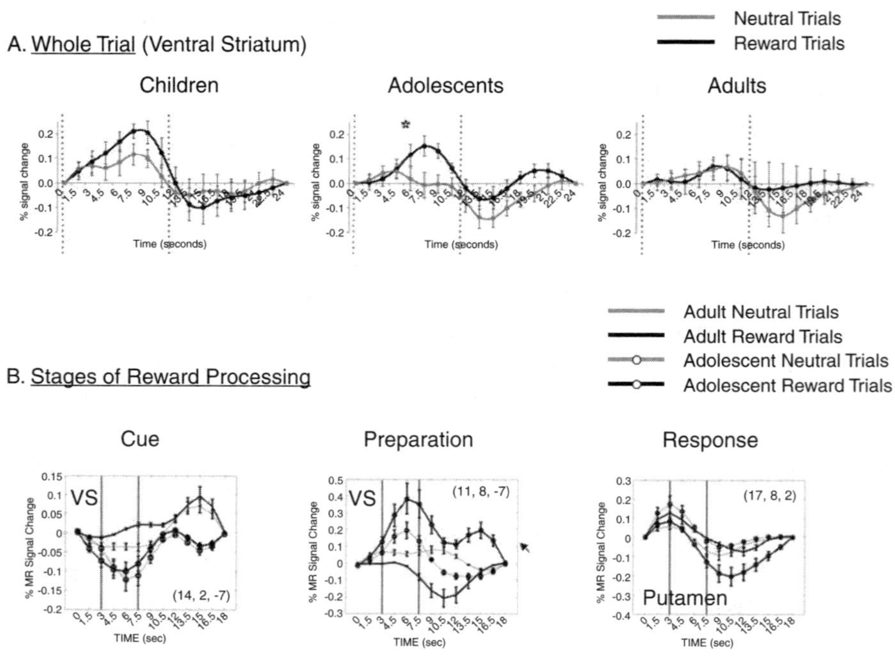

Figure 4.2. (A). Adolescents show greater activity in ventral striatum (VS) when considering a whole reward trial versus neutral trial. From "Developmental Changes in Brain Function Underlying the Influence of Reward Processing on Inhibitory Control," by A. Padmanabhan, C. F. Geier, S. J. Ordaz, T. Teslovich, and B. Luna, 2011, *Developmental Cognitive Neuroscience, 1,* p. 525. Copyright 2011 by Elsevier. Adapted with permission. (B). When considering stages of reward processing it is evident that this increase occurs during the response preparation period. Adults show increased VS activity compared with adolescents in the initial period when the reward cue is being assessed. From "Immaturities in Reward Processing and Its Influence on Inhibitory Control in Adolescence," by C. F. Geier, R. Terwilliger, T. Teslovich, K. Velanova, and B. Luna, 2010, *Cerebral Cortex, 20,* pp. 1620–1623. Copyright 2010 by Oxford University Press. Adapted with permission.

abstract incentive cue, which may undermine motivation or may point to unique phases of reward processing that may have different developmental trajectories (Geier et al., 2010). These results suggest that adolescents have differential engagement of the VS, which typically expresses as an increased engagement of the VS, reflecting sensitivity to detection, valuation, and prediction of rewards but can also result in suboptimal recruitment of reward circuitry in specific reward contingencies or during specific phases of reward processing.

In our own studies (Geier et al., 2010; Padmanabhan et al., 2011), we have used a rewarded antisaccade (AS) task to assess developmental change in reward sensitivity and its interaction with a basic component of cognitive control, response inhibition. At the start of each rewarded AS trial, participants are presented with cues that signal whether corrected performance on the forthcoming trial will result in the accrual, loss, or no gain of points leading to a monetary reward. This stage is when cue information is processed regarding potential incentives. Next, the incentive cue disappears and is replaced by a central red fixation. Participants are told beforehand that they should prepare to inhibit a response at this time. This second stage serves as an instruction cue that is known from single-cell nonhuman primate studies to engage preparatory oculomotor control regions, including the frontal eye field (FEF), supplementary eye field, and parietal eye field, that determine a correct inhibitory response (Everling & Munoz, 2000). Importantly, this stage is also one when anticipation of an upcoming reward takes place. Finally, the fixation cue disappears and a small filled circle appears at an unpredictable peripheral location. This is the motor response stage, when participants must not look at the stimulus when it appears, instead generating an eye movement to the exact opposite location. In this task, reward accrual is contingent on the ability to inhibit a prepotent saccadic response to the suddenly appearing visual target (Hallett, 1978). Developmental differences were investigated during these separate stages of reward processing: reward assessment (processing of the rewarded/neutral cue), response preparation/reward anticipation (presentation of fixation/instruction cue), and response (correct inhibitory response; Geier et al., 2010).

Behaviorally, both reaction time and performance (correct inhibitory response rates) improved during rewarded versus neutral trials (Geier et al., 2010; Geier & Luna, 2012). The fMRI results indicated that adults, but not adolescents, showed prompt recruitment of the VS during the initial stage of reward cue assessment (see Figure 4.2b). By the response preparation period, however, adolescents but not adults showed robust engagement of the VS, reaching higher levels of activation than adults. Importantly, in parallel to relative greater recruitment of the VS, adolescents also showed greater engagement of oculomotor control regions including the FEF and intraparietal sulcus than did adults (see Figure 4.3). In single-cell nonhuman primate studies, these regions have been found to increase activity during the preparatory period determining a successful inhibitory eye movement response (Everling & Munoz, 2000). Given that adolescents performed at adult levels only during incentive trials, when they recruit oculomotor control regions to a greater level than adults, and not in neutral trials, reflects the greater effort that adolescents exert to engage inhibitory control. The parallel increased recruitment of VS and oculomotor regions during reward trials suggests that VS activity may support enhanced recruitment of circuitry that enables reward receipt. This extends prior interpretation of the relationship between VS function and control processes, which is most often

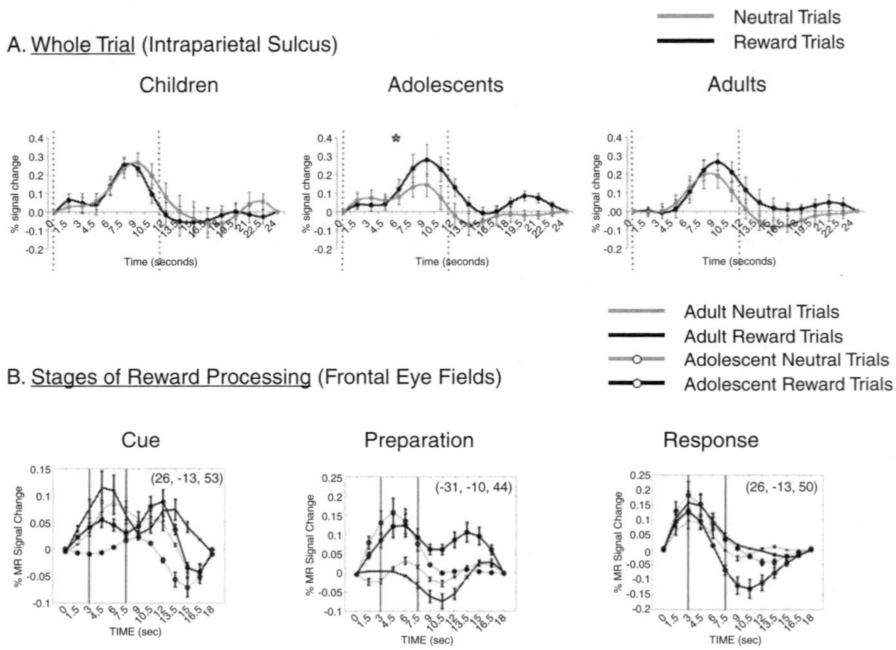

Figure 4.3. Adolescents show greater activity in regions that support cognitive control of eye movements during a rewarded antisaccade task. (A). When considering the whole reward trial, adolescents compared with adults show increased recruitment of the intraparietal sulcus, known to support voluntary saccade inhibition in reward versus neutral trials. From "Developmental Changes in Brain Function Underlying the Influence of Reward Processing on Inhibitory Control," by A. Padmanabhan, C. F. Geier, S. J. Ordaz, T. Teslovich, and B. Luna, 2011, *Developmental Cognitive Neuroscience, 1,* p. 525. Copyright 2011 by Elsevier. Adapted with permission. (B). More specifically, adolescents compared with adults show greater engagement of the frontal eye fields, which are core to the ability to suppress an impending saccade during preparation to make a correct inhibitory response. From "Immaturities in Reward Processing and Its Influence on Inhibitory Control in Adolescence," by C. F. Geier, R. Terwilliger, T. Teslovich, K. Velanova, and B. Luna, 2010, *Cerebral Cortex, 20,* pp. 1620–1623. Copyright 2010 by Oxford University Press. Adapted with permission.

characterized in a top-down manner with the VS (and reward processes more generally) being regulated by prefrontal-mediated executive systems. The VS may play a role in integrating reward information to affect response behavior. As such, adolescents' heightened reward responses may be viewed as "adaptive" in that reward approach is enhanced. However, adolescents' engagement of reward and motor systems closer to the response stage (preparation vs. cue, as in adults) may lead to a more "impulsive" system in the context of reward motivation.

Although there is general consensus that adolescents often show heightened responses in the VS, specific elements of reward-related decision making contributing to VS activation may be developing along different timelines in the adolescent period. In an elegant study, Cohen et al. (2010) found that when *decision value* (the value assigned to a potential choice) and *prediction error* (the difference between the expected value and actual outcome of a choice or behavior) are considered independently, there is evidence that the peak in adolescent hyperactivity in the VS may be due to the processing of underlying prediction errors separate from the decision-making process per se. That is, the magnitude of the reward itself does not affect adolescent behavior as much as the anticipation of a reward in relation to reward receipt. In addition, heightened responses in the VS in adolescence to rewarding stimuli may in part be linked to hormonal changes associated with puberty, as early puberty has been found to be associated with increased striatal activity (subsequently declining with more advanced puberty) and has been linked with testosterone levels (Forbes & Dahl, 2010; Op de Macks et al., 2011).

In contrast to the directionality of immature VS responding, several studies have also shown decreased engagement of the OFC (Galvan et al., 2006; Geier et al., 2010; van Leijenhorst, Zamoli, et al., 2010) in adolescents relative to adults, suggesting more limited executive assessment, regulation of incentives, or both. In addition, adolescents with higher reported risk taking show less recruitment of the OFC, as well as other prefrontal regions (Galvan, Hare, Voss, Glover, & Casey, 2007; Shad, Bidesi, Chen, Ernst, & Rao, 2011; van Leijenhorst, Crone, & Bunge, 2006), suggesting a mechanism by which limitations in engaging executive control may lead to increased reward-driven behavior. Supporting the findings in OFC, considerable evidence suggests increased engagement of more distributed prefrontal regions (dorsolateral prefrontal cortex, dlPFC; ventromedial prefrontal cortex, vmPFC) concurrent with the transition from adolescence to adulthood (Hwang et al., 2010). Choosing high-risk options to obtain low-magnitude rewards has been found to decrease from adolescence to adulthood and is mediated by prefrontal activity (van Leijenhorst, Gunther Moor, et al., 2010). From childhood to later adulthood, the engagement of sustained attention networks that overlap with reward regions increases with reward contingencies (e.g., dlPFC and vmPFC, dorsal striatal, and temporal-parietal regions; Smith, Halari, Giampetro, Brammer, & Rubia, 2011; van Leijenhorst, Gunther Moor, et al., 2010), while stimulus saliency networks, including posterior cingulate and inferior temporal regions, decreased. In one imaging study using a decision-making task where subjects could choose a safe bet or take a gamble, adolescents and adults demonstrated similar behavior (Paulsen, Platt, Huettel, & Brannon, 2011). However, brain regions in the decision-making network that support processes such as integrating contextual information and previous outcomes, including the insula, the hippocampus, and the amygdala, show increased activation through adolescence into adulthood (Paulsen et al., 2011). These results suggest that with increasing age, the influence of reward enhances top-down executive processing circuits, supporting mature, adult levels of goal-directed behavior. Effective decision making in the context of motivational cues necessitates successful integration of frontal executive systems and their influence on striatal reward systems. Indeed, increased connectivity between the vmPFC and striatum, as well as frontoparietal and insular brain regions, has been found to be associated with decreased impulsive choices on a temporal discounting paradigm (Christakou, Brammer, & Rubia, 2011). Prefrontally guided functional connections supporting cognitive control have been found to increase in number and in strength (Hwang et al., 2010; Stevens et al., 2007) through adolescence as has the integrity of white matter frontally guided connections (Asato et al., 2010). The effective modulation of subcortical processes may support adult-level decision making and, ultimately, decreases in risk-taking behavior (but also see Berns, Moore, & Capra, 2009).

Taken together, these studies suggest two key components that are unique in the adolescent period. First, adolescents have a predisposition for greater sensitivity to reward contingencies, engaging areas of the reward circuitry (VS) that heighten motivation and engaging motor action systems that may result in more impulsive responses in the context of rewards. Second, prefrontal systems that support the ability to generate executive decisions are available, permitting the generation of voluntary decision making. However, though available, executive processes are still sluggish, possibly undermining the assessment of reward contingencies in the context of planned behavior and the ability to readily provide control of reflexive responses, undermining controlled, reward-related decision making.

One limitation of developmental fMRI studies of reward processing is that they typically use monetary incentives. However, monetary incentives may be valued differently across development (e.g., $25 may be valued more highly by an adolescent than an adult who has more ready access to money). This could potentially confound interpretation of the effects of rewards on behavior, as a more valued reward may induce greater motivation and improved performance. Geier and Luna (2012) explored this notion in a behavioral study aimed at minimizing reward value differences between adolescents and adults. In this study, participants chose their own reward prior to testing (maximizing individual-level subjective value), and instead of monetary rewards, points toward a prize were offered, setting up a "fixed economy" where the range of points was standardized across all subjects. Even in this context, although adolescents committed more cognitive control errors than adults, their error rates improved with increasing rewards, suggesting greater sensitivity to reward. This was in contrast to the adults, whose performance did not change with different reward amounts.

As a final point, in addition to considering age-related differences in how adolescents value the same reward relative to adults, it is important to consider age-related differences in how types of rewards are valued. For instance, Chein, Albert, O'Brien, Uckert, and Steinberg (2011) found that the presence of peers engaged the reward circuitry in adolescents to a greater extent than in adults, which was associated with increased risk taking in a driving task. These results suggest that not only do adolescents show greater reward sensitivity but also certain types of incentives (e.g., social reward) may be particularly salient motivators during this period. Adolescence is a period of social reorientation during which there is a predilection for social experiences that support the development of adult independent skills, including establishing peer groups and increasing interests in forming romantic relationships (Blakemore, 2008; Forbes & Dahl, 2010).

In sum, the studies reviewed above demonstrate that adolescents exhibit heightened responses in core regions of the reward system, likely reflecting sensitivity to incentives, which may vary according to value magnitude and type. Recruitment of the reward system may engage action processes that facilitate reward receipt but may also contribute to impulsive decisions and actions in the context of rewards. Cognitive systems are available supporting the production of executive decisions. The cognitive systems are still limited in important ways, such as in performance monitoring and error processing, which in the presence of reward-driven action may undermine the system's ability to process context to inform optimal decision making.

RELEVANCE TO THE JUVENILE JUSTICE SYSTEM

In the past few years, there has been attention on how developmental neuroscience findings can and has informed the juvenile justice system, particularly as it relates to sentencing such as the death penalty and life without parole for juveniles (Scott & Steinberg, 2008). Although these are inherently ethical questions, the role that neuroscience plays in providing important biologically based evidence to inform decisions at the level of the U.S. Supreme Court has been increasingly considered (*Graham v. Florida*, 2010; *Miller v. Alabama*, 2012; *Roper v. Simmons*, 2005). First, it is important to emphasize that developmental neuroscience findings describe the adolescent *period* when considering adolescents as a group; the findings do not apply at the individual level. There is great variability in both behavioral and fMRI findings undermining the ability to inform *individual* legal cases in the determination of guilt or the ability to be rehabilitated. Even if in the future fMRI evidence can inform propensities at the individual level, the risk of a false positive, incorrectly identifying an individual as a life criminal, would still limit its applicability.

Developmental neuroscience evidence of specific immaturities in brain processes supporting decision making provides a biological model supporting what psychology has already revealed about limitations in adolescent behavior and what has been surmised intuitively in society. As such, this biologically based information does not provide novel insights so much as it strengthens the impact of the information. The fMRI evidence depicting increased activity in the VS during reward processing and limitations in engaging executive circuitry in adolescents, combined with immaturities in brain structure and neurotransmitter function, substantiates the behavioral profile of increased motivational reactivity coupled with limitations in executive decision making during this period of development. The implication is that age may be a mitigating circumstance when considering the culpability (*Graham v. Florida*, 2010; *Miller v. Alabama*, 2012; *Roper v. Simmons*, 2005). This evidence does not speak to guilt or exonerate responsibility but provides insight into an important factor that underlies a risk-taking act that resulted in a crime. As such, neuroscience evidence of immaturities in the adolescent brain has been found to be particularly relevant in informing the extent of sentencing. The fact that a crime had been committed during a period of development when there are biologically based vulnerabilities to risk taking implies that a behavior may not have occurred if the individual was mature and that given time to develop, this propensity may be resolved. Sentences such as the death penalty or life without parole assume that the individual will not change his or her propensity for crime. In the majority of individuals antisocial behavior may be limited only to the adolescent period (Moffitt, 1993). In addition, the processes that underlie increased sensation seeking in adolescence also support enhanced learning. DA supports not only reward processing but also learning contextual associations (Cools, 2011; Wise, 2004). Although an enhanced ability to learn contextual associations can lead to establishing bad habits, such as substance abuse in adolescence, it can also support a period when rehabilitation may be particularly effective. Hence, juveniles may be more amenable to rehabilitation and have a greater ability to be reintegrated in society.

The neuroscience evidence of immaturities in the adolescent brain supporting decision making does not imply that adolescents are unable to make responsible decisions. In fact, most adolescents make responsible decisions and do not engage in risk-taking behavior. Adult-level executive systems are starting to reach adult-like levels of function, although limitations still remain in terms of the efficiency of engaging distributed networks that support top-down control of behavior. Adolescents are slower to engage and maintain an executive mode of control and may be prone to errors. When sensitivity to motivational cues is increased, the limitations in accessing the control network may be further compromised. Hence, adolescent immaturities are more pertinent to impulsive acts that occur without the ability to plan and consider consequences. In the context of being able to deliberate a decision, especially with guidance from a mature individual, the time to exert the available adult-level executive systems allows the adolescent to guide a responsible decision and consider long-term consequences.

THE ADAPTIVE ADOLESCENT PERIOD

Although the term *immaturity* makes reference to the adolescent brain as a suboptimal adult brain, this period can also be viewed as adaptive and, as such, the adolescent brain can be seen as operating in an optimal manner for the demands of such a developmental stage. As adolescents gain access to mature-level cognitive processes, they are able to make decisions that are independent of the guidance of adults. Increases in motivational drives encourage adolescents to make independent decisions that allow them to explore new contexts and learn new abilities that are of particular fit to them individually. One area of growth is in the social domain as adolescents establish social circles and romantic relationships, which are also influenced by hormonal changes during puberty (Forbes & Dahl, 2010). These decisions are essential in establishing a foundation for moving away from the proverbial "nest" and being able to establish adult roles. The ability to access cognitive processes that support executive decision making (despite increased sensitivity to rewarded stimuli) provides an important platform to encourage the acquisition of independent skills. Viewed in this manner, the adolescent brain is in fact optimal for the critical task of this stage of development—beginning to establish independence for a successful adulthood.

CONCLUSION

Neuroimaging evidence indicates that the adolescent period is unique in its hyperreactivity to reward incentives in the context of having access to adult-level cognitive tools that are still strengthening and not yet optimally reliable. Gray matter is still thinning throughout the cortex, supporting more efficient processing needed for complex neuronal computations that support processes underlying executive control. White matter tracts are still myelinating, speeding neuronal transmission needed for the engagement of distributed networks that support integrated information processing and ready top-down control of behavior. Importantly, the reward system is hyperactive as there is a peak of DA availability. Taken together, the adolescent period is one in which independent executive decisions can be made, but the period may be suboptimal in the ability to maintain a controlled executive state and integrate errors, especially when reward contingencies are in place. Thus, the adolescent period is one of heightened risk taking. The transitional nature of this reward-driven and reactive period of development is particularly informative to the juvenile justice system when considering lifelong sentences that assume an unchanging profile. On the other hand, adolescent access to adult-level executive tools allows for responsible decisions to be made in optimal circumstances. Finally, the adolescent brain is not to be viewed as a suboptimal adult brain but rather as a stage in brain maturation that is optimal for fostering the acquisition of independent skills and social networks essential for adult survival.

Sensation/novelty-seeking behaviors peak during adolescence and likely contribute to well-documented increases in risk-taking behaviors during this period of development. Concurrent with these behavioral changes are a number of neurobiological changes influencing both affective and cognitive processes, resulting in an increased sensitivity to reward contingencies in the context of maturing executive control systems. Brain maturational changes in gray and white matter during adolescence enhance neuronal processing supporting complex cognitive computations. Connectivity between distal brain areas strengthens, allowing integration of networks supporting top-down control of behavior. Furthermore, neurochemical changes occur, including a peak in dopamine availability, which may critically underlie peaks in sensation-seeking behavior. Functional neuroimaging studies, showing increased recruitment of reward processing regions and immature engagement of prefrontal regions in adolescence compared with adults, are in agreement with brain structural imaging studies showing continued maturation of fronto-striatal systems supporting reward processing. Taken together, the literature suggests that adolescents are especially influenced by reward contingencies, which can lead to vulnerability to biased and, at times, suboptimal decision making. A different yet complementary perspective suggests that an adolescent sensation-seeking period may also be adaptive as it encourages exploration of one's environment, novel social interactions, and the acquisition of skills supporting independence into adulthood. The juvenile justice system is increasingly informed by developmental neuroscience, which provides a model for adolescent vulnerabilities for risk taking that can result in crime. This research underscores the nature of this developmental stage, which can be pertinent to questions of culpability, sentencing, and rehabilitation.

REFERENCES

Adriani, W., Chiarotti, F., & Laviola, G. (1998). Elevated novelty seeking and peculiar d-amphetamine sensitization in periadolescent mice compared with adult mice. *Behavioral Neuroscience, 112,* 1152–1166. doi:10.1037/0735-7044.112.5.1152

Adriani, W., & Laviola, G. (2000). A unique hormonal and behavioral hyporesponsivity to both forced novelty and d-amphetamine in periadolescent mice. *Neuropharmacology, 39,* 334–346. doi:10.1016/S0028-3908(99)00115-X

Andersen, S. L., Thompson, A. P., Krenzel, E., & Teicher, M. H. (2002). Pubertal changes in gonadal hormones do not underlie adolescent dopamine receptor overproduction. *Psychoneuroendocrinology, 27,* 683–691. doi:10.1016/S0306-4530(01)00069-5

Anderson, S. A., Classey, J. D., Conde, F., Lund, J. S., & Lewis, D. A. (1995). Synchronous development of pyramidal neuron dendritic spines and parvalbumin-immunoreactive chandelier neuron axon terminals in layer III of monkey prefrontal cortex. *Neuroscience, 67,* 7–22. doi:10.1016/0306-4522(95)00051-J

Apicella, P., Ljungberg, T., Scarnati, E., & Schultz, W. (1991). Responses to reward in monkey dorsal and ventral striatum. *Experimental Brain Research, 85,* 491–500. doi:10.1007/BF00231732

Asato, M. R., Terwilliger, R., Woo, J., & Luna, B. (2010). White matter development in adolescents: A DTI study. *Cerebral Cortex, 20,* 2122–2131. doi:10.1093/cercor/bhp282

Badanich, K. A., Adler, K. J., & Kirstein, C. L. (2006). Adolescents differ from adults in cocaine conditioned place preference and cocaine-induced dopamine in the nucleus accumbens septi. *European Journal of Pharmacology, 550,* 95–106. doi:10.1016/j.ejphar.2006.08.034

Bechara, A., Damasio, A. R., Damasio, H., & Anderson, S. W. (1994). Insensitivity to future consequences following damage to human prefrontal cortex. *Cognition, 50,* 7–15. doi:10.1016/0010-0277(94)90018-3

Benes, F. M., Taylor, J. B., & Cunningham, M. C. (2000). Convergence and plasticity of monoaminergic systems in the medial prefrontal cortex during the postnatal period: Implications for the development of psychopathology. *Cerebral Cortex, 10,* 1014–1027. doi:10.1093/cercor/10.10.1014

Berns, G. S., Moore, S., & Capra, C. M. (2009). Adolescent engagement in dangerous behaviors is associated with increased white matter maturity of frontal cortex. *PLoS ONE, 4,* e6773. doi:10.1371/journal.pone.0006773

Bjork, J. M., Knutson, B., Fong, G. W., Caggiano, D. M., Bennett, S. M., & Hommer, D. W. (2004). Incentive-elicited brain activation in adolescents: Similarities and differences from young adults. *The Journal of Neuroscience, 24,* 1793–1802. doi:10.1523/JNEUROSCI.4862-03.2004

Bjork, J. M., Lynne-Landsman, S. D., Sirocco, K., & Boyce, C. A. (2012). Brain maturation and risky behavior: The promise and the challenges of neuroimaging-based accounts. *Child Development Perspectives, 6,* 385–391. doi:10.1111/cdep.12001

Bjork, J. M., Smith, A. R., Chen, G., & Hommer, D. W. (2010). Adolescents, adults and rewards: Comparing motivational neurocircuitry recruitment using fMRI. *PLoS ONE, 5,* e11440. doi:10.1371/journal.pone.0011440

Bjorklund, D. F., & Harnishfeger, K. K. (1995). The evolution of inhibition mechanisms and their role in human cognition and behavior. In F. N. Dempster & C. J. Brainerd (Eds.), *Interference & inhibition in cognition* (pp. 141–173). San Diego, CA: Academic Press. doi:10.1016/B978-012208930-5/50006-4

Blakemore, S. J. (2008). The social brain in adolescence. *Nature Reviews Neuroscience, 9,* 267–277. doi:10.1038/nrn2353

Breiter, H. C., Aharon, I., Kahneman, D., Dale, A., & Shizgal, P. (2001). Functional imaging of neural responses to expectancy and experience of monetary gains and losses. *Neuron, 30,* 619–639. doi:10.1016/S0896-6273(01)00303-8

Brenhouse, H. C., Sonntag, K. C., & Andersen, S. L. (2008). Transient D1 dopamine receptor expression on prefrontal cortex projection neurons: Relationship to enhanced motivational salience of drug cues in adolescence. *The Journal of Neuroscience, 28,* 2375–2382. doi:10.1523/JNEUROSCI.5064-07.2008

Brown, M. R., Vilis, T., & Everling, S. (2007). Frontoparietal activation with preparation for antisaccades. *Journal of Neurophysiology, 98,* 1751–1762. doi:10.1152/jn.00460.2007

Bunge, S. A., Dudukovic, N. M., Thomason, M. E., Vaidya, C. J., & Gabrieli, J. D. (2002). Immature frontal lobe contributions to cognitive control in children: Evidence from fMRI. *Neuron, 33,* 301–311. doi:10.1016/S0896-6273(01)00583-9

Caviness, V. S., Kennedy, D. N., Bates, J. F., & Makris, N. (1996). The developing human brain: A morphometric profile. In R. W. Thatcher, G. R. Lyon, J. Rumsey, & N. A. Krasnegor (Eds.), *Developmental neuroimaging: Mapping the development of brain and behavior* (pp. 3–14). New York, NY: Academic Press.

Chambers, R. A., Taylor, J. R., & Petenza, M. N. (2003). Developmental neurocircuitry of motivation in adolescence: A critical period of addiction vulnerability. *The American Journal of Psychiatry, 160,* 1041–1052. doi:10.1176/appi.ajp.160.6.1041

Chein, J., Albert, D., O'Brien, L., Uckert, K., & Steinberg, L. (2011). Peers increase adolescent risk taking by enhancing activity in the brain's reward circuitry. *Developmental Science, 14,* F1–F10. doi:10.1111/j.1467-7687.2010.01035.x

Chikama, M., McFarland, N. R., Amaral, D. G., & Haber, S. N. (1997). Insular cortical projections to functional regions of the striatum correlate with cortical cytoarchitectonic organization in the primate. *Journal of Neuroscience, 17*(24), 9686–9705.

Christakou, A., Brammer, M., & Rubia, K. (2011). Maturation of limbic corticostriatal activation and connectivity associated with developmental changes in temporal discounting. *NeuroImage, 54,* 1344–1354. doi:10.1016/j.neuroimage.2010.08.067

Ciesielski, K. T., Lesnik, P. G., Savoy, R. L., Grant, E. P., & Ahlfors, S. P. (2006). Developmental neural networks in children performing a Categorical N-Back Task. *NeuroImage, 33,* 980–990. doi:10.1016/j.neuroimage.2006.07.028

Cohen, J. R., Asarnow, R. F., Sabb, F. W., Bilder, R. M., Bookheimer, S. Y., Knowlton, B. J., & Poldrack, R. A. (2010). A unique adolescent response to reward prediction errors. *Nature Neuroscience, 13,* 669–671. doi:10.1038/nn.2558

Cools, R. (2008). Role of dopamine in the motivational and cognitive control of behavior. *The Neuroscientist, 14,* 381–395. doi:10.1177/1073858408317009

Cools, R. (2011). Dopaminergic control of the striatum for high-level cognition. *Current Opinion in Neurobiology, 21,* 402–407. doi:10.1016/j.conb.2011.04.002

Crone, E. A., Wendelken, C., Donohue, S., van Leijenhorst, L., & Bunge, S. A. (2006). Neurocognitive development of the ability to manipulate information in working memory. *Proceedings of the National Academy of Sciences of the United States of America, 103,* 9315–9320. doi:10.1073/pnas.0510088103

Delgado, M. R., Locke, H. M., Stenger, V. A., & Fiez, J. A. (2003). Dorsal striatum responses to reward and punishment: Effects of valence and magnitude manipulations. *Cognitive, Affective & Behavioral Neuroscience, 3,* 27–38. doi:10.3758/CABN.3.1.27

Delgado, M. R., Nystrom, L. E., Fissell, C., Noll, D. C., & Fiez, J. A. (2000). Tracking the hemodynamic responses to reward and punishment in the striatum. *Journal of Neurophysiology, 84,* 3072–3077.

Diamond, A., & Goldman-Rakic, P. S. (1989). Comparison of human infants and rhesus monkeys on Piaget's AB task: Evidence for dependence on dorsolateral prefrontal cortex. *Experimental Brain Research, 74,* 24–40. doi:10.1007/BF00248277

Di Martino, A., Scheres, A., Margulies, D. S., Kelly, A. M., Uddin, L. Q., Shehzad, Z., . . . Milham, M. P. (2008). Functional connectivity of human striatum: A resting state FMRI study. *Cerebral Cortex, 18*(12), 2735–2747.

Elliott, R., Newman, J. L., Longe, O. A., & Deakin, J. F. (2003). Differential response patterns in the striatum and orbitofrontal cortex to financial reward in humans: A parametric functional magnetic resonance imaging study. *The Journal of Neuroscience, 23*, 303–307.

Eluvathingal, T. J., Hasan, K. M., Kramer, L., Fletcher, J. M., & Ewing-Cobbs, L. (2007). Quantitative diffusion tensor tractography of association and projection fibers in normally developing children and adolescents. *Cerebral Cortex, 17*, 2760–2768. doi:10.1093/cercor/bhm003

Erickson, S. L., & Lewis, D. A. (2002). Postnatal development of parvalbumin- and GABA transporter-immunoreactive axon terminals in monkey prefrontal cortex. *The Journal of Comparative Neurology, 448*, 186–202. doi:10.1002/cne.10249

Ernst, M., Nelson, E. E., Jazbec, S., McClure, E. B., Monk, C. S., Leibenluft, E., . . . Pine, D. S. (2005). Amygdala and nucleus accumbens in responses to receipt and omission of gains in adults and adolescents. *NeuroImage, 25*, 1279–1291. doi:10.1016/j.neuroimage.2004.12.038

Everling, S., & Munoz, D. P. (2000). Neuronal correlates for preparatory set associated with pro-saccades and anti-saccades in the primate frontal eye field. *The Journal of Neuroscience, 20*, 387–400.

Fair, D. A., Dosenbach, N. U., Church, J. A., Cohen, A. L., Brahmbhatt, S., Miezin, F. M., . . . Schlaggar, B. L. (2007). Development of distinct control networks through segregation and integration. *Proceedings of the National Academy of Sciences of the United States of America, 104*, 13507–13512. doi:10.1073/pnas.0705843104

Forbes, E. E., & Dahl, R. E. (2010). Pubertal development and behavior: Hormonal activation of social and motivational tendencies. *Brain and Cognition, 72*, 66–72. doi:10.1016/j.bandc.2009.10.007

Fudge, J. L., Kinishio, K., Walsh, P., Richard, C., & Haber, S. N. (2002). Amygdaloid projections to ventromedial striatal subterritories in the primate. *Neuroscience, 110* (2), 257–275.

Fuster, J. M. (1989). *The Prefrontal Cortex* (Vol. 2). New York: Raven Press.

Fuster, J. M. (2002). Frontal lobe and cognitive development. *Journal of Neurocytology, 31*, 373–385. doi:10.1023/A:1024190429920

Galvan, A., Hare, T., Voss, H., Glover, G., & Casey, B. J. (2007). Risk-taking and the adolescent brain: Who is at risk? *Developmental Science, 10*, F8–F14. doi:10.1111/j.1467-7687.2006.00579.x

Galvan, A., Hare, T. A., Parra, C. E., Penn, J., Voss, H., Glover, G., & Casey, B. J. (2006). Earlier development of the accumbens relative to orbitofrontal cortex might underlie risk-taking behavior in adolescents. *The Journal of Neuroscience, 26*, 6885–6892. doi:10.1523/JNEUROSCI.1062-06.2006

Geier, C. F., Garver, K., Terwilliger, R., & Luna, B. (2009). Development of working memory maintenance. *Journal of Neurophysiology, 101*, 84–99. doi:10.1152/jn.90562.2008

Geier, C. F., & Luna, B. (2009). The maturation of incentive processing and cognitive control. *Pharmacology, Biochemistry and Behavior, 93*, 212–221. doi:10.1016/j.pbb.2009.01.021

Geier, C. F., & Luna, B. (2012). Developmental effects of incentives on response inhibition. *Child Development, 83*, 1262–1274. doi:10.1111/j.1467-8624.2012.01771.x

Geier, C. F., Terwilliger, R., Teslovich, T., Velanova, K., & Luna, B. (2010). Immaturities in reward processing and its influence on inhibitory control in adolescence. *Cerebral Cortex, 20*, 1613–1629. doi:10.1093/cercor/bhp225

Giedd, J. N., Blumenthal, J., Jeffries, N. O., Castellanos, F. X., Liu, H., Zijdenbos, A., . . . Rappaport, J. L. (1999). Brain development during childhood and adolescence: A longitudinal MRI study. *Nature Neuroscience, 2*, 861–863. doi:10.1038/13158

Giorgio, A., Watkins, K. E., Douaud, G., James, A. C., James, S., De Stefano, N., . . . Johansen-Berg, H. (2008). Changes in white matter microstructure during adolescence. *NeuroImage, 39*, 52–61. doi:10.1016/j.neuroimage.2007.07.043

Gogtay, N., Giedd, J. N., Lusk, L., Hayashi, K. M., Greenstein, D., Vaituzis, A. C., . . . Thompson, P. M. (2004). Dynamic mapping of human cortical development during childhood through early adulthood. *Proceedings of the National Academy of Sciences of the United States of America, 101*, 8174–8179. doi:10.1073/pnas.0402680101

Goldman-Rakic, P. S. (1987). Circuitry of primate prefrontal cortex and regulation of behavior by representational memory. In V. B. Mountcastle (Ed.), *Handbook of physiology, section 1. The nervous system, vol. v. Higher functions of the brain, part 1* (pp. 373–417). Bethesda, MD: American Physiology Society.

Goldman-Rakic, P. S., & Brown, R. M. (1982). Postnatal development of monoamine content and synthesis in the cerebral cortex of rhesus monkeys. *Brain Research, 254*, 339–349.

Graham v. Florida, 560 U.S. _____ (2010).

Haber, S. N., Kunishio, K., Mizobuchi, M., & Lynd-Balta, E. (1995). The orbital and medial prefrontal circuit through the primate basal ganglia. *The Journal of Neuroscience, 15* (7 Pt 1), 4851–4867.

Hallett, P. E. (1978). Primary and secondary saccades to goals defined by instructions. *Vision Research, 18*, 1279–1296. doi:10.1016/0042-6989(78)90218-3

Hare, T. A., O'Doherty, J., Camerer, C. F., Schultz, W., & Rangel, A. (2008). Dissociating the role of the orbitofrontal cortex and the striatum in the computation of goal values and prediction errors. *The Journal of Neuroscience, 28*, 5623–5630. doi:10.1523/JNEUROSCI.1309-08.2008

Hedner, T., Iversen, K., & Lundborg, P. (1984). Central GABA mechanisms during postnatal development in the rat: Neurochemical characteristics. *Journal of Neural Transmission, 59*, 105–118. doi:10.1007/BF01255409

Heron, M. (2012). Deaths: Leading causes for 2008. *National Vital Statistics Report, 6*, 1–94.

Hikosaka, O., Nakumura, K., & Nakahara, H. (2006). Basal ganglia orient eyes to reward. *Journal of Neurophysiology, 95*, 567–584. doi:10.1152/jn.00458.2005

Huttenlocher, P. R. (1990). Morphometric study of human cerebral cortex development. *Neuropsychologia, 28*, 517–527. doi:10.1016/0028-3932(90)90031-I

Huttenlocher, P. R., & Dabholkar, A. S. (1997). Regional differences in synaptogenesis in human cerebral cortex. *The Journal of Comparative Neurology, 387*, 167–178. doi:10.1002/(SICI)1096-9861(19971020)387:2<167::AID-CNE1 >3.0.CO;2-Z

Hwang, K., Hallquist, M. N., & Luna, B. (2012). The development of hub architecture in the human functional brain network. *Cerebral Cortex*. Advance online publication. doi:10.1093/cercor/bhs227

Hwang, K., & Luna, B. (2011). The development of brain connectivity supporting prefrontal cortical functions. In D. T. Stuss & R. T. Knight (Eds.), *Principle of frontal lobe functions* (2nd ed.). New York, NY: Oxford University Press.

Hwang, K., Velanova, K., & Luna, B. (2010). Strengthening of top-down frontal cognitive control networks underlying the development of inhibitory control: An fMRI effective connectivity study. *The Journal of Neuroscience, 30*, 15535–15545. doi:10.1523/JNEUROSCI.2825-10.2010

Johnson, M. H. (1995). The inhibition of automatic saccades in early infancy. *Developmental Psychobiology, 28*, 281–291. doi:10.1002/dev.420280504

Klingberg, T., Forssberg, H., & Westerberg, H. (2002). Increased brain activity in frontal and parietal cortex underlies the development of visuospatial working memory capacity during childhood. *Journal of Cognitive Neuroscience, 14*, 1–10. doi:10.1162/089892902317205276

Knutson, B., & Cooper, J. C. (2005). Functional magnetic resonance imaging of reward prediction. *Current Opinion in Neurology, 18*, 411–417. doi:10.1097/01.wco.0000173463.24758.f6

Knutson, B., Westdorp, A., Kaiser, E., & Hommer, D. (2000). FMRI visualization of brain activity during a monetary incentive delay task. *NeuroImage, 12*, 20–27. doi:10.1006/nimg.2000.0593

Kringelbach, M. L. (2005). The human orbitofrontal cortex: Linking reward to hedonic experience. *Nature Reviews Neuroscience, 6*, 691–702. doi:10.1038/nrn1747

Lambe, E. K., Krimer, L. S., & Goldman-Rakic, P. S. (2000). Differential postnatal development of catecholamine and serotonin inputs to identified neurons in prefrontal cortex of rhesus monkey. *The Journal of Neuroscience, 20*, 8780–8787.

Laviola, G., Adriani, W., Terranova, M. L., & Gerra, G. (1999). Psychobiological risk factors for vulnerability to psychostimulants in human adolescents and animal models. *Neuroscience and Biobehavioral Reviews, 23*, 993–1010. doi:10.1016/S0149-7634(99)00032-9

Lebel, C., Walker, L., Leemans, A., Phillips, L., & Beaulieu, C. (2008). Microstructural maturation of the human brain from childhood to adulthood. *NeuroImage, 40*, 1044–1055. doi:10.1016/j.neuroimage.2007.12.053

Lewis, D. A. (1997). Development of the prefrontal cortex during adolescence: Insights into vulnerable neural circuits in schizophrenia. *Neuropsychopharmacology, 16,* 385–398. doi:10.1016/S0893-133X(96)00277-1

Lewis, D. A., Melchitzky, D. S., & Burgos, G. G. (2002). Specificity in the functional architecture of primate prefrontal cortex. *Journal of Neurocytology, 31,* 265–276. doi:10.1023/A:1024174026286

Lidow, M. S., & Rakic, P. (1992). Scheduling of monoaminergic neurotransmitter receptor expression in the primate neocortex during postnatal development. *Cerebral Cortex, 2,* 401–416. doi:10.1093/cercor/2.5.401

Luciana, M., & Nelson, C. A. (1998). The functional emergence of prefrontally-guided working memory systems in four- to eight-year-old children. *Neuropsychologia, 36,* 273–293. doi:10.1016/S0028-3932(97)00109-7

Luciana, M., Wahlstrom, D., Porter, J. N., & Collins, P. F. (2012). Dopaminergic modulation of incentive motivation in adolescence: Age-related changes in signaling, individual differences, and implications for the development of self-regulation. *Developmental Psychology, 48,* 844–861. doi:10.1037/a0027432

Luna, B., Thulborn, K. R., Munoz, D. P., Merriam, E. P., Garver, K. E., Minshew, N. J., . . . Sweeney, J. A. (2001). Maturation of widely distributed brain function subserves cognitive development. *NeuroImage, 13,* 786–793. doi:10.1006/nimg.2000.0743

Mathews, I. Z., & McCormick, C. M. (2007). Female and male rats in late adolescence differ from adults in amphetamine-induced locomotor activity, but not in conditioned place preference for amphetamine. *Behavioural Pharmacology, 18,* 641–650. doi:10.1097/FBP.0b013e3282effbf5

McClure, S. M., York, M. K., & Montague, P. R. (2004). The neural substrates of reward processing in humans: The modern role of fMRI. *The Neuroscientist, 10,* 260–268. doi:10.1177/1073858404263526

McCutcheon, J. E., White, F. J., & Marinelli, M. (2009). Individual differences in dopamine cell neuroadaptations following cocaine self-administration. *Biological Psychiatry, 66,* 801–803. doi:10.1016/j.biopsych.2009.04.018

Miller v. Alabama, 567 U.S. ____ (2012).

Moffitt, T. E. (1993). Adolescence-limited and life-course-persistent antisocial behavior: A developmental taxonomy. *Psychological Review, 100,* 674–701. doi:10.1037/0033-295X.100.4.674

Montague, D. M., Lawler, C. P., Mailman, R. B., & Gilmore, J. H. (1999). Developmental regulation of the dopamine D1 receptor in human caudate and putamen. *Neuropsychopharmacology, 21,* 641–649. doi:10.1016/S0893-133X(99)00062-7

Nelson, C. A., Monk, C. S., Lin, J., Carver, L. J., Thomas, K. M., & Truwitt, C. L. (2000). Functional neuroanatomy of spatial working memory in children. *Developmental Psychology, 36,* 109–116. doi:10.1037/0012-1649.36.1.109

O'Doherty, J. P. (2004). Reward representations and reward-related learning in the human brain: Insights from neuroimaging. *Current Opinion in Neurobiology, 14,* 769–776. doi:10.1016/j.conb.2004.10.016

Olesen, P. J., Macoveanu, J., Tegner, J., & Klingberg, T. (2007). Brain activity related to working memory and distraction in children and adults. *Cerebral Cortex, 17,* 1047–1054. doi:10.1093/cercor/bhl014

Op de Macks, Z. A., Gunther Moor, B.. Overgaauw, S., Guroglu, B., Dahl, R. E., & Crone, E. A. (2011). Testosterone levels correspond with increased ventral striatum activation in response to monetary rewards in adolescents. *Developmental Cognitive Neuroscience, 1,* 517–529. doi:10.1016/j.dcn.2011.06.003

Padmanabhan, A., Geier, C. F., Ordaz, S. J., Teslovich, T., & Luna, B. (2011). Developmental changes in brain function underlying the influence of reward processing on inhibitory control. *Developmental Cognitive Neuroscience, 1,* 517–529. doi:10.1016/j.dcn.2011.06.004

Paulsen, D. J., Platt, M. L., Huettel, S. A., & Brannon, E. M. (2011). Decision-making under risk in children, adolescents, and young adults. *Frontiers in Psychology, 2*(72). doi:10.3389/fpsyg.2011.00072

Reyna, V. F., & Brainerd, C. J. (2011). Dual processes in decision making and developmental neuroscience: A fuzzy-trace model. *Developmental Review, 31,* 180–206. doi:10.1016/j.dr.2011.07.004

Roesch, M. R., & Olson, C. R. (2003). Impact of expected reward on neuronal activity in prefrontal cortex, frontal and supplementary eye fields and premotor cortex. *Journal of Neurophysiology, 90,* 1766–1789. doi:10.1152/jn.00019.2003

Roesch, M. R., & Olson, C. R. (2004). Neuronal activity related to reward value and motivation in primate frontal cortex. *Science, 304,* 307–310. doi:10.1126/science.1093223

Roper v. Simmons, 543 U.S. 551 (2005).

Rosenberg, D. R., & Lewis, D. A. (1994). Changes in the dopaminergic innervation of monkey prefrontal cortex during late postnatal development: A tyrosine hydroxylase immunohistochemical study. *Biological Psychiatry, 36,* 272–277. doi:10.1016/0006-3223(94)90610-6

Rosenberg, D. R., & Lewis, D. A. (1995). Postnatal maturation of the dopaminergic innervation of monkey prefrontal and motor cortices: A tyrosine hydroxylase immunohistochemical analysis. *The Journal of Comparative Neurology, 358,* 383–400. doi:10.1002/cne.903580306

Rubia, K., Smith, A. B., Woolley, J., Nosarti, C., Heyman, I., Taylor, E., & Brammer, M. (2006). Progressive increase of frontostriatal brain activation from childhood to adulthood during event-related tasks of cognitive control. *Human Brain Mapping, 27,* 973–993. doi:10.1002/hbm.20237

Rushworth, M. F., Noonan, M. P., Boorman, E. D., Walton, M. E., & Behrens, T. E. (2011). Frontal cortex and reward-guided learning and decision-making. *Neu-*

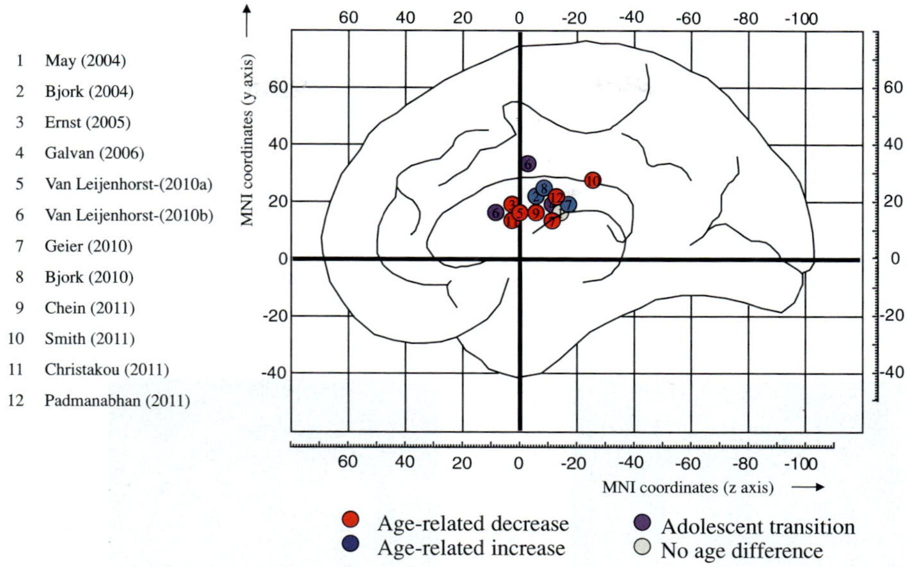

Color Plate 1. Meta-analysis of available reward processing studies in adolescence, with a specific focus on the ventral striatum.

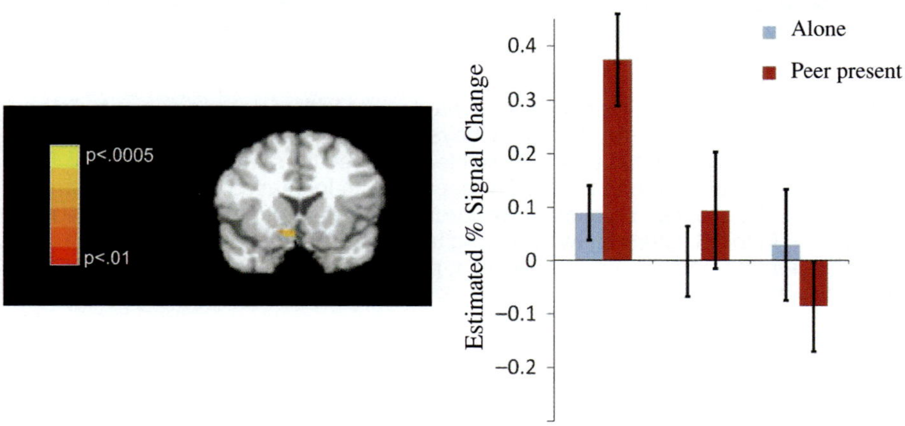

Color Plate 2. Left panel: Age (adolescents, young adults, adults) × Social Condition (peer present vs. alone) interaction in the right ventral striatum (vs. MNI peak coordinates, x = 9, y = 12, z = –8). Right panel: Mean estimated BOLD signal change (beta coefficients) in adolescents, young adults, and adults under ALONE (blue bars) and PEER PRESENT (red bars) conditions. Error bars indicate standard error of the mean. Adapted from "Peers Increase Adolescent Risk Taking by Enhancing Activity in the Brain's Reward Circuitry," by J. Chein, D. Albert, L. O'Brien, K. Uckert, and L. Steinberg, 2011, *Developmental Science, 14,* p. F6. Copyright 2011 by Wiley-Blackwell. Adapted with permission.

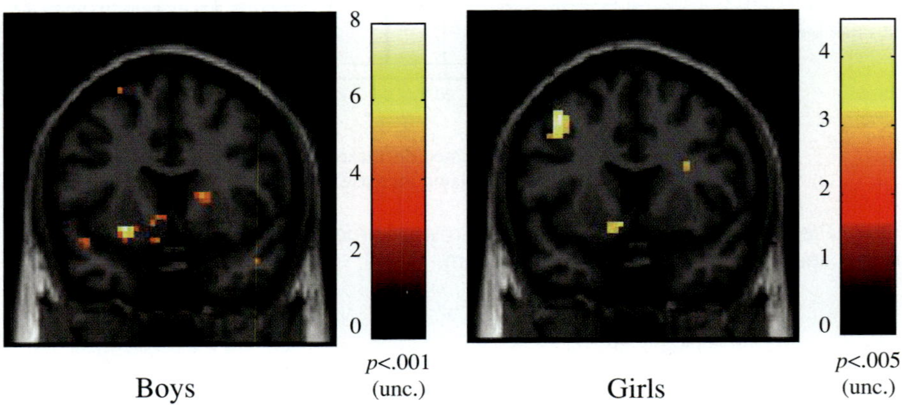

Color Plate 3. Regions of activation for reward > loss with testosterone as predictor included the bilateral ventral striatum in boys (left) and left ventral striatum in girls (right), at a threshold of $p < .005$, uncorrected. Colored bars represent *t* values. Adapted from “Testosterone Levels Correspond With Increased Ventral Striatum Activation in Response to Monetary Rewards in Adolescents,” by Z. A. Op de Macks, B. Gunther Moor, S. Overgaauw, B. Guroglu, R. E. Dahl, and E. A. Crone, 2011, *Developmental Cognitive Neuroscience, 1,* p. 512. Copyright 2011 by Elsevier. Adapted with permission.

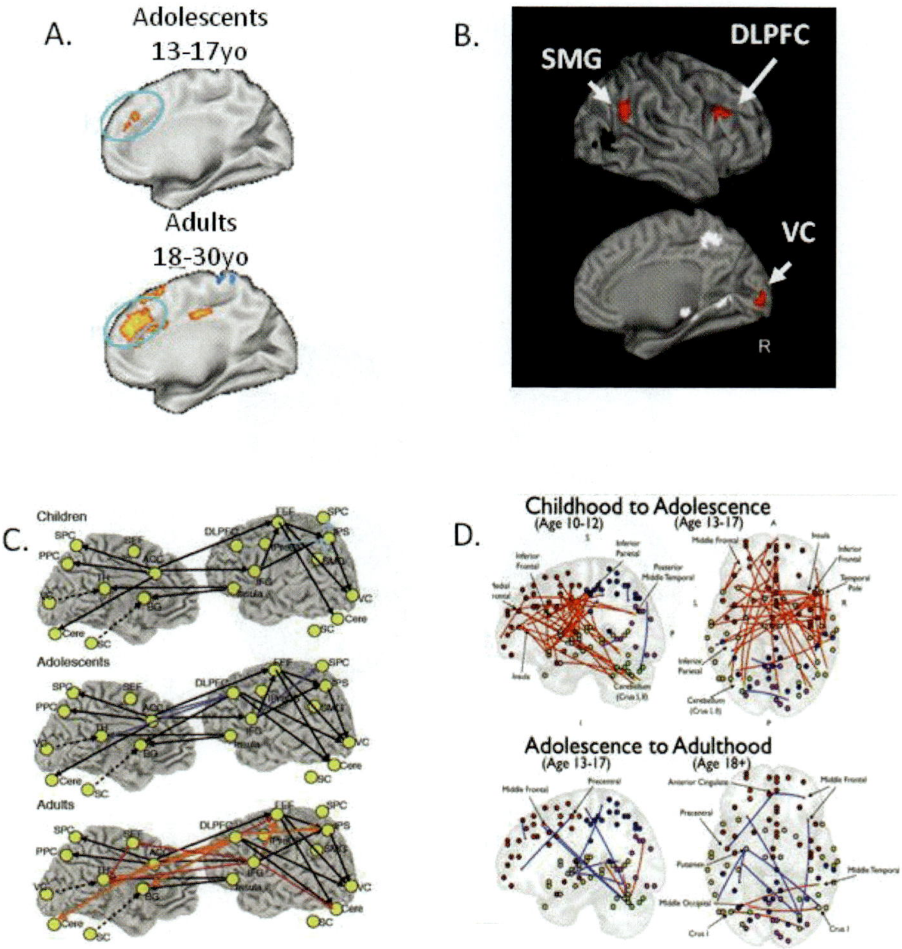

Color Plate 4. fMRI studies delineating changes in brain function underlying cognitive development. (A). Adolescents show decreased recruitment of dorsal anterior cingulate cortex (dACC) during inhibitory errors reflecting limitations in performance monitoring. From "Maturational Changes in Anterior Cingulate and Frontoparietal Recruitment Support the Development of Error Processing and Inhibitory Control," by K. Velanova, M. E. Wheeler, and B. Luna, 2008, *Cerebral Cortex,* 18, p. 2516. Copyright 2008 by Oxford University Press. Adapted with permission. (B). Adolescents show decreased recruitment of the frontoposterior network supporting the maintenance of cognitive control (Velanova et al., 2009). (C). Granger effective connectivity indicates that prefrontal top-down connectivity becomes established by adolescence and subsequently strengthens into adulthood (Hwang et al., 2010). (D). Resting state connectivity shows that while the foundational hub architecture of the brain is already established in childhood, prefrontal hub to non-hub connections become established from childhood to adolescence subsequently showing small refinements integrating cerebellar hubs. From "The Development of Hub Architecture in the Human Functional Brain Network," by K. Hwang, M. N. Hallquist, and B. Luna, 2012, *Cerebral Cortex.* Advance online publication. Copyright 2012 by Oxford University Press. Adapted with permission.

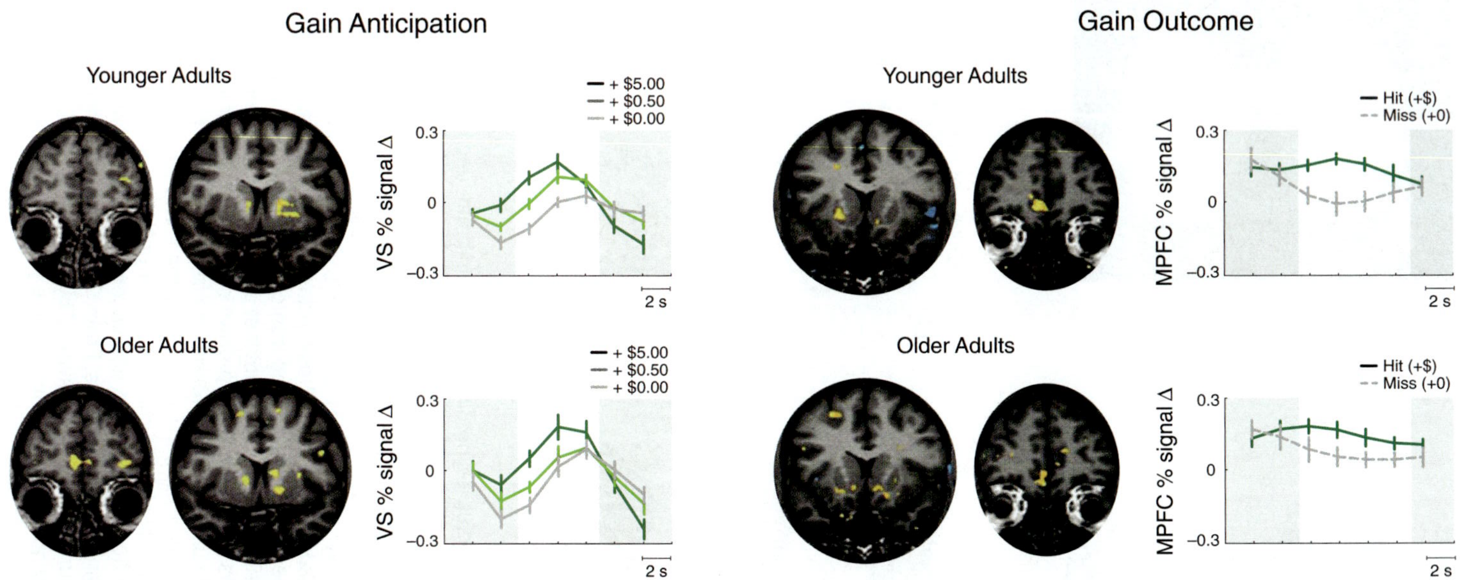

Color Plate 5. Ventral striatal functional activity is modulated by magnitude during anticipation of monetary gains in both younger and older adults (left panel). Medial prefrontal regions show similar differences in signal change between gain and nongain outcomes in both younger and older adults (right panel). All statistical brain maps displayed are thresholded at $p < .0001$ uncorrected. All error bars on timecourses are SEM (standard error of the mean).

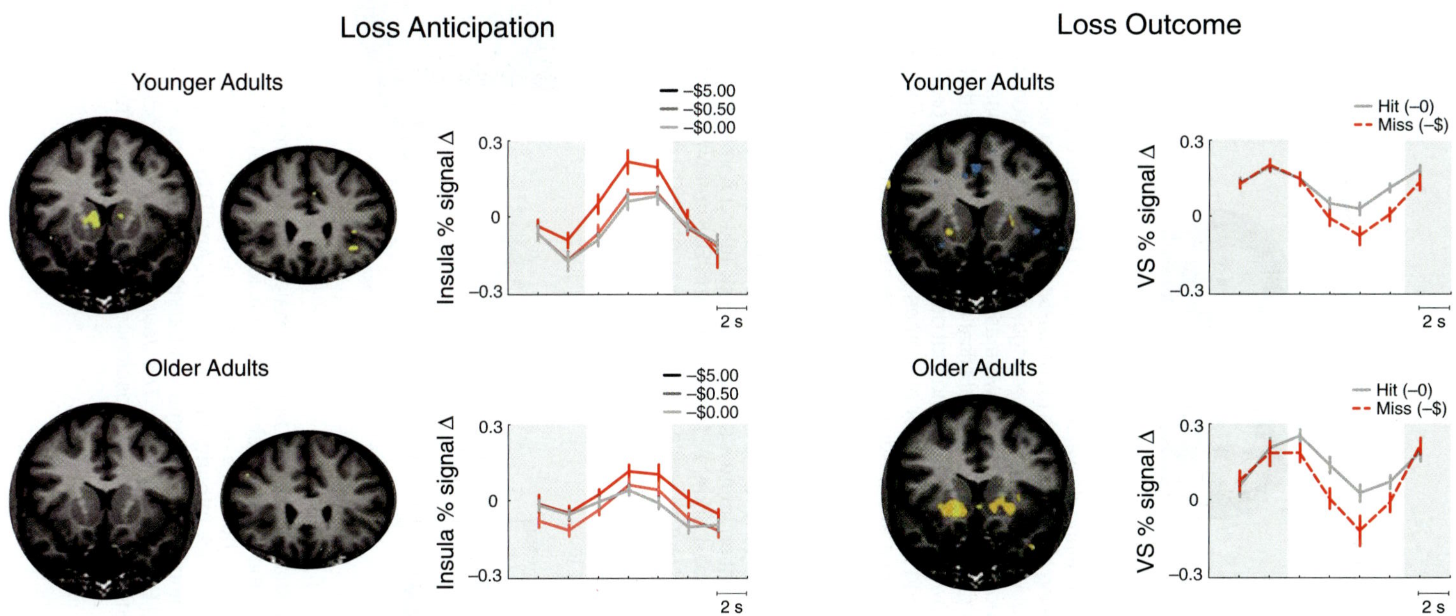

Color Plate 6. Functional activity in the caudate and insula is modulated by magnitude during anticipation of monetary gains in younger but not older adults (left panel). In contrast, medial prefrontal and ventral striatal regions show similar differences in signal change between nonloss and loss outcomes in both younger and older adults (right panel). All statistical brain maps displayed are thresholded at $p < .0001$ uncorrected. All error bars on timecourses are SEM (standard error of the mean).

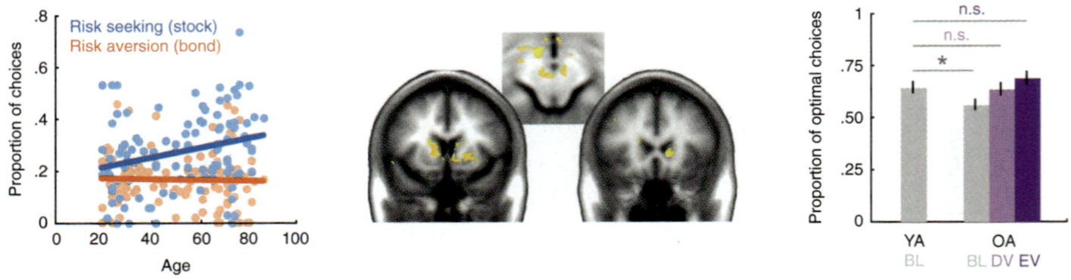

Color Plate 7. In a risky financial investment task (N = 110), older adults make more mistakes when choosing assets that are probabilistically associated with rewards (selection of stocks) but do not differ from younger adults in risk aversion (selection of bonds). These behavioral age differences were associated with increased neural variability with age in the striatum (N = 53). Statistical maps are thresholded at $p < .0001$, uncorrected. In a follow-up study, we found that decision aids which provided a visual depiction of the running history of prior outcomes (discrete value, DV) or a summary of prior performance and prediction of future performance (integrated value, IV) increased performance in older adults to the performance level of younger adults at baseline (BL). From "Variability in Nucleus Accumbens Activity Mediates Age-Related Suboptimal Financial Risk Taking," by G. R. Samanez-Larkin, C. M. Kuhnen, D. J. Yoo, and B. Knutson, 2010, *The Journal of Neuroscience, 30,* pp. 1429–1430. Copyright 2010 by the Society for Neuroscience. Adapted with permission. And from "Expected Value Information Improves Financial Risk Taking Across the Adult Life Span," by G. R. Samanez-Larkin, A. D. Wagner, and B. Knutson, 2011, *Social Cognitive and Affective Neuroscience, 6,* p. 214. Copyright 2010 by Oxford University Press. Adapted with permission.

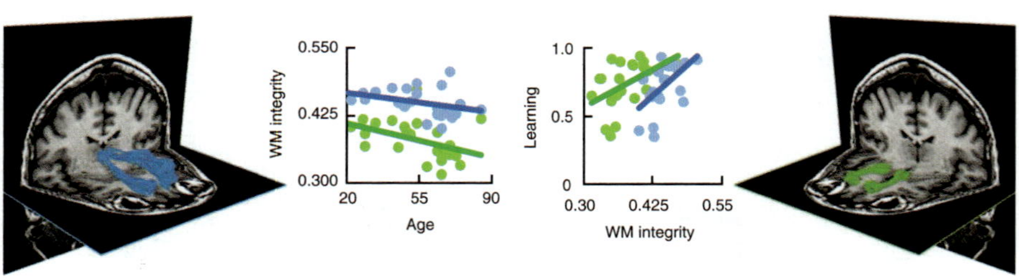

Color Plate 8. White matter integrity from the thalamus to the medial prefrontal cortex (left, blue) and the medial prefrontal cortex to the ventral striatum (right, green) is associated with both age and reward learning performance. From "Frontostriatal White Matter Integrity Mediates Adult Age Differences in Probabilistic Reward Learning," by G. R. Samanez-Larkin, S. M. Levens, L. M. Perry, R. F. Dougherty, and B. Knutson, 2012, *The Journal of Neuroscience, 32,* p. 5335. Copyright 2012 by the Society for Neuroscience. Adapted with permission.

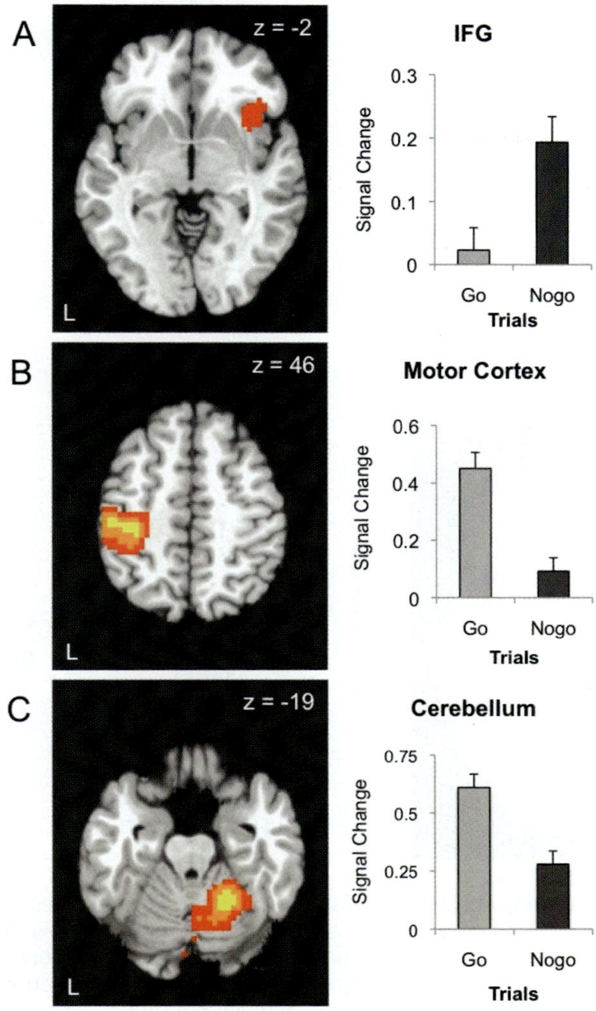

Color Plate 9. Activation maps and percent change in magnetic resonance (MR) signal during the "hot" go/no-go task as a function of go and no-go trials. (A). The right inferior frontal cortex was associated with correct inhibition of a response (no-go) relative to making a correct response (go). (Left) Activation map depicting right inferior frontal gyrus activation, thresholded at $p < .05$, whole-brain corrected displayed on a representative high-resolution T1 weighted axial image. (Right) Percent change in MR signal for go and no-go trials in the inferior frontal gyrus. (B). The left primary motor cortex was associated with making a correct response (go) relative to correctly withholding a response. (Left) Activation map depicting activation in left precentral gyrus, thresholded at $p < .05$, whole-brain corrected displayed on a representative high-resolution T1 weighted axial image. (Right) Percent change in MR signal for go and no-go trials in the left precentral gyrus. (C). The cerebellum was associated with making a correct response (go) relative to correctly withholding a response. (Left) Activation map depicting cerebellum activation, thresholded at $p < .05$, whole-brain corrected displayed on a representative high resolution T1 weighted axial image. (Right) Percent change in MR signal for go and no-go trials in the cerebellum. Error bars represent 1 standard error above and below the mean. From "Behavioral and Neural Correlates of Delay of Gratification 40 Years Later," by B. J. Casey et al., 2011. *Proceedings of the National Academy of Sciences of the United States of America,* 108, p. 15000. Copyright 2011 by the National Academy of Sciences. Adapted with permission.

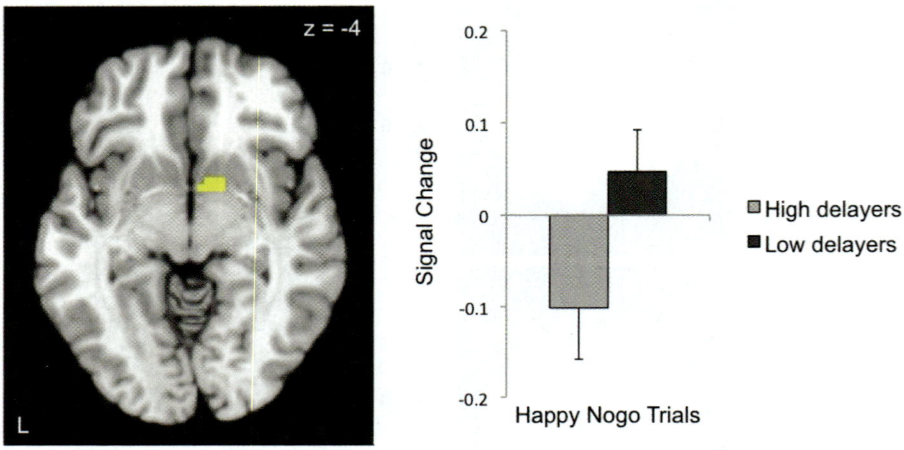

Color Plate 10. Low delay ability in early childhood predicts greater recruitment of ventral striatum to happy no-go trials (i.e., when inhibiting responses to positive social cues) 40 years later. (Left) Activation map for the three-way interaction of task, emotion, and delay group depicting ventral striatum activity thresholded at $p < .05$, small volume corrected displayed on a representative high-resolution T1 weighted axial image. (Right) Percent change in magnetic resonance (MR) signal to happy no-go trials in high and low delayers. Error bars represent 1 standard error above and below the mean. From "Behavioral and Neural Correlates of Delay of Gratification 40 Years Later," by B. J. Casey et al., 2011. *Proceedings of the National Academy of Sciences of the United States of America,* 108, p. 15001. Copyright 2011 by the National Academy of Sciences. Adapted with permission.

ron, *70*(6), 1054–1069. doi: S0896-6273(11)00395-3[pii]10.1016/j.neuron.2011.05.014

Scherf, K. S., Sweeney, J. A., & Luna, B. (2006). Brain basis of developmental change in visuospatial working memory. *Journal of Cognitive Neuroscience*, *18*, 1045–1058. doi:10.1162/jocn.2006.18.7.1045

Schultz, W. (2000). Multiple reward signals in the brain. *Nature Reviews Neuroscience*, *1*, 199–207. doi:10.1038/35044563

Schultz, W., Preuschoff, K., Camerer, C., Hsu, M., Fiorillo, C. D., Tobler, P. N., & Bossaerts, T. (2008). Explicit neural signals reflecting reward uncertainty. *Philosophical Transactions of the Royal Society of London. Series B, Biological Sciences*, *363*, 3801–3811. doi:10.1098/rstb.2008.0152

Scott, E. S., & Steinberg, L. (2008). *Rethinking juvenile justice*. Boston, MA: Harvard University Press.

Seeman, P., Bzowej, N. H., Guan, H. C., Bergeron, C., Becker, L. E., Reynolds, G. P., . . . Tourtellotte, W. W. (1987). Human brain dopamine receptors in children and aging adults. *Synapse*, *1*(5), 399–404. doi:10.1002/syn.890010503

Selemon, L. D., & Goldman-Rakic, P. S. (1985). Longitudinal topography and interdigitation of corticostriatal projections in the Rhesus monkey. *Journal of Neuroscience*, *5*, 776–794.

Shad, M. U., Bidesi, A. P., Chen, L. A., Ernst, M., & Rao, U. (2011). Neurobiology of decision making in depressed adolescents: A functional magnetic resonance imaging study. *Journal of the American Academy of Child & Adolescent Psychiatry*, *50*, 612–621. doi:10.1016/j.jaac.2011.03.011

Smith, A. B., Halari, R., Giampetro, V., Brammer, M., & Rubia, K. (2011). Developmental effects of reward on sustained attention networks. *NeuroImage*, *56*, 1693–1704. doi:10.1016/j.neuroimage.2011.01.072

Somerville, L. H., & Casey, B. (2010). Developmental neurobiology of cognitive control and motivational systems. *Current Opinion in Neurobiology*, *20*, 236–241. doi:10.1016/j.conb.2010.01.006

Sowell, E. R., Thompson, P. M., Holmes, C. J., Jernigan, T. L., & Toga, A. W. (1999). In vivo evidence for post-adolescent brain maturation in frontal and striatal regions. *Nature Neuroscience*, *2*, 859–861. doi:10.1038/13154

Spear, L. P. (2000). The adolescent brain and age-related behavioral manifestations. *Neuroscience & Biobehavioral Reviews*, *24*, 417–463. doi:10.1016/S0149-7634(00)00014-2

Spear, L. P. (2010). *The behavioral neuroscience of adolescence*. New York, NY: Norton.

Spear, L. P., & Brake, S. C. (1983). Periadolescence: Age-dependent behavior and psychopharmacological responsivity in rats. *Developmental Psychobiology*, *16*, 83–109. doi:10.1002/dev.420160203

Spear, L. P., Shalaby, I. A., & Brick, J. (1980). Chronic administration of haloperidol during development: Behavioral and psychopharmacological effects. *Psychopharmacology*, *70*, 47–58. doi:10.1007/BF00432369

Steinberg, L., Albert, D., Cauffman, E., Banich, M., Graham, S., & Woodlard, J. (2008). Age differences in sensation seeking and impulsivity as indexed by behavior and self-report: Evidence for a dual systems model. *Developmental Psychology, 44*, 1764–1778. doi:10.1037/a0012955

Stevens, M. C., Kiehl, K. A., Pearlson, G. D., & Calhoun, V. D. (2007). Functional neural networks underlying response inhibition in adolescents and adults. *Behavioural Brain Research, 181*, 12–22. doi:10.1016/j.bbr.2007.03.023

Thomas, K. M., King, S. W., Franzen, P. L., Welsh, T. F., Berkowitz, A. L., Noll, D. C., . . . Casey, B. J. (1999). A developmental functional MRI study of spatial working memory. *NeuroImage, 10*, 327–338. doi:10.1006/nimg.1999.0466

Thut, G., Schultz, W., Roelcke, U., Nienhusmeier, M., Missimer, J., Maguire, R. P., . . . Leenders, K. L. (1997). Activation of the human brain by monetary reward. *Neuroreport, 8*, 1225–1228. doi:10.1097/00001756-199703240-00033

Tseng, K. Y., & O'Donnell, P. (2005). Post-pubertal emergence of prefrontal cortical up states induced by D1-NMDA co-activation. *Cerebral Cortex, 15*, 49–57. doi:10.1093/cercor/bhh107

van Leijenhorst, L., Crone, E. A., & Bunge, S. A. (2006). Neural correlates of developmental differences in risk estimation and feedback processing. *Neuropsychologia, 44*, 2158–2170. doi:10.1016/j.neuropsychologia.2006.02.002

van Leijenhorst, L., Gunther Moor, B., Op de Macks, Z. A., Rombouts, S. A., Westenberg, P. M., & Crone, E. A. (2010). Adolescent risky decision-making: Neurocognitive development of reward and control regions. *NeuroImage, 51*, 345–355. doi:10.1016/j.neuroimage.2010.02.038

van Leijenhorst, L., Zanolie, K., Van Meel, C. S., Westenberg, P. M., Rombouts, S. A., & Crone, E. A. (2010). What motivates the adolescent? Brain regions mediating reward sensitivity across adolescence. *Cerebral Cortex, 20*(1), 61—69. doi:10.1093/cercor/bhp078

Velanova, K., Wheeler, M. E., & Luna, B. (2008). Maturational changes in anterior cingulate and frontoparietal recruitment support the development of error processing and inhibitory control. *Cerebral Cortex, 18*, 2505–2522. doi:10.1093/cercor/bhn012

Velanova, K., Wheeler, M. E., & Luna, B. (2009). The maturation of task set–related activation supports late developmental improvements in inhibitory control. *The Journal of Neuroscience, 29*, 12558–12567. doi:10.1523/JNEUROSCI.1579-09.2009

Wahlstrom, D., Collins, P., White, T., & Luciana, M. (2010). Developmental changes in dopamine neurotransmission in adolescence: Behavioral implications and issues in assessment. *Brain and Cognition, 72*, 146–159. doi:10.1016/j.bandc.2009.10.013

Wahlstrom, D., White, T., & Luciana, M. (2010). Neurobehavioral evidence for changes in dopamine system activity during adolescence. *Neuroscience and Biobehavioral Reviews, 34*, 631–648. doi:10.1016/j.neubiorev.2009.12.007

Wise, R. A. (2002). Brain reward circuitry: Insights from unsensed incentives. *Neuron, 36*, 229–240. doi:10.1016/S0896-6273(02)00965-0

Wise, R. A. (2004). Dopamine, learning and motivation. *Nature Reviews Neuroscience, 5*, 483–494. doi:10.1038/nrn1406

Yakovlev, P. I., & Lecours, A. R. (1967). The myelogenetic cycles of regional maturation of the brain. In A. Minkowski (Ed.), *Regional development of the brain in early life* (pp. 3–70). Oxford, England: Blackwell Scientific.

5

REWARD PROCESSING AND RISKY DECISION MAKING IN THE AGING BRAIN

GREGORY R. SAMANEZ-LARKIN AND BRIAN KNUTSON

This chapter reviews studies that have examined how age influences psychological and neural responses to financial incentives and risk. The findings suggest that although processing of basic rewards may be maintained across the adult life span, learning about new rewards may decline as a function of age. These behavioral changes can be linked to relative preservation of striatal function in the face of age-related declines in the connectivity of the prefrontal cortex to the striatum. This frontostriatal disconnection may impair risky decision making, both in the laboratory and in the real world. These novel findings inform theory about how affect and cognition combine to guide

G.R.S.L. is currently supported by a Pathway to Independence Award (K99-AG042596) from the National Institute on Aging. Much of our own work that is discussed in this chapter was supported by grants from the National Institute on Aging (R21-AG030778 to B.K.; F31-AG032804 and F32-AG039131 to G.R.S.L.) and the FINRA Investor Education Foundation. A portion of this chapter is from *Incentive Processing in the Aging Brain: Individual Differences in Value-Based Learning and Decision Making Across the Adult Life Span* (Doctoral Dissertation, Stanford University). Retrieved from http://purl.stanford.edu/vy834vv5149. Adapted with permission.

http://dx.doi.org/10.1037/14322-006
The Neuroscience of Risky Decision Making, by V. F. Reyna and V. Zayas (Editors)

choice, and they imply that a deeper understanding of how the aging brain processes incentives may eventually inform the design of more targeted and effective decision aids for individuals of all ages.

As global demographics shift toward an increase in the proportion of older adults in the population, older adults will control correspondingly more global resources. Will they allocate those resources in the same way they might have earlier in life, or will the very process of aging influence the manner in which financial decisions are approached and negotiated? Although stereotypes about the effects of aging on financial risk taking abound (such as the notion that risk aversion globally increases with age), relatively little evidence has been collected either to verify or refute these commonly held beliefs. Even less is known about what psychological and neural mechanisms might underlie age differences in risky decision making. In this chapter, we review the emerging literature on the influence of aging on incentive processing and financial risk taking, correlated neural substrates, and generalizations to real-world behavior, with a goal of identifying fruitful directions for future research.

Multiple psychological factors, both cognitive and affective, contribute to decision making. An extensive body of research suggests that fluid cognitive capacities such as attention, working memory, and executive control decline with age (Salthouse, 2004), while leaving crystallized cognitive capacities relatively spared (Park et al., 2002). Neuroscience research has linked declines in fluid cognitive capacity to changes in medial temporal and lateral prefrontal cortical function (Hedden & Gabrieli, 2004). In contrast to these fluid cognitive declines, affective processing remains intact in old age, and emerging neuroscience research has begun to link these affective variables to changes in striatal, insular, and prefrontal function (Samanez-Larkin & Carstensen, 2011). Yet, few studies have investigated how age-related changes in cognition, affect, or associated neural circuits influence incentive processing and risky decision making (Samanez-Larkin, 2010).

Over the past several years, we have conducted a series of studies in an initial attempt to examine individual differences in reward processing across the adult life span using an interdisciplinary and translational approach. This approach combines psychological theory, imaging methods from neuroscience, and experimental tasks from behavioral economics and finance to examine decision making in the laboratory and in the real world. Overall, the results reveal a pattern of age differences in the function of neural systems that support aspects of incentive processing and risky decision making. These studies and related work from other laboratories have explored individual differences across a range of reward-related tasks ranging from basic anticipatory and consummatory responses to incentive cues, to probabilistic reward learning, to risky decision making about investments.

PROCESSING OF MONETARY GAINS AND LOSSES

The development of event-related functional magnetic resonance imaging (fMRI) in the early 1990s allowed investigators to visualize second-to-second changes in cortical and subcortical brain function, illuminating neural responses not only in response to events but also during anticipation of those events. Coupled with calibrated tasks involving monetary incentives, researchers could for the first time visualize subcortical responses during anticipation of uncertain gains and losses (Knutson & Cooper, 2005). These experiments were recently extended to studies of human aging. These studies suggested that older adults showed similar subcortical ventral striatal responses similar to those of younger adults when anticipating monetary gains (e.g., in the context of cued reaction time tasks such as the monetary incentive delay task; Knutson, Adams, Fong, & Hommer, 2001; Knutson & Greer, 2008; Samanez-Larkin et al., 2007; see Color Plate 5). Younger and older adults also showed similar neural responses to reward outcomes in the medial prefrontal cortex and ventral striatum (Cox, Aizenstein, & Fiez, 2008; Samanez-Larkin et al., 2007; Samanez-Larkin, Kuhnen, Yoo, & Knutson, 2010; Color Plate 5). Together, these findings provided initial evidence that basic neural responses to the anticipation and receipt of monetary gains are relatively preserved from young adulthood to old age.

A strikingly different pattern, however, emerged during anticipation of monetary losses. Specifically, older adults showed reduced reactivity in the dorsal striatum and anterior insula than younger adults while anticipating monetary loss (Samanez-Larkin et al., 2007). This age difference was also reflected in self-reported affect, such that older adults reported lower levels of anticipatory negative arousal when anticipating losses than did younger adults. This diminished negative arousal during loss anticipation for older adults replicated in an independent sample (Nielsen, Knutson, & Carstensen, 2008). Interestingly, the age differences did not extend to loss outcomes—when older adults actually lost money, they showed neural and affective reactions to loss outcomes similar to those of younger adults (see Color Plate 6).

This age-related asymmetry in gain and loss anticipation coheres with a large body of behavioral research suggesting an age-related "positivity" effect (Carstensen & Mikels, 2005; Mather & Carstensen, 2005). Socioemotional selectivity theory (Carstensen, 2006; Carstensen & Mikels, 2005) posits that as time horizons shrink across adulthood, humans are increasingly motivated to optimize well-being. In fact, cross-sectional and longitudinal experience sampling research has repeatedly demonstrated that emotional experience in everyday life becomes less negative across adulthood (Carstensen, Pasupathi, Mayr, & Nesselroade, 2000; Carstensen et al., 2011). A similar age by valence interaction emerges in studies of attention and memory (Carstensen & Mikels, 2005; Mather & Carstensen, 2005) and appears to extend to incentive anticipation. By extension, diminished negativity during anticipation of losses (but not in response to loss outcomes) may result from older adults avoiding anxiety associated with potential losses unless they actually occur (however, see Wood, Busemeyer, Koling, Cox, & Davis, 2005, for evidence that positivity effects may sometimes extend to outcomes). Whether this suppression of anticipatory anxiety is strategic or more automatic remains an open question. Alternatively, regulation may grow more automatic and require less effort with age (Samanez-Larkin & Carstensen, 2011).

Reduced loss anticipation may enhance the well-being of older adults and may also contribute to age differences in some, but not all, decisions. In fact, a recent study found similarly reduced insula activation in older compared to younger adults when they were offered unfair divisions of money in an ultimatum game (Harlé & Sanfey, 2012). Older adults showed reduced insular activity (previously associated with heightened negative affect) but still rejected more unfair offers than did younger adults. Thus, it remains unclear whether reduced insular responsiveness influences affective experience only or whether it also directly alters learning and decision making. In the monetary incentive delay paradigms mentioned above, performance is typically controlled via adaptive target durations, so that all subjects succeed (or "hit") on approximately two thirds of trials. Thus changes in loss anticipation have no consequence for task performance. It is possible that reduced neural anticipation of loss in old age only emerges when loss anticipation is not required for performance—a possibility we return to later.

In contrast to research suggesting that neural responses to monetary gains are relatively preserved over adulthood, another early study of adult age differences in reward processing drew the opposite conclusion: older adults show reduced neural anticipation of monetary gains and so are less motivated than younger adults (Schott et al., 2007). A number of important differences between these studies may account for their differential findings. First, Schott et al. (2007) used very small magnitude rewards (€0.50) on each trial. They reported an age difference such that ventral striatal signals in older adults did not distinguish between €0.50 and €0.00 during anticipation. In fact, a similar effect is observed in Samanez-Larkin et al., 2007 (see the $0.50 and $0.00 lines in Color Plate 5.). However, in the Samanez-Larkin et al. (2007) study, the $5.00 cues elicited high levels of neural activity in both age groups. Thus, it is possible that low-magnitude rewards were not large enough to elicit strong neural responses. In other studies, low-magnitude rewards produce striatal signals with much lower levels of test–retest reliability than elicited by higher-magnitude rewards (Wu, Samanez-Larkin, & Knutson, 2012). Second, Schott et al. used symbolic cues that did not explicitly communicate reward magnitude on each trial during anticipation. Associations between the cue shapes and reward value were verbally communicated to subjects during the task instructions, but, at some level, the association between these symbolic cues and their value had to be learned. Older adults may not have encoded these cue–reward associations as strongly as younger adults. Such an alternative account predicts that the older adults should have had lower levels of striatal signal during the cue phase (anticipation) but higher levels of striatal signal during the outcome phase (due to a larger reward prediction error)—which exactly matches the observed pattern of findings. Thus, the study may reveal more about the influence of aging on reward learning than about basic incentive processing and motivation. Accordingly, we now turn to studies that explicitly focus on adult age differences in reward learning.

GAIN AND LOSS LEARNING

In contrast to the studies suggesting relative preservation of basic reward processing across adulthood, the literature on reward learning reveals more consistent age differences in performance and associated neural activity. For instance, older adults show reduced ventral striatal activation during probabilistic reward learning in fMRI studies (Mell et al., 2009). Electrophysiological studies have similarly shown reduced activity in frontal cortical regions during probabilistic reward learning in older adults (Eppinger, Hämmerer, & Li, 2011; Eppinger, Kray, Mock, & Mecklinger, 2008; Hämmerer, Li, Müller, & Lindenberger, 2011). Some have suggested that these age differences may be due to older adults' difficulty in dynamically computing prediction errors in novel environments (Eppinger et al., 2011), and some evidence exists to support this account. Specifically, in fMRI studies, striatal activity appears functionally intact in older adults during simple reward-based tasks that do not require novel learning, but more variable and less associated with reward prediction error signals (Samanez-Larkin, 2010) during tasks that require learning in the same individuals and brain regions. These variable responses appear to generalize to some risk-taking tasks, as discussed in the next section on risky decisions.

Recently, theorists have begun to debate whether learning about gains versus losses differentially changes with age. Some evidence suggests that older adults are more sensitive to positive than to negative feedback during probabilistic learning than are younger adults (Denburg, Recknor, Bechara, & Tranel, 2006; Wood et al., 2005). Others have suggested the opposite: that older adults are more sensitive to negative than to positive feedback (Hämmerer et al., 2011). However, one study often cited as providing evidence for increases in learning from negative feedback with age (Frank & Kong, 2008) did not include a younger adult group. Therefore, those findings cannot provide evidence for an age by valence interaction across adulthood. Instead, they suggest that a subset of older adults show a stronger bias toward learning from losses, whereas late middle-aged and young-older adults did not show the same bias. In contrast, healthy young adults and healthy older adults show no valence bias, consistent with an absence of an age by valence interaction in reward learning over much of the adult life span (Frank, Seeberger, & O'Reilly, 2004; Lighthall, Gorlick, Schoeke, Frank, & Mather, 2013). If a shift toward negativity occurs, it appears to occur much later in old age (e.g., after age 80; Frank & Kong, 2008; J. R. Simon, Howard, & Howard, 2010), when investigators must be careful to control for potential confounds related to declining health. A slight nonlinear increase in negativity near the end of life is in fact consistent with the larger literature on emotional experience in everyday life (Carstensen et al., 2011).

Overall, across probabilistic reward learning tasks, investigators have most consistently reported main effects of age without qualification by valence (Eppinger et al., 2011). By implication, the majority of age differences in reward learning tasks may relate to more general difficulties with probabilistic learning. In probabilistic learning tasks, the uncertainty of the outcome on any individual trial may introduce risk. Might these age-related learning impairments also contribute to adult age differences in risky decision making? The tasks described thus far did not systematically vary the level of risk among options or include certain alternatives, but recent studies have begun to explore age differences in choice among risky and safe options.

RISKY DECISION MAKING

Risky decisions involve choices between options in which at least one alternative has an uncertain outcome. To test societal stereotypes of older adults as being more risk averse than younger adults, a long history of behavioral research has focused on aging and risk aversion, beginning with studies of cautiousness in responding (Botwinick, 1969; Calhoun & Hutchison, 1981; Okun, 1976). A critical review of this work suggests that stereotypes of age-related risk aversion are not supported by findings from well-controlled experimental tasks (Mather, 2006). The past several decades of this research were recently reviewed in a meta-analysis. The meta-analysis, which focused on gambling tasks and risky investment choices, found no evidence for systematic adult age differences in risk preferences (Mata, Josef, Samanez-Larkin, & Hertwig, 2011). Rather, the findings identified a subset of tasks in which older adults choose to avoid risk, but other tasks in which older adults choose to seek risk more often than younger adults (Mata et al., 2011). Notably, in many of these tasks, the expression of this "risk preference" is opposite of the reward maximizing strategy. Thus, in these tasks, apparent age differences in risk preferences may instead result from cognitive limitations (Henninger, Madden, & Huettel, 2010). Consistent with this account, tasks that require subjects to learn from recent experience show larger age differences in performance than do tasks in which performance does not depend on learning (Mata et al., 2011).

Few neuroimaging studies involving choices between high- and low-risk options have compared younger and older adults. In an early study, which included a risky decision making task that does not require learning, older adults behaviorally chose more low-risk options and showed greater insula activation during choice (Lee, Leung, Fox, Gao, & Chan, 2008). However, one important limitation of this study was that the older adult group included only nine subjects. The small sample size makes it difficult to evaluate the generalizability of either the behavior or brain activity observed in the older sample, especially in light of the results of the meta-analysis described above. Also, insula activation showed high variability between subjects—particularly in older adults. The unequal variance between groups implies strong individual differences in the older group, which may violate assumptions of conventional statistical comparisons. Thus, wide generalizations based on these findings may be premature.

Another study of adult age differences in risky decision making used a different task that elicits a mix of both low-risk and high-risk choices within each individual across the task (Kuhnen & Knutson, 2005). This investment task (the BIAS Task) was designed to emulate everyday financial decisions by requiring subjects to make a series of choices between "safe" bonds and "risky" stocks. Reward maximization requires rapid learning from probabilistic feedback throughout the task. Given the task structure, a "rational actor" (i.e., Bayesian updating, risk-neutral agent) should begin each task round by choosing the safe asset (bond) and then should shift over time to a risky asset (stock) when the expected value of choosing that risky asset exceeds the fixed expected value of the safe asset. Individual choices that deviate from those of the rational actor can be classified as risk averse (i.e., the choice of a bond over a better stock) or risk seeking (i.e., the choice of an uncertain stock over a bond or alternative stock). In a large community sample of young, middle-aged, and older adults, we found no age differences in risk aversion but did find age differences in risk seeking (see Color Plate 7a; Samanez-Larkin et al., 2010). Age differences specifically surfaced during trials in which older adults chose risky assets—a pattern that replicated in two other groups who participated in the task outside the MRI scanner (Samanez-Larkin et al., 2010; Samanez-Larkin, Wagner, & Knutson, 2011). Consistent with a neurocomputational account (S.-C. Li, 2005; S.-C. Li, Lindenberger, & Sikström, 2001), age differences in risky choice were mediated by a neural measure of functional variability in ventral striatal activity (see Color Plate 7b; Samanez-Larkin et al., 2010). This neural variability[1] increased with age in the midbrain and striatum, and the age-related variability effects replicated in an entirely independent study which used a different task that did not involve reward (Garrett, Kovacevic, McIntosh, & Grady, 2010).

The study suggests that variability in neural signals that compute and represent expected value in a dynamic environment may increase with age. Consistent with this account, related behavioral evidence suggests that older adults have more difficulty estimating the specific value of ambiguous stimuli during reward learning tasks (e.g., whether a nonrewarded outcome should be weighted positively or negatively following a gain or loss cue; Eppinger & Kray, 2011). Together, these findings suggest that apparent age differences in risk preference may instead relate to differences in learning ability. In support of this conclusion, neuroimaging studies of decisions that do not require rapid learning from recent experience show similar patterns of neural activity in striatal (Samanez-Larkin, Mata, et al., 2011) and prefrontal (Hosseini et al., 2010) regions of both younger and older adults.

RESOLVING AN APPARENT PARADOX

The combined findings on basic reward processing, reward learning, and risky decision making raises a puzzling question. How can the same striatal regions that appear to be functionally intact in basic reward tasks show functional irregularities in learning and decision tasks? One solution to this apparent contradiction may be that a broader neural network lies at the source of the age differences in striatal activity during learning and decision making. For instance, while basic striatal function may remain preserved over the adult life span, prefrontal input may change. Functionally, such a disconnection might not impair basic motivation but may instead misdirect that motivation away from appropriate but novel goals (Knutson, Fong, Bennett, Adams, & Hommer, 2003).

The highly interconnected anatomy of reward circuitry has been extensively characterized in both human and nonhuman primates (Cohen, Schoene-Bake, Elger, & Weber, 2009; Draganski et al., 2008; Haber, 2003;

[1]Note that the vast majority of fMRI studies compare mean signal between different task conditions. Signal variability may be an important, overlooked individual difference measure relevant to understanding age differences in brain function.

Haber & Knutson, 2010). If connections from the medial prefrontal cortex to the ventral striatum are compromised in aging, they might influence reward learning and risk taking. The recent development of diffusion tensor imaging tractography allows investigators to visualize the "integrity" (a combination of fiber density, axonal diameter, and myelination) of even subcortical tracts such as those implicated in reward processing. In a recent study, we examined the structural integrity of reward circuitry using diffusion tensor imaging in a group of younger, middle-aged, and older adults who also completed a probabilistic reward learning task (Samanez-Larkin, Levens, Perry, Dougherty, & Knutson, 2012). Analyses focused on a ventromedial circuit from the ventral tegmental area in the midbrain to the ventral striatum through the pallidum to the thalamus, from the thalamus to the medial prefrontal cortex, and from the frontal cortex back into the ventral striatum. Findings specifically indicated that the integrity of pathways connecting the thalamus to the prefrontal cortex and the prefrontal cortex to the ventral striatum was reduced in older age and was also associated with reward learning (see Color Plate 8; Samanez-Larkin et al., 2012). These findings suggest that one source of the age-related striatal functional variability observed in prior studies may arise from structural degradation of prefrontal input to the striatum, which might compromise reward learning. Interestingly, these frontostriatal pathways primarily utilize the neurotransmitter glutamate. While the vast majority of research and theory about age differences in neurochemical signaling has focused on dopamine (Braver & Barch, 2002; S.-C. Li, Lindenberger, & Bäckman, 2010), these findings emphasize the importance of also considering interactions with other neurochemical systems (Mora, Segovia, & Del Arco, 2007; Segovia, Porras, Del Arco, & Mora, 2001). Notably, age differences in reward learning are distinct from traditional impairments in explicit memory—in terms of both associated neural circuits (i.e., ventromedial frontostriatal networks versus lateral frontal and medial temporal networks) and psychological processes (e.g., feedback-driven learning versus working memory; Samanez-Larkin, Wagner, & Knutson, 2011).

In summary, apparently contradictory findings may reflect age differences in broader prefrontal networks associated with increased task demands rather than more general deficits in striatal activity associated with motivation. Thus, what appear to be motivational deficits may instead result from cognitive deficits. Although some have claimed that basic motivational function declines with age (Eppinger, Nystrom, & Cohen, 2012), this claim is inconsistent with decades of behavioral research on the psychology of aging (Carstensen, 2006; Carstensen, Mikels, & Mather, 2005; Charles & Carstensen, 2010) as well as a growing number of neuroscience studies (Samanez-Larkin, 2011; Samanez-Larkin & Carstensen, 2011).

INDIVIDUAL DIFFERENCES IN OLD AGE

Studies of adult age differences in risky decision making often find that individual differences increase with age (Eppinger & Kray, 2011). Even in tasks in which decision making appears to decline on average with age, many older individuals show no deficits whatsoever compared with healthy young adults. For instance, using the Iowa gambling task (Denburg, Tranel, & Bechara, 2005), researchers found that although some older individuals took more risks and made fewer returns than younger adults, others performed as well as young adults. These findings raise at least two possibilities: (a) either a subset of older adults retains function from young adulthood to old age, or (b) changes in motivation and cognition across adulthood alter the specific processes that guide decision making in some older individuals.

Although no longitudinal studies have definitively tested these alternative accounts, some suggestive cross-sectional evidence supports the latter account. For instance, in the Iowa gambling task, which involves risky choice, memory, and learning, the mechanisms that determine performance may change across the life span in the subset of individuals who continue to perform well. Interestingly, older adults who perform as well as younger adults seem to be guided by physiological responses (e.g., assessed with skin conductance) during anticipation of gains. In stark contrast, younger adults in the same circumstances appear to be guided instead by physiological responses during the anticipation of loss (Denburg et al., 2006). Thus, these findings are consistent with an age-related shift in the processing of positive relative to negative information (Carstensen & Mikels, 2005; Mather & Carstensen, 2005) and further imply that some older adults leverage this appetitive motivation in the service of making successful risky decisions.

DECISION MAKING DOES NOT GLOBALLY DECLINE WITH AGE

A number of decision-making scenarios show that older adults perform just as well or even better than younger adults (Castel, 2005; Hosseini et al., 2010; Kovalchik, Camerer, Grether, Plott, & Allman, 2005; Kühn et al., 2011; Y. Li, Baldassi, Johnson, & Weber, 2011; Löckenhoff, 2011; Mata & Nunes, 2010; Mata et al., 2012; Mather, 2006; Mienaltowski, 2011; Mikels et al., 2010; Nielsen et al., 2008; Reyna & Brainerd, 2011; Roalf, Mitchell, Harbaugh, & Janowsky, 2012; Roesch, Bryden, Cerri, Haney, & Schoenbaum, 2012; Samanez-Larkin, Mata, et al., 2011; Scheibe, Mata, & Carstensen, 2011; N. W. Simon et al., 2010; Spaniol, Voss, Bowen, & Grady, 2011; Strough, Karns, & Schlosnagle, 2011; Worthy, Gorlick, Pacheco, Schnyer,

& Maddox, 2011). Many of these scenarios involve decisions that do not require learning in a novel environment (however, see Worthy et al., 2011) but instead require accumulation of experience, crystallized intelligence, gist memory, or emotional and motivational processing.

ENHANCING CHOICE THROUGH DECISION AIDS

In decision scenarios in which older adults do not perform as well as younger adults, research might ideally identify opportunities for effective intervention. The research reviewed above suggests that age differences in risky decision making may be related to difficulty in computing dynamic representations of expected value in a novel environment. Thus, in subsequent work, we sought to determine whether targeted decision aids could improve the financial risk taking of older adults (Samanez-Larkin, Wagner, & Knutson, 2011). We found that presentation of explicit expected value information (either in the form of a graphical representation of all trial outcomes or a summary measure of prior and projected earnings) improved decision making in both younger and older adults. Remarkably, providing expected value information improved the performance of older adults to match that of younger adults at baseline (see Color Plate 7c). These findings imply that providing simplified information about expected value may improve financial decision making across the adult life span. Similar benefits of "informed" choice have also been reported in children (Van Duijvenvoorde, Jansen, Bredman, & Huizenga, 2012).

Although these results are encouraging, this research is many steps away from broad implementation outside the laboratory. Some evidence suggests that these and related behavioral interventions may have limited effectiveness in older individuals. For example, describing an expected value computation strategy and exposing subjects to repeated training with this strategy evokes less behavioral change in older than in younger adults (Westbrook, Martins, Yarkoni, & Braver, 2012), since older adults tend to shift away from the suggested strategy over time. Research has yet to clarify whether this shift is related to memory decay or a subjective perception that the suggested strategy lacks efficacy.

New decision strategies may prove more difficult to train after a lifetime of experience with other strategies. In fact, in old age it may be more adaptive for individuals to stick with simpler strategies (Worthy & Maddox, 2012). Some evidence suggests that in many real-world decision scenarios, more simple (or "satisficing") strategies do not diminish decision quality for older individuals (Mata & Nunes, 2010). Importantly, the extent to which age differences in decision quality emerge in the real world depends on the context or environment in which the decisions are made (Mata et al., 2012).

Although decision aids (Samanez-Larkin, Wagner, & Knutson, 2011; Van Duijvenvoorde et al., 2012) may provide more reliable support than strategic training, they may be more limited in application. In many real-world circumstances, prior outcomes and expected values cannot be easily recorded, computed, or displayed. However, precise computations of value may not be required in most scenarios. In fact, some have argued that getting the gist rather than exact verbatim details is most critical in real-world scenarios (e.g., Reyna & Farley, 2006; Reyna & Lloyd, 2006). Overall, initial findings seem promising enough to imply that experimentally informed implementation of decision aids at a broader societal level represents a viable long-term research goal.

EXTENDING FINDINGS TO THE REAL WORLD

An important focus of our research on reward processing, reward learning, risky decision making, and aging involves extending performance measures from the laboratory to the real world. Interestingly, individuals who make fewer "mistakes" in our laboratory financial investment task (or more choices in line with those of a risk-neutral, Bayesian-updating actor) also accumulate more assets in the real world (Samanez-Larkin et al., 2010). In a related probabilistic learning task, we found that individual differences in learning to acquire gains were associated with accumulation of financial assets, whereas individual differences in learning to avoid losses were distinctly associated with avoidance of financial debt—which was reflected in individuals' credit scores (Knutson, Samanez-Larkin, & Kuhnen, 2011). Findings from this study also indicated that overall probabilistic learning ability was associated with a more general measure of financial well-being—the debt-to-asset ratio (Knutson et al., 2011), and all of these effects remained significant after controlling for age and intelligence quotient. These studies not only provide evidence for the ecological validity of laboratory-based incentive tasks, but also may help to identify individuals with specific vulnerabilities that compromise financial decision making in the real world (Denburg et al., 2007). Unfortunately, older adults are disproportionately targeted by financial fraud (SaveAndInvest.org, 2011). In current work, we are studying older individuals who are at heightened risk for making financial mistakes based on prior fraud victimization. We are also examining how potential vulnerability to financial fraud may relate to affective or cognitive individual differences in neural activity and behavior across adulthood.

CONCLUSION

Basic motivational processes and associated brain function appear to remain relatively intact across much of adulthood and into old age (Samanez-Larkin, 2010; Samanez-Larkin & Carstensen, 2011). In simple incentive processing tasks with low cognitive demands, younger and older adults show similar patterns of subcortical activity. In risky decision making tasks, contrary to societal stereotypes, risk tolerance appears relatively stable across adulthood (Mata et al., 2011), with some evidence that individual differences may increase later in life (Eppinger & Kray, 2011; Spaniol & Wegier, 2012). Rather than systematically increasing with age, suboptimal risky decisions in older adults seem more linked to cognitive demands of particular decision scenarios. Subcortical regions like the ventral striatum that reliably activate in reward tasks with low cognitive demands begin to show irregular activity in decision tasks with higher cognitive demands. Related studies of broader network structure suggest that these specific decision impairments may relate more closely to circuit dysfunction in general, and to frontostriatal connectivity in particular (Samanez-Larkin et al., 2012).

Taken together, these and other findings suggest that aging does not uniformly degrade decision making. Many studies find little evidence of declining decision quality in either some or all older adults as compared with younger adults (Samanez-Larkin, 2011). Future research should explore both contexts in which older adults may show suboptimal choice as well as situations in which decision making remains stable or even improves with age (Y. Li et al., 2011; Löckenhoff, 2011; Strough et al., 2011). Future research should also strive to establish the ecological validity of laboratory findings. Currently, few studies have directly examined adult age differences in risky economic decision making in the real world (Agarwal, Driscoll, Gabaix, & Laibson, 2009; Korniotis & Kumar, 2011; Mata & Nunes, 2010). Researchers can and should integrate laboratory measures (including brain imaging) with real-world measures of decision making to more fully characterize how decision making changes across the life span.

Although the research reviewed here encompasses a broad range of processes, the field is still young and will surely continue to grow in coming years. An integrative decision neuroscience approach has tremendous potential to have both scientific and societal impact. Given the current and unique moment in human history in which demographic changes are drastically increasing the age of decision makers around the globe, scientists have the potential to make major contributions to improving the well-being of humans of all ages.

REFERENCES

Agarwal, S., Driscoll, J. C., Gabaix, X., & Laibson, D. I. (2009). The age of reason: Financial decisions over the life-cycle with implications for regulation. *Brookings Papers on Economic Activity, 40*, 51–117. doi:10.1353/eca.0.0067

Botwinick, J. (1969). Disinclination to venture response versus cautiousness in responding: Age differences. *The Journal of Genetic Psychology, 115*, 55–62. doi: 10.1080/00221325.1969.10533870

Braver, T. S., & Barch, D. M. (2002). A theory of cognitive control, aging cognition, and neuromodulation. *Neuroscience and Biobehavioral Reviews, 26*, 809–817. doi:10.1016/S0149-7634(02)00067-2

Calhoun, R. E., & Hutchison, S. L. (1981). Decision-making in old age: Cautiousness and rigidity. *The International Journal of Aging & Human Development, 13*, 89–98. doi:10.2190/LFUA-4KR0-B0QX-M584

Carstensen, L. L. (2006). The influence of a sense of time on human development. *Science, 312*, 1913–1915. doi:10.1126/science.1127488

Carstensen, L. L., & Mikels, J. A. (2005). At the intersection of emotion and cognition: Aging and the positivity effect. *Current Directions in Psychological Science, 14*, 117–121. doi:10.1111/j.0963-7214.2005.00348.x

Carstensen, L. L., Mikels, J. A., & Mather, M. (2005). Aging and the intersection of cognition, motivation and emotion. In J. E. Birren & K. W. Schaie (Eds.), *Handbook of the psychology of aging* (6th ed.; pp. 343–362.). San Diego, CA: Academic Press.

Carstensen, L. L., Pasupathi, M., Mayr, U., & Nesselroade, J. R. (2000). Emotional experience in everyday life across the adult life span. *Journal of Personality and Social Psychology, 79*, 644–655. doi:10.1037/0022-3514.79.4.644

Carstensen, L. L., Turan, B., Scheibe, S., Ram, N., Ersner-Hershfield, H., Samanez-Larkin, G. R., . . . Nesselroade, J. K.. (2011). Emotional experience improves with age: Evidence based on over 10 years of experience sampling. *Psychology and Aging, 26*, 21–33. doi:10.1037/a0021285

Castel, A. D. (2005). Memory for grocery prices in younger and older adults: The role of schematic support. *Psychology and Aging, 20*, 718–721. doi:10.1037/0882-7974.20.4.718

Charles, S. T., & Carstensen, L. L. (2010). Social and emotional aging. *Annual Review of Psychology, 61*, 383–409. doi:10.1146/annurev.psych.093008.100448

Cohen, M. X., Schoene-Bake, J.-C., Elger, C. E., & Weber, B. (2009). Connectivity-based segregation of the human striatum predicts personality characteristics. *Nature Neuroscience, 12*(1), 32–34. doi:10.1038/nn.2228

Cox, K. M., Aizenstein, H. J., & Fiez, J. A. (2008). Striatal outcome processing in healthy aging. *Cognitive, Affective & Behavioral Neuroscience, 8*, 304–317. doi:10.3758/CABN.8.3.304

Denburg, N. L., Cole, C. A., Hernandez, M., Yamada, T. H., Tranel, D., Bechara, A., & Wallace, R. B. (2007). The orbitofrontal cortex, real-world decision-making, and normal aging. *Annals of the New York Academy of Sciences*. doi:10.1196/annals.1401.031

Denburg, N. L., Recknor, E. C., Bechara, A., & Tranel, D. (2006). Psychophysiological anticipation of positive outcomes promotes advantageous decision-making in normal older persons. *International Journal of Psychophysiology, 61*(1), 19–25. doi:10.1016/j.ijpsycho.2005.10.021

Denburg, N. L., Tranel, D., & Bechara, A. (2005). The ability to decide advantageously declines prematurely in some normal older persons. *Neuropsychologia, 43*, 1099–1106. doi:10.1016/j.neuropsychologia.2004.09.012

Draganski, B., Kherif, F., Kloppel, S., Cook, P. A., Alexander, D. C., Parker, G. J. M., . . . Frackowiak, R. S. J. (2008). Evidence for segregated and integrative connectivity patterns in the human basal ganglia. *The Journal of Neuroscience, 28*, 7143–7152. doi:10.1523/JNEUROSCI.1486-08.2008

Eppinger, B., Hämmerer, D., & Li, S.-C. (2011). Neuromodulation of reward-based learning and decision making in human aging. *Annals of the New York Academy of Sciences, 1235*(1), 1–17. doi:10.1111/j.1749-6632.2011.06230.x

Eppinger, B., & Kray, J. (2011). To choose or to avoid: Age differences in learning from positive and negative feedback. *Journal of Cognitive Neuroscience, 23*(1), 41–52. doi:10.1162/jocn.2009.21364

Eppinger, B., Kray, J., Mock, B., & Mecklinger, A. (2008). Better or worse than expected? Aging, learning, and the ERN. *Neuropsychologia, 46*, 521–539. doi:10.1016/j.neuropsychologia.2007.09.001

Eppinger, B., Nystrom, L. E., & Cohen, J. D. (2012). Reduced sensitivity to immediate reward during decision-making in older than younger adults. *PLoS ONE, 7*(5), e36953. doi:10.1371/journal.pone.0036953

Frank, M. J., & Kong, L. (2008). Learning to avoid in older age. *Psychology and Aging, 23*, 392–398. doi:10.1037/0882-7974.23.2.392

Frank, M. J., Seeberger, L. C., & O'Reilly, R. C. (2004). By carrot or by stick: Cognitive reinforcement learning in parkinsonism. *Science, 306*, 1940–1943. doi:10.1126/science.1102941

Garrett, D. D., Kovacevic, N., McIntosh, A. R., & Grady, C. L. (2010). Blood oxygen level–dependent signal variability is more than just noise. *The Journal of Neuroscience, 30*, 4914–4921. doi:10.1523/JNEUROSCI.5166-09.2010

Haber, S. N. (2003). The primate basal ganglia: Parallel and integrative networks. *Journal of Chemical Neuroanatomy, 26*, 317–330. doi:10.1016/j.jchemneu.2003.10.003

Haber, S. N., & Knutson, B. (2010). The reward circuit: linking primate anatomy and human imaging. *Neuropsychopharmacology, 35*(1), 4–26. doi:10.1038/npp.2009.129

Hämmerer, D., Li, S.-C., Müller, V., & Lindenberger, U. (2011). Life span differences in electrophysiological correlates of monitoring gains and losses during probabilistic reinforcement learning. *Journal of Cognitive Neuroscience, 23*, 579–592. doi:10.1162/jocn.2010.21475

Harlé, K. M., & Sanfey, A. G. (2012). Social economic decision-making across the lifespan: An fMRI investigation. *Neuropsychologia, 50*, 1416–1424. doi:10.1016/j.neuropsychologia.2012.02.026

Hedden, T., & Gabrieli, J. D. E. (2004). Insights into the ageing mind: A view from cognitive neuroscience. *Nature Reviews Neuroscience, 5*, 87–96. doi:10.1038/nrn1323

Henninger, D. E., Madden, D. J., & Huettel, S. A. (2010). Processing speed and memory mediate age-related differences in decision making. *Psychology and Aging, 25*, 262–270. doi:10.1037/a0019096

Hosseini, S. M. H., Rostami, M., Yomogida, Y., Takahashi, M., Tsukiura, T., & Kawashima, R. (2010). Aging and decision making under uncertainty: Behavioral and neural evidence for the preservation of decision making in the absence of learning in old age. *NeuroImage, 52*, 1514–1520. doi:10.1016/j.neuroimage.2010.05.008

Knutson, B., Adams, C. M., Fong, G. W., & Hommer, D. (2001). Anticipation of increasing monetary reward selectively recruits nucleus accumbens. *The Journal of Neuroscience, 21*, RC159).

Knutson, B., & Cooper, J. C. (2005). Functional magnetic resonance imaging of reward prediction. *Current Opinion in Neurology, 18*, 411–417. doi:10.1097/01.wco.0000173463.24758.f6

Knutson, B., Fong, G. W., Bennett, S. M., Adams, C. M., & Hommer, D. (2003). A region of mesial prefrontal cortex tracks monetarily rewarding outcomes: Characterization with rapid event-related fMRI. *NeuroImage, 18*, 263–272. doi:10.1016/S1053-8119(02)00057-5

Knutson, B., & Greer, S. M. (2008). Anticipatory affect: Neural correlates and consequences for choice. *Philosophical Transactions of the Royal Society of London. Series B, Biological Sciences, 363*, 3771–3786. doi:10.1098/rstb.2008.0155

Knutson, B., Samanez-Larkin, G. R., & Kuhnen, C. M. (2011). Gain and loss learning differentially contribute to life financial outcomes. *PLoS ONE, 6*, e24390. doi:10.1371/journal.pone.0024390

Korniotis, G. M., & Kumar, A. (2011). Do older investors make better investment decisions? *The Review of Economics and Statistics*, 93(1), 244–265. doi:10.1162/REST_a_00053

Kovalchik, S., Camerer, C. F., Grether, D., Plott, C., & Allman, J. M. (2005). Aging and decision making: A comparison between neurologically healthy elderly and young individuals. *Journal of Economic Behavior & Organization*, 58(1), 79–94. doi:10.1016/j.jebo.2003.12.001

Kühn, S., Schmiedek, F., Schott, B. H., Ratcliff, R., Heinze, H.-J., Düzel, E., . . . Lövden, M. (2011). Brain areas consistently linked to individual differences in perceptual decision-making in younger as well as older adults before and after training. *Journal of Cognitive Neuroscience, 23*, 2147–2158. doi:10.1162/jocn.2010.21564

Kuhnen, C. M., & Knutson, B. (2005). The neural basis of financial risk taking. *Neuron, 47*, 763–770. doi:10.1016/j.neuron.2005.08.008

Lee, T. M. C., Leung, A. W. S., Fox, P. T., Gao, J.-H., & Chan, C. C. H. (2008). Age-related differences in neural activities during risk taking as revealed by functional MRI. *Social Cognitive and Affective Neuroscience, 3*(1), 7–15. doi:10.1093/scan/nsm033

Li, S.-C. (2005). Neurocomputational perspectives linking neuromodulation, processing noise, representational distinctiveness, and cognitive aging. In R. Cabeza, L. Nyberg & D. Park (Eds.), *Cognitive neuroscience of aging: Linking cognitive and cerebral aging* (pp. 354–379). New York, NY: Oxford University Press.

Li, S.-C., Lindenberger, U., & Bäckman, L. (2010). Dopaminergic modulation of cognition across the life span. *Neuroscience and Biobehavioral Reviews, 34*, 625–630. doi:10.1016/j.neubiorev.2010.02.003

Li, S.-C., Lindenberger, U., & Sikström, S. (2001). Aging cognition: From neuromodulation to representation. *Trends in Cognitive Sciences*, 5, 479–486. doi: 10.1016/S1364-6613(00)01769-1

Li, Y., Baldassi, M., Johnson, E. J., & Weber, E. U. (2011). *Compensating cognitive capabilities, decision performance, and aging.* Unpublished manuscript. Columbia University, New York, NY.

Lighthall, N. R., Gorlick, M. A., Schoeke, A., Frank, M. J., & Mather, M. (2013). Stress modulates reinforcement learning in younger and older adults. *Psychology and Aging*. doi:10.1037/a0029823

Löckenhoff, C. E. (2011). Age, time, and decision making: From processing speed to global time horizons. *Annals of the New York Academy of Sciences, 1235*(1), 44–56. doi:10.1111/j.1749-6632.2011.06209.x

Mata, R., Josef, A. K., Samanez-Larkin, G. R., & Hertwig, R. (2011). Age differences in risky choice: A meta-analysis. *Annals of the New York Academy of Sciences, 1235*(1), 18–29. doi:10.1111/j.1749-6632.2011.06200.x

Mata, R., & Nunes, L. (2010). When less is enough: Cognitive aging, information search, and decision quality in consumer choice. *Psychology and Aging, 25*, 289–298. doi:10.1037/a0017927

Mata, R., Pachur, T., von Helversen, B., Hertwig, R., Rieskamp, J., & Schooler, L. (2012). Ecological rationality: A framework for understanding and aiding the aging decision maker. *Frontiers in Neuroscience*, 6, 19. doi:10.3389/fnins.2012.00019

Mather, M. (2006). A review of decision-making processes: Weighing the risks and benefits of aging. In L. L. Carstensen & C. R. Hartel (Eds.), *When I'm 64* (pp. 145–173). Washington, DC: The National Academies Press.

Mather, M., & Carstensen, L. L. (2005). Aging and motivated cognition: The positivity effect in attention and memory. *Trends in Cognitive Sciences*, 9, 496–502. doi:10.1016/j.tics.2005.08.005

Mell, T., Wartenburger, I., Marschner, A., Villringer, A., Reischies, F. M., & Heekeren, H. R. (2009). Altered function of ventral striatum during reward-based decision making in old age. *Frontiers in Human Neuroscience*, 3, 34. doi:10.3389/neuro.09.034.2009

Mienaltowski, A. (2011). Everyday problem solving across the adult life span: Solution diversity and efficacy. *Annals of the New York Academy of Sciences*, *1235*(1), 75–85. doi:10.1111/j.1749-6632.2011.06207.x

Mikels, J. A., Löckenhoff, C. E., Maglio, S. J., Goldstein, M. K., Garber, A., & Carstensen, L. L. (2010). Following your heart or your head: Focusing on emotions versus information differentially influences the decisions of younger and older adults. *Journal of Experimental Psychology: Applied*, *16*(1), 87–95. doi:10.1037/a0018500

Mora, F., Segovia, G., & Del Arco, A. (2007). Glutamate-dopamine-GABA interactions in the aging basal ganglia. *Brain Research Reviews*, *52*, 340–353. doi:10.1016/j.brainresrev.2007.10.006

Nielsen, L., Knutson, B., & Carstensen, L. L. (2008). Affect dynamics, affective forecasting, and aging. *Emotion*, 8, 318–330. doi:10.1037/1528-3542.8.3.318

Okun, M. A. (1976). Adult age and cautiousness in decision: A review of the literature. *Human Development*, *19*, 220–233. doi:10.1159/000271530

Park, D. C., Lautenschlager, G., Hedden, T., Davidson, N. S., Smith, A. D., & Smith, P. K. (2002). Models of visuospatial and verbal memory across the adult life span. *Psychology and Aging*, *17*, 299–320. doi:10.1037/0882-7974.17.2.299

Reyna, V. F., & Brainerd, C. J. (2011). Dual processes in decision making and developmental neuroscience: A fuzzy-trace model. *Developmental Review*, *31*, 180–206. doi:10.1016/j.dr.2011.07.004

Reyna, V. F., & Farley, F. (2006). Risk and rationality in adolescent decision making: Implications for theory, practice, and public policy. *Psychological Science in the Public Interest*, *7*(1), 1–44. doi:10.1111/j.1529-1006.2006.00026.x

Reyna, V. F., & Lloyd, F. J. (2006). Physician decision making and cardiac risk: Effects of knowledge, risk perception, risk tolerance, and fuzzy processing. *Journal of Experimental Psychology: Applied*, *12*, 179–195. doi:10.1037/1076-898X.12.3.179

Roalf, D. R., Mitchell, S. H., Harbaugh, W. T., & Janowsky, J. S. (2012). Risk, reward, and economic decision making in aging. *The Journals of Gerontology: Series B: Psychological Sciences and Social Sciences*, *67*, 289–298. doi:10.1093/geronb/gbr099

Roesch, M. R., Bryden, D. W., Cerri, D. H., Haney, Z. R., & Schoenbaum, G. (2012). Willingness to wait and altered encoding of time-discounted reward in the orbitofrontal cortex with normal aging. *The Journal of Neuroscience*, *32*, 5525–5533. doi:10.1523/JNEUROSCI.0586-12.2012

Salthouse, T. A. (2004). What and when of cognitive aging. *Current Directions in Psychological Science, 13*, 140–144. doi:10.1111/j.0963-7214.2004.00293.x

Samanez-Larkin, G. R. (2010, April 22). *Incentive processing in the aging brain: Individual differences in value-based learning and decision making across the adult life span* (Doctoral dissertation, Stanford University). Retrieved from http://purl.stanford.edu/vy834vv5149

Samanez-Larkin, G. R. (2011). *Decision making over the life span*. Hoboken, NJ: Wiley-Blackwell.

Samanez-Larkin, G. R., & Carstensen, L. L. (2011). Socioemotional functioning and the aging brain. In J. Decety & J. T. Cacioppo (Eds.), *The handbook of social neuroscience* (pp. 507–521). New York, NY: Oxford University Press. doi:10.1093/oxfordhb/9780195342161.013.0034

Samanez-Larkin, G. R., Gibbs, S. E. B., Khanna, K., Nielsen, L., Carstensen, L. L., & Knutson, B. (2007). Anticipation of monetary gain but not loss in healthy older adults. *Nature Neuroscience, 10*, 787–791. doi:10.1038/nn1894

Samanez-Larkin, G. R., Kuhnen, C. M., Yoo, D. J., & Knutson, B. (2010). Variability in nucleus accumbens activity mediates age-related suboptimal financial risk taking. *The Journal of Neuroscience, 30*, 1426–1434. doi:10.1523/JNEUROSCI.4902-09.2010

Samanez-Larkin, G. R., Levens, S. M., Perry, L. M., Dougherty, R. F., & Knutson, B. (2012). Frontostriatal white matter integrity mediates adult age differences in probabilistic reward learning. *The Journal of Neuroscience, 32*, 5333–5337. doi:10.1523/JNEUROSCI.5756-11.2012

Samanez-Larkin, G. R., Mata, R., Radu, P. T., Ballard, I. C., Carstensen, L. L., & McClure, S. M. (2011). Age differences in striatal delay sensitivity during intertemporal choice in healthy adults. *Frontiers in Neuroscience, 5*, 126. doi:10.3389/fnins.2011.00126

Samanez-Larkin, G. R., Wagner, A. D., & Knutson, B. (2011). Expected value information improves financial risk taking across the adult life span. *Social Cognitive and Affective Neuroscience, 6*, 207–217. doi:10.1093/scan/nsq043

SaveAndInvest.org. (2011). *Fighting Fraud 101*. Retrieved from http://www.saveandinvest.org/web/groups/sai/@sai/documents/sai_original_content/p036701.pdf

Scheibe, S., Mata, R., & Carstensen, L. L. (2011). Age differences in affective forecasting and experienced emotion surrounding the 2008 US presidential election. *Cognition and Emotion, 25*, 1029–1044. doi:10.1080/02699931.2010.545543

Schott, B. H., Niehaus, L., Wittmann, B. C., Schütze, H., Seidenbecher, C. I., Heinze, H.-J., & Düzel, E. (2007). Aging and early-stage Parkinson's disease affect separable neural mechanisms of mesolimbic reward processing. *Brain: A Journal of Neurology, 130*, 2412–2424. doi:10.1093/brain/awm147

Segovia, G., Porras, A., Del Arco, A., & Mora, F. (2001). Glutamatergic neurotransmission in aging: A critical perspective. *Mechanisms of Ageing and Development, 122*(1), 1–29. doi:10.1016/S0047-6374(00)00225-6

Simon, J. R., Howard, J. H., & Howard, D. V. (2010). Adult age differences in learning from positive and negative probabilistic feedback. *Neuropsychology, 24*, 534–541. doi:10.1037/a0018652

Simon, N. W., Lasarge, C. L., Montgomery, K. S., Williams, M. T., Mendez, I. A., Setlow, B., & Bizon, J. L. (2010). Good things come to those who wait: Attenuated discounting of delayed rewards in aged Fischer 344 rats. *Neurobiology of Aging, 31*, 853–862. doi:10.1016/j.neurobiolaging.2008.06.004

Spaniol, J., Voss, A., Bowen, H. J., & Grady, C. L. (2011). Motivational incentives modulate age differences in visual perception. *Psychology and Aging, 26*, 932–939. doi:10.1037/a0023297

Spaniol, J., & Wegier, P. (2012). Decisions from experience: Adaptive information search and choice in younger and older adults. *Frontiers in Neuroscience, 6*, 36. doi:10.3389/fnins.2012.00036

Strough, J., Karns, T. E., & Schlosnagle, L. (2011). Decision-making heuristics and biases across the life span. *Annals of the New York Academy of Sciences, 1235*(1), 57–74. doi:10.1111/j.1749-6632.2011.06208.x

Van Duijvenvoorde, A. C. K., Jansen, B. R. J., Bredman, J. C., & Huizenga, H. M. (2012). Age-related changes in decision making: Comparing informed and non-informed situations. *Developmental Psychology, 48*(1), 192–203. doi:10.1037/a0025601

Westbrook, A., Martins, B. S., Yarkoni, T., & Braver, T. S. (2012). Strategic insight and age-related goal-neglect influence risky decision-making. *Frontiers in Neuroscience, 6*, 68. doi:10.3389/fnins.2012.00068

Wood, S., Busemeyer, J., Koling, A., Cox, C. R., & Davis, H. (2005). Older adults as adaptive decision makers: Evidence from the Iowa gambling task. *Psychology and Aging, 20*, 220–225. doi:10.1037/0882-7974.20.2.220

Worthy, D. A., Gorlick, M. A., Pacheco, J. L., Schnyer, D. M., & Maddox, W. T. (2011). With age comes wisdom: decision making in younger and older adults. *Psychological Science, 22*, 1375–1380. doi:10.1177/0956797611420301

Worthy, D. A., & Maddox, W. T. (2012). Age-based differences in strategy use in choice tasks. *Frontiers in Neuroscience, 5*, 145. doi:10.3389/fnins.2011.00145

Wu, C. C., Samanez-Larkin, G. R., & Knutson, B. (2012). *Neural markers of incentive anticipation are associated with affective traits*. Working Paper.

III

NEUROPSYCHOLOGY

6

MIND AND BRAIN IN DELAY OF GRATIFICATION

VIVIAN ZAYAS, WALTER MISCHEL, AND GAYATHRI PANDEY

A central focus of psychological and behavioral sciences is to identify the factors that enable and hinder delay of gratification. In this chapter, we review findings from the original preschool delay of gratification work that identify key attentional–cognitive control strategies that enable (vs. hinder) delay. We also describe recent behavioral and neuroscientific findings that investigate the link between preschool delay of gratification abilities and adult mechanisms of cognitive control. This work suggests that dispositional abilities to delay gratification are subserved by individual differences in the functioning of prefrontal cortical and limbic neural systems. We end by discussing the implications of this work for theory and future research.

Delay of gratification, the ability to forgo an immediate reward for the sake of obtaining a more desirable but delayed reward, has been shown to predict successful outcomes in diverse and consequential domains, such as academics and work, close relationships, and physical and mental well-being (Mischel, Shoda, & Rodriguez, 1989; Mischel et al., 2011). Moreover,

http://dx.doi.org/10.1037/14322-007
The Neuroscience of Risky Decision Making, by V. F. Reyna and V. Zayas (Editors)

the extent to which behaviors are guided by momentary rewards without consideration of future costs increases the likelihood for drug abuse, risky sexual behaviors, obesity, criminality, and consumer debt (e.g., Bogg & Roberts, 2004; Moffitt et al., 2011; Polivy, 1998; Tangney, Baumeister, & Boone, 2004).

Considerable attention has been devoted to identifying the biological, psychological, social, and cultural factors, and the interactions among them, that enable some individuals to successfully delay gratification and make doing so difficult for others (Ainslie, 1975; Blair, 2010; Blair & Raver, 2012; Evans & Kim, 2013; Hackman, Farah, & Meaney, 2010; Mischel et al., 1989). Here, we focus on the psychological and neural mechanisms that facilitate or hinder the ability to resist temptation. We first review the classic work finding that individual differences in the ability to delay gratification observed in early childhood show remarkable stability over the life span and across situations, predicting a wide array of adaptive life outcomes in adolescence and adulthood. Next, we review findings from experimental work on delay of gratification that identified key attentional–cognitive processes that enable delay of gratification, specifically distraction (directing attention away from tempting, appetitive, consummatory, visceral, or "hot" aspects of the situation) and reconstrual or reappraisal (focusing on qualities of rewards that are more informational, abstract, and "cooler"). We then briefly describe recent findings from our research team on the cognitive and neural circuitry that may subserve dispositional abilities to delay gratification throughout the life span.

We conclude by highlighting a key implication of the extant findings on delay of gratification to date. An important consequence of enacting self-control strategies is that they dampen the extent to which representations of temptations, which are inherently appetitive and consummatory (or hot), are active in working memory. In so doing, they decrease the psychological pull of the temptation in the situation—even in the face of actual, objective temptations. Although effortful cognitive control is a prerequisite for the enactment of self-control strategies, such as distraction and reconstrual, such an act makes delaying gratification less effortful and indeed much easier. It enables more "willpower" with less sweat if, as William James (1890/1950) put it long ago, certain preliminaries are met.

DELAY OF GRATIFICATION

The preschool delay of gratification paradigm (Mischel, Ebbesen, & Zeiss, 1972; Mischel et al., 1989) has garnered the attention of scholars from diverse disciplines in social, developmental, cognitive, and clinical psychology, as well as behavioral economics and philosophy, because it captures a quintessential self-control dilemma: Does one choose a smaller reward available immediately, such as taking a toke of a cigarette, eating a piece of the forbidden chocolate cake, or splurging on a trip to Paris, or wait for a larger reward available at a later time, such as achieving physical health, a lean physique, or financial security for the golden years? And equally important, the delay of gratification paradigm also provides a window into *how* one follows through with the decision once made.

In the classic delay of gratification situation, preschoolers are told that the experimenter needs to leave the room to prepare for an upcoming task and are presented with the choice of receiving one smaller treat (cookie, marshmallow, little pretzel stick) immediately or a larger treat (twice the amount of the treat selected) when the experimenter returns (e.g., Mischel & Ayduk, 2004; Mischel et al., 1972, 1989). Despite its simplicity, the delay of gratification situation poses the child with a conflict: Does she choose what she desires *now* or does she wait (an unknown amount of time) for what she desires in the *future?* Once she chooses, is she able to make good on her commitment?

Although the majority of preschoolers clearly express to the experimenter their intention to wait for the larger, delayed treats, only a subset of children are actually able to wait the entire 15-minute period. Despite their best intentions, waiting becomes very difficult in the face of temptation, and preschoolers experience increasing frustration as they continue to wait. Thus, many fall short of their stated goal. On average, preschoolers succumb to the immediate temptation within 1 minute of the start of the delay period (although 15 minutes were needed to obtain the reward; Mischel & Ebbesen, 1970).

Remarkably, individual differences in the ability of preschoolers to resist eating the tempting treats or ringing the bell to end the delay period predict a multitude of long-term outcomes. Those preschoolers who were able to delay gratification showed greater cognitive, self-regulatory, and coping competence later in life (Shoda, Mischel, & Peake, 1990). As adolescents, these preschoolers were also perceived to be more cognitively and socially competent, coping better with frustration and stress and achieving higher scholastic performance (Mischel et al., 1989). As adults, they were less likely to use cocaine (e.g., Ayduk et al., 2000; Mischel & Ayduk, 2004) and more likely to have a lower body mass index (Schlam, Wilson, Shoda, Mischel, & Ayduk, 2013). Such findings are consistent with results obtained in other cross-sectional and longitudinal studies that have used different samples and different assessments of delay ability (Bonato & Boland, 1983; Bruce et al., 2011; Francis & Susman, 2009; Kubzansky, Martin, & Buka, 2009; Moffitt et al., 2011; Seeyave et al., 2009).

The fact that preschool delay of gratification ability predicts successful outcomes in diverse domains (from academics to health) suggests that success in delaying gratification at age 4 taps into more general cognitive capacities (e.g., attentional control, inhibitory control, working memory) involved in the regulation of feelings, thoughts, and behaviors for the sake of achieving long-term goals. In particular, in order to wait for the larger reward, the preschooler must be able to regulate feelings, thoughts, and behaviors associated with the frustration elicited by waiting in the presence of the readily available rewards. Such capacities for regulating psychological and behavioral responses for the sake of long-term goals are needed to succeed in diverse life domains, as one must be able to effectively cope with the inevitable setbacks that arise during goal pursuit.

Given this, Ayduk et al. (2000) reasoned that the ability to regulate aversive states, as reflected by the delay of gratification ability, may be particularly beneficial for individuals who possess chronic personal vulnerabilities that increase their likelihood of experiencing aversive, negative states. To test the hypothesis that delay ability serves a protective function among vulnerable groups, in two studies, using two different cohorts, individuals were assessed in the delay of gratification paradigm in childhood, and they were assessed again on dispositional rejection sensitivity (RS) as well as various interpersonally relevant outcome measures (aggression, peer rejection, drug use) in adulthood approximately 20 years later. Past work has shown that high RS individuals, who are predisposed to anxiously or angrily expect, readily perceive, and intensely react to social rejection, are more likely to report destructive personal and interpersonal outcomes, such as depression, verbal and nonverbal signs of anger, and physical aggression (Ayduk, Downey, & Kim, 2001; Ayduk, Downey, Testa, Yen, & Shoda, 1999; Downey & Feldman, 1996; Downey, Freitas, Michaelis, & Khouri, 1998; Downey, Lebolt, Rincon, & Freitas, 1998). In Ayduk et al.'s (2000) work, high RS individuals who were also low in preschool delay ability showed the predictable negative consequences of RS. They reported lower self-esteem and self-worth, less effective coping ability, lower education levels, and greater cocaine and crack use. However, critically, high RS individuals who were high in preschool delay ability did *not* show the same negative consequences. Their outcomes were essentially indistinguishable from low RS individuals (Ayduk et al., 2000). Similar findings have been obtained in other samples (Ayduk et al., 2008) and with behavioral measures of reactivity, such as the startle response (Gyurak & Ayduk, 2007). Moreover, as will be discussed in later sections on the neural correlates subserving delay ability, the rostral anterior cingulate cortex (rACC), an area of the brain associated with emotional control (Etkin, Egner, Peraza, Kandel, & Hirsh,

2006), is implicated in the buffering effects of attentional control (Gyurak, Goodkind, Kramer, Miller, & Levenson, 2012).

COGNITIVE STRATEGIES THAT ENABLE DELAY OF GRATIFICATION

What are the strategies that enable some individuals to resist temptation while other individuals succumb? Before addressing the psychological and neural processes that enable or hinder delaying of gratification, it is fruitful to first ask a more basic question: Why is delaying gratification even difficult? Although this question may appear overly simplistic, it offers insights into the strategies that may enable delay ability.

Part of the reason that waiting for a larger reward is difficult is because immediately available rewards are *concrete* and delayed rewards are *abstract*. As such, immediate rewards are highly salient, easily processed, more likely to automatically capture attention and elicit appetitive behaviors, and more difficult to ignore and resist (Carretié, Hinojosa, Martín-Loeches, Mercado, & Tapia, 2004). Immediate rewards are also perceived as subjectively more valuable (e.g., Ainslie, 1975). In contrast, delayed rewards are hypothetical, inherently less salient, less motivating, and perceived as less valuable. Thus, when evaluating between a small reward now versus a larger reward at a later time, people prefer the former, reflecting the famous proverb that a "bird in the hand is worth two in the bush."

Not surprisingly then, by default—in the absence of any attempts at self-regulation—in quintessential self-control dilemmas, exposures to temptations automatically activate hot, appetitive aspects of the mental representation of the immediate rewards and spontaneously elicit actions directed toward them (Metcalfe & Mischel, 1999). These impulsive tendencies must somehow be regulated in order to obtain the desired but delayed reward.

Starting in the 1970s, a series of experiments focused on identifying the cognitive strategies that enabled preschoolers to delay immediate gratification and wait for the larger, more desired reward (e.g., Mischel et al., 2011). This work identified various strategies that affected a given individual's ability to resist temptation. The simplest strategy was to minimize the extent to which one attends to the tempting stimulus, either by ignoring it completely or through distraction in which one directs attention away from aspects of the situation that elicit appetitive, concrete, or hot representations. A more complex strategy involved dampening the power of the tempting stimulus via reframing (reconstruing or reappraising) the meaning of the stimulus to focus on the informational, abstract, or "cool" aspects of the situation instead of the default appetitive, concrete, or hot aspects.

Effect of Distraction Strategies on Delay of Gratification

In several experiments, strategies such as ignoring and distraction that dampened the salience of the tempting stimulus led to greater delay ability. For example, if children took part in the delay of gratification procedure when the rewards were out of sight, they waited longer compared with the standard condition in which the rewards were plainly in sight (Mischel & Ebbesen, 1970). Thus, an externally enacted strategy of restructuring the physical situation such that the tempting aspects of the situation were less visible and unavailable for processing made the task of delaying easier. Likewise, if children were provided with a distraction (e.g., given a fun toy to play with), they were able to wait longer than did children who were not provided with a distraction (Mischel et al., 1972). The effectiveness of this strategy was not limited to external distractions. Subjective, internal thoughts were equally effective. When children were simply given the instruction to "think fun," the children's own thoughts served as sufficient distraction, facilitating delay and successfully thwarting the aversive aspects of the immediate situation (Mischel et al., 1972).

Most interesting were findings showing that in the absence of any explicit instructions, preschoolers' *spontaneous* enactment of attentional–control strategies during the standard delay of gratification task in which all the rewards were fully visible meaningfully predicted delay time (Rodriguez, Mischel, & Shoda, 1989). Children's spontaneous behavior during the delay period was meticulously coded in terms of whether they directed their attention toward the immediately available tempting reward or toward nontempting aspects of the situation. The proportion of time spontaneously spent directing attention away from the rewards and toward other nontempting aspects of the situation was a strong predictor ($r = .49$) of delay time.

Effect of Reappraisal on Delay of Gratification

A second strategy enabling delay of gratification is reappraisal. Reconstruing or reframing the tempting stimuli in terms of its cooler, informational, and abstract features instead of its naturally salient hot, appetitive, or consummatory features enabled preschoolers to wait longer for the delayed rewards (e.g., Mischel et al., 1972, 1989; Mischel & Ayduk, 2004; Mischel & Underwood, 1974). For example, preschoolers who were instructed to imagine the treats in terms of their cool, abstract, and informational features (e.g., marshmallows look like white puffy clouds) waited longer than those who imagined the treats in terms of their hot, concrete, and appetitive features (e.g., the sweet taste of marshmallows; Mischel & Baker, 1975). Interestingly, although the actual presence of the treats increases the salience of the hot aspects of the situation and thus hinders delay of gratification ability, the *symbolic* presence of the treat (a photograph of the treat) increases the salience of the cool aspects of the rewards and thus promotes delaying gratification (Mischel & Moore, 1973). The specificity of the reward is important. Viewing the photograph of the reward one is waiting for (e.g., two marshmallows) is more motivating than viewing the photograph of an irrelevant reward (e.g., toy).

Integrating Key Findings From the Experimental and Longitudinal Work

In short, both the experimental and the longitudinal work speak to the strategies that allow individuals to delay gratification. On the one hand, the longitudinal findings suggest that there are important, naturally existing, individual differences in delay ability; that this variability predicts consequential outcomes in adolescence and adulthood in diverse life domains; and that individual differences in the spontaneous use of attentional–control strategies (occurring in the absence of any explicit instructions) is a key strategy predicting delay of gratification (e.g., Eigsti et al., 2006; Rodriguez et al., 1989). On the other hand, the experimental work suggests that regardless of the particular strategy (ignore, distraction, reconstrual) and whether it was enacted externally by the structure of the situation (obscure the treats from sight) or internally by the preschooler's own efforts (think about the marshmallows as clouds), providing preschoolers with self-control strategies served to dampen the salience of the tempting stimulus, and this in turn enabled delay.

Collectively, the experimental and longitudinal work also move away from a purely trait, dispositional conceptualization of delay of gratification ability toward a focus on cognitive strategies and processes. Because such strategies can be acquired and practiced, they are promising routes for increasing delay of gratification ability. Specifically, the preschooler who might have succumbed to the tempting aspects of the situation if left to her own devices might be able to wait for the larger reward if she was provided with an appropriate strategy, such as engaging in a distracting activity or focusing on the cool, cognitive, and abstract qualities of the treats. Similarly, the opposite is also likely: The preschooler who might have been able to delay gratification in the absence of any explicit instructions may find it more difficult to wait for the larger reward if she is provided with an inappropriate strategy, such as focusing on the immediate reward or its hot, appetitive (consummatory), and concrete features (Metcalfe & Mischel, 1999; Mischel & Ayduk, 2004). The critical point is that because the experimental work shows that for the majority of children (those with high as well as low delay ability) the appropriate strategy can be enacted if made temporarily accessible via external or internal strategies, it is possible for children who are not spontaneously adept at delaying gratification to learn to enact more appropriate strategies and improve their overall ability to delay gratification.

A Hot/Cool Systems Approach to Delay of Gratification

The hot/cool framework (Metcalfe & Mischel, 1999) was developed to integrate diverse findings from the delay of gratification work and to delineate more precisely the mechanisms by which strategies, such as distraction and reappraisal, subserve delay of gratification (Mischel & Ayduk, 2002, 2004; Metcalfe & Mischel, 1999). Similar to other two-system models of related constructs, such as risky decision making (Reyna & Farley, 2006; Reyna & Rivers, 2008), temporal discounting (McClure, Laibson, Loewenstein, & Cohen, 2004), impulsivity (Steinberg et al., 2008), and addictions (Bechara, 2005; Everitt, Dickinson, & Robbins, 2001; Everitt & Robbins, 2005), the hot/cool framework is based on the idea that there are two modes of information processing (e.g., Lieberman, Gaunt, Gilbert, & Trope, 2002; Smith & DeCoster, 2000): a cool cognitive system involved in more deliberative and reflective processing and a hot emotional system that is primarily involved in the spontaneous evaluation of rewards and punishments.

Although the hot/cool framework was first developed as a heuristic, with no commitment to their anatomical structures, a hope was that these metaphors might reflect more tangible cognitive and neural processes. As reflected by the contributions in the present volume, an explosion of research in cognitive neuroscience over the past two decades has been turning this idea into a reality (e.g., Heatherton, 2011; Lieberman, 2007; Ochsner & Gross, 2007). Although an extensive review of the literature is beyond the scope of this chapter, here we present a brief description of these two systems, their characteristics and neural substrates, and how variations in the functioning of these neural systems may affect people's tendency (due to both dispositional and situational influences) to delay gratification. We then turn to recent work from our research team identifying the adult cognitive and neural correlates of preschool delay of gratification.

Hot Limbic System and Cool Cognitive System

The hot, impulsive, or "go" system (also referred to in different frameworks as "System 1," automatic, spontaneous, experiential, associative) is seen early in development (Eisenberger, Smith, Sadovsky, & Spinrad, 2004; Rothbart, Ellis, & Posner, 2004). It is primarily stimulus-triggered and affective in nature, and it operates quickly, with little effort, deliberation, or control. As such, it provides a rudimentary analysis of the potential rewards and threats in the environment (e.g., Cacioppo & Gardner, 1999; Compton, 2003), especially those that are primary reinforcers and punishers, and enables fast-acting responsive behaviors (e.g., moving toward rewards and away from threats). Research from cognitive neuroscience has routinely implicated limbic structures (e.g., Cunningham et al., 2004), such as the amygdala (e.g., Armony & LeDoux, 2000; Bechara, 2005; Breiter et al., 1996; Metcalfe & Jacobs, 1996, 1998; Morris, Öhman, & Dolan, 1998; Phelps & LeDoux, 2005), nucleus accumbens (Galvan et al., 2005), and ventral striatum (Delgado, Locke, Stenger, & Fiez, 2003; Delgado, Nystrom, Fissell, Noll, & Fiez, 2000; Knutson, Adams, Fong, & Hommer, 2001), with the hot system.

The cool, cognitive, or "know" system (also referred to in different frameworks as "System 2," deliberate, rational, rule-based, reflective) is responsible for a number of abilities that are commonly referred to as *cognitive control, executive functions*, *central executive*, and *attentional bias* (e.g., Baddeley, 1986; Cohen & Servan-Schreiber, 1992; Desimone & Duncan, 1995; Shallice, 1988). In contrast to the hot system, the cool system develops later, emerging by around the age of 4 (Mischel, 1974; see also Eisenberger et al., 2004; Rothbart et al., 2004). This system is typically viewed as the seat of free will and self-regulation (Moffitt et al., 2011). It enables an individual to inhibit automatic, reflexive stimulus-triggered responses; to reflect on and manipulate (maintain, enhance, and suppress) information in working memory, including mental representations of goals and events not present in the immediate situation; to devise and implement plans for achieving future goals (Baddeley, 1998); and to facilitate effective and appropriate response selection (Rowe, Toni, Josephs, Frackowiak, & Passingham, 2000). An expansive neuroimaging literature provides evidence that various cognitive control functions are governed by structures in the prefrontal cortex (PFC; Jackson et al., 2003; Miller & Cohen, 2001; Ochsner & Gross, 2007; O'Reilly, 2006), such as the inferior frontal gyrus (IFG), which is involved in maintaining information in working memory and in executing planned action, and the lateral PFC, which is involved in representations of abstract rules (Bunge & Zelazo, 2006), as well as the anterior cingulate cortex, which is hypothesized to serve conflict-monitoring functions that signal recruitment of PFC control mechanisms (Botvinick, Braver, Barch, Carter, & Cohen, 2001; Etkin et al., 2006; Heatherton, 2011; Kerns et al., 2004).

Relative Activation of the Hot and Cool System as Mechanisms Underlying Delay of Gratification

A key assumption of the hot/cool framework is that delay of gratification is governed by continuous interactions between the hot and cool systems (for a discussion, see Metcalfe & Mischel, 1999). From this perspective, a given stimulus in the environment can be represented in terms of its concrete, appetitive, or hot features or in terms of abstract, informational, or cool features. Accordingly a given stimulus can activate these features within a person's mind, which are represented as a neural network, and are referred to simply as "hot spots" of the hot system and "cool nodes" of the cool system. Furthermore, the hot spots of the hot system and the cool nodes of the cool system are connected with one another, such that activation of cool nodes (e.g., thinking about a marshmallow as a cloud) can lead to a decrease in the activation of hot nodes (e.g., focusing on the sensory eliciting qualities of eating a marshmallow). Thus, the extent to which one engages in greater activation of the cool (vs. hot) system, for example by means of distraction and reappraisal strategies, facilitates the ability to wait for the delayed rewards. In contrast, the extent to which activation of the hot system is dominant, for example, by increased salience of the temptations, hinders delay. This idea of two continuously interacting systems whose relative activations have implications for decision making and behavior resonates with those of other scholars in the related domains of delay discounting and impulsivity (e.g., Blais & Weber, 2001; Figner & Weber, 2011; McClure et al., 2004; Mellers, Schwartz, & Weber, 1997; Weber, 2001; Zaleskiewicz, 2001).

Not surprisingly, research in cognitive neuroscience is increasingly focusing on interactions among neural structures subserving the processes that enable delay of gratification and the relative balance between activation of limbic structures associated with the processing of affective stimuli and the PFC structures recruited in regulation of cognition, affect, and behavior (Bechara, 2005; Heatherton, 2011; LeDoux, 1996; McClure et al., 2004, 2007; Ochsner et al., 2004; Sanfey, Hastie, Colvin, & Grafman, 2003; Sanfey, Loewenstein, McClure, & Cohen, 2006; Somerville & Casey, 2010). Recent studies show that directing attention away from emotionally salient features of a situation reduces activation in emotion-generative neural regions, such as the amygdala and insula (Bantick et al., 2002; McRae et al., 2010). Thus, similar to the role of distraction in dampening the tempting aspects of the rewards in the original delaying of gratification experiments, in recent cognitive neuroscience studies, directing attention away from appetitive stimuli (via shifting gaze or working memory load manipulations) minimizes the extent to which the stimulus is encoded in working memory. Moreover, a recent study recording event-related potentials investigated whether attentional deployment is effective even *after* the affective cue is encoded into working memory. Thiruchselvam, Hajcak, and Gross (2012) had participants view an emotion-arousing image (e.g., car crash) and hold the image in working memory. After the image was in memory, they were instructed to either focus their attention to a neutral aspect of the representation or an arousing aspect of the representation. Even though the emotion-arousing image had already been encoded in working memory, attention deployment to neutral aspects of the representation led to reduced self-reported mood and dampened late positive potential, a neural measure of emotional responding.

Neuroimaging work has also looked at the effect of reconstruing the meaning of a situation on the activation of neural systems involved in the processing of affective stimuli and its regulation. For example, Ochsner et al. (2004) showed that reappraising a negative stimulus (e.g., snake) in more neutral terms increased activation of the cingulate and PFC, which is implicated in the cool system, and decreased the activation of the amygdala. This suggests that the PFC and cingulate play a critical role in the reappraisal strategies attributed to the cool system, and that enactment of such strategies decreases the sensitivity of the hot system, as reflected by decreased activation of the amygdala in response to the negative stimulus.

Individual Differences

Contextual factors, both those generated internally by one's own thoughts and those generated externally by cues available in the situation, can influence the relative momentary activation of the hot versus cool systems and thus a person's ability to delay. But individuals also differ in the chronic and stable activations of these two systems. Exposure to environmental factors throughout development can lead to greater dominance of one system over the other. Chronic stress, for example, through its effects on the hippocampus (Sapolsky, 1996) or PFC (Brown, Henning, & Wellman, 2005; Vyas, Bernal, & Chattarji, 2003), could increase the chronic activation of the hot system (McEwen & Gianaros, 2010). In contrast, routine enactment of attentional–control and other self-regulation strategies and cognitive capacities, including higher working memory capacity (Barkley, 1997; Hinson, Jameson, & Whitney, 2003), could lead to greater chronic activation of the cool system (Ayduk et al., 2000; Fishbach & Trope, 2005). Biological predispositions, physiology, drug use, and disease could also affect the extent to which one system is more chronically active relative to the other. Regardless of the source, individual differences in the neural structures associated with either the hot or the cool systems, and their interconnections, are expected to contribute to chronic, trait-like, dispositional differences in the ability to delay gratification (Metcalfe & Mischel, 1999; Mischel & Ayduk, 2004). Indeed, individual differences in the structure and function of these neural systems may mediate the remarkable predictive ability of preschool delay on later life outcomes.

Research has routinely found evidence that some individuals are particularly sensitive to the hot aspects of temptations. For example, through use of a "cue reactivity" paradigm in which participants are exposed to images of primary reinforcers, obese individuals, smokers, and drug addicts show stronger activation of the mesolimbic reward system in response to temptations (e.g., image of cigarettes for smokers; Childress et al., 1999; David et al., 2007; Rothemund et al., 2007). Moreover, increased sensitivity to rewards has implications for control mechanisms. For example, the typical PFC–amygdala coupling, which is observed during attempts at emotion regulation in nonclinical samples, is not observed in clinical populations (e.g., major depressive disorder, bipolar personality disorder; Johnstone, van Reekum, Urry, Kalin, & Davidson, 2007). Instead of the inverse coupling suggesting PFC down-regulation of limbic areas in nonclinical samples, both PFC and amygdala activation are high in clinical samples. Similarly, in the addiction literature, addictive behaviors may emerge from a dysregulation in neural systems in which there is an interplay between a hypersensitive limbic system that is highly reactive to rewards along with a hypoactive prefrontal system (Bechara, 2005) that fails to down-regulate affect (Demos, Kelley, & Heatherton, 2011). Such dynamics may account for difficulties in delay of gratification.

Another recent line of inquiry by Gyurak et al. (2012) has been examining individual differences in the cognitive and neural systems by which delay ability (and other related capacities such as executive control) might serve as a protective factor especially for those with chronic vulnerabilities to adaptively regulate negative emotions and thoughts. Although this work is not able to investigate the developmental issue, because all measures were assessed concurrently, it is implicating the role of the rACC, which is involved in the monitoring of errors and the signaling of the need for control. Greater activation of the dorsal ACC in a task requiring inhibition of threatening stimuli has been linked to individual differences in self-reported attentional control (Bishop, Jenkins, & Lawrence, 2007). In the Gyurak et al. (2007) study, participants viewed images depicting social rejection (a woman sitting alone in a room) as well as equally negatively valenced images of a nonsocial nature. Among participants with low self-esteem (a disposition that is similar to high RS in being highly sensitive to rejection), those who also had high attentional control reported less arousal after viewing images of social rejection than did those with low attentional control. Moreover, results of the functional magnetic resonance imaging (fMRI) analysis indicated that those with low self-esteem and high attentional control engaged the rACC, an area of the brain associated with emotional control, more than their low-self-esteem and low-attentional-control counterparts. Activation in the rACC fully mediated the relationship between the interaction of self-esteem and attentional control and self-reported arousal, suggesting that the rACC activation underlies the buffering effects of attentional control.

Preschool Delay of Gratification and Adult Cognitive and Neural Mechanisms

Despite the growing body of research speaking to the cognitive and neural mechanisms of the hot and cool systems underlying self-control and related constructs (Hare, Camerer, & Rangel, 2009; Heatherton, 2011; McClure et al., 2004), only recently have studies begun to directly investigate the developmental question of how preschool delay ability relates to adult cognitive and neural processes. Given that the ability to wait for larger rewards depends on how one selectively attends to and mentally represents aspects of the tempting situation, and that enacting these strategies depends on the ability to recruit cognitive control, a straightforward prediction is that preschool delay would be a precursor, or marker, of the cognitive and neural systems underlying cognitive control in adulthood.

In a multisite, multidisciplinary endeavor, our research team has begun to tackle this developmental question. This work has involved following up with individuals who took part in the delay of gratification at age 4 and now in adulthood having the same individuals complete behavioral measures while fMRI scans are obtained. We briefly review key findings from this new wave of delay of gratification research here.

Behavioral Findings: Predicting Adult Impulse Control From Preschool Attentional–Control Strategies

In a follow-up to an existing longitudinal study, we investigated whether performance in the delay of gratification situation at age 4 predicts performance on a standard measure of impulse control (go/no-go task) at age 18 (Eigsti et al., 2006). We reasoned that dispositional abilities in delaying gratification reflect, in part, individual differences in the relative activation of the cool or "no-go" system over the hot (or go) system and that such stable differences make it easier for individuals to enact strategies that dampen the salience of the appetitive, hot, or go-related representations in self-control situations. Thus, not surprisingly, we chose to use a well-established task of impulse control, the go/no-go task, which despite striking differences at the surface level bears some resemblance to the preschool delay of gratification task (Casey et al., 1997; Fillmore & Rush, 2002; Fillmore, Rush, & Hays, 2002; Kaufman, Ross, Stein, & Garavan, 2003).

In the go/no-go task, participants are instructed to respond to target (go) stimuli by pressing a response key, but to *not* press a response key to other nontarget (no-go) stimuli. The ability to successfully refrain from making responses on no-go trials (reflected by false alarm rate on no-go trials) and the efficiency with which an individual is able to make a response on go trials (reflected by reaction times on go trials), are behavioral indicators of the ability to successfully and efficiently inhibit a response. Past work using the go/no-go task has found that children ages 7 to 12 show greater difficulty than adults (twice as many errors overall and slower reaction time; Durston, Thomas, Yang, et al., 2002), consistent with the idea that impulse control becomes more efficient with development (Davidson, Amso, Anderson, & Diamond, 2006; Keating & Bobbitt, 1978; see also Chapter 3, this volume).

Given that the original delay of gratification work showed that preschoolers' ability to delay gratification was affected by contextual factors (e.g., when rewards are obscured from sight, delaying is easier than when rewards are visible), we aimed to mimic this contextual effect in the go/no-go paradigm. Specifically, we included a parametric manipulation of the number of preceding consecutive go trials. This parametric manipulation essentially primes the go response, which, in turn, increases conflict between the two response options (to go or *not* to go) and thus increases the need for greater cognitive control to accurately and efficiently perform the task. For example, inhibiting a go response following only one go trial is easier than inhibiting a go response after five consecutive go trials. Indeed, as the number of preceding consecutive go trials increases, the proportion of false alarms on no-go trials increases (Durston, Thomas, Worden, Yang, & Casey, 2002), as do reaction times on go trials (Liston et al., 2006).

In our follow-up, we therefore asked the following: Would preschoolers' ability to enact strategies that allow them to delay gratification predict their ability, as adults, to effectively and efficiently refrain from responding to irrelevant stimuli in the go/no-go task? The results from the follow-up study revealed a clear and remarkable convergence between the spontaneous attentional–control strategies enacted by preschoolers in the delay of gratification situation and their adult impulse control abilities as reflected by the go/no-go task (Eigsti et al., 2006). As shown in Figure 6.1, those who at age 4 directed their attention away from tempting aspects of the situation (i.e., *low temptation focus*), compared with those who directed their attention toward tempting aspects of the situation (i.e., *high temptation focus*), were more efficient at suppressing prepotent responses in the go/no-go task in adulthood. Specifically, consistent with other research showing that longer reaction times on go trials is a behavioral marker of difficulty with impulse control (Liston et al., 2006), the low temptation focus group was faster on go responses without making more errors. Moreover, the predictive ability of individual differences in preschool attentional–control strategies was most pronounced in conditions in which a go trial was preceded by a greater number of consecutive go trials, which presumably required greater impulse control. The results showed that the difference between preschoolers with low temptation focus and high temptation focus increased linearly as the need for impulse control increased (i.e., when the go stimulus had been preceded by five or six consecutive go trials). Overall, the results indicate that for individuals who as preschoolers

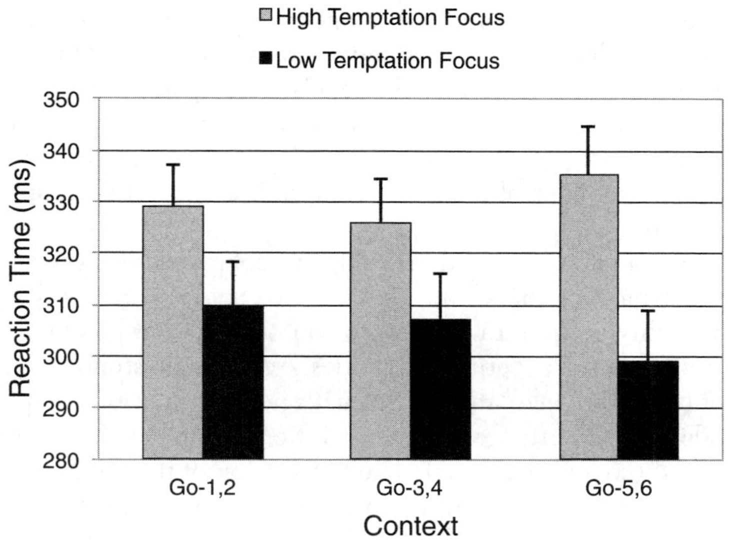

Figure 6.1. Mean reaction times on go trials as a function of preschool attentional-control (high vs. low temptation focus) and as a function of the number of consecutive preceding go trials. Bars represent 1 standard error above and below the mean. Those who at age 4 showed better attentional control (low temptation focus) were faster at responding to go trials, compared with those with worse attentional control at age 4 (high temptation focus). This difference between effective versus ineffective attentional control at age 4 was most pronounced in conditions in which resisting a prepotent impulse was greatest (i.e., with greater number of consecutive preceding go trials). ms = milliseconds. From "Attentional Control in Preschool Predicts Cognitive Control at Age Eighteen," by L.-M. Eigsti et al., 2006. *Psychological Science,* 17, p. 482. Copyright 2006 by Wiley-Blackwell. Adapted with permission.

spontaneously enacted ineffective attentional–control strategies (high temptation focus) to perform the go/no-go task accurately as adults, they needed to compensate by slowing down their speed of responding, particularly in the most difficult trials (i.e., following a large number of consecutive go trials).

Neural Correlates: Implicating the PFC and the Limbic System

Given that performance on the go/no-go task has been well characterized as involving activation in frontostriatal regions of the brain (Booth et al., 2003; Casey et al., 1997; Davidson et al., 2004; Durston, Thomas, Worden, et al., 2002; Durston, Thomas, Yang, et al., 2002; Durston et al., 2003; Konishi et al., 1999; Vaidya et al., 1998), the behavioral findings from the Eigsti et al. (2006) follow-up provocatively suggest that preschool delay ability may serve as an early marker of the functional integrity of this circuitry. In recent work involving a different cohort (Casey et al., 2011), we provide the first empirical support for this proposition.

In this study, participants had completed the delay of gratification procedure at age 4 during the 1960s and 1970s as well as various self-report measures of self-control in their 20s and 30s. Participants were grouped into those who exhibited consistently above-average self-control throughout the various assessments (*high delay* group) and those who exhibited consistently below-average self-control (*low delay* group). A subset of this sample agreed to take part in the follow-up study.

In the first part of the study, participants completed two versions of the go/no-go task: a cool and a hot version. The cool version was designed to assess the ability to inhibit responses to cool stimuli, that is, stimuli that do not inherently possess appetitive properties. Accordingly, stimuli were photographs of individual men and women with neutral emotional expressions. One gender served as the go stimuli, and the opposite gender served as the no-go stimuli (counterbalanced). The hot version of the go/no-go task was designed to assess the ability to inhibit responses to stimuli that inherently possess appetitive properties. Thus, the hot go/no-go task was identical to the cool go/no-go task except that the go stimuli were photographs of faces with emotional expressions (e.g., happy) and the no-go stimuli were photographs of faces with a different emotional expression (e.g., fearful). Happy faces are appetitive and automatically trigger approach-related responses (Hare, Tottenham, Davidson, Glover, & Casey, 2005), whereas fearful faces trigger attentional vigilance (Davis & Whalen, 2001) and defensive responses when encountered in situations of anxiety (Grillon & Charney, 2011).

Given a growing body of research distinguishing between hot and cool executive functions (Figner, Mackinlay, Wilkening, & Weber, 2009; Somerville & Casey, 2010; see also Chapter 3, this volume), we predicted that preschool delay ability would affect performance most strongly in the hot (vs. cool) go/no-go task. Moreover, we reasoned that trials in which participants were instructed to go on fearful faces and to *not* go on happy faces would be particularly difficult, because this condition required inhibiting the appetitive appeal of happy faces. Thus, we predicted that preschool delay ability would be particularly diagnostic in these more difficult trials.

As shown in Figure 6.2, left panel, at the behavioral level, the high delay group and the low delay group did not differ appreciably in their ability to withhold a response in the cool go/no-go task, as expected. However, the high delay group, compared with the low delay group, was much more effective at withholding a response in the hot version of the task. Specifically, the primary difference between the high and low delayers emerged in situations in which they were required to inhibit a behavioral response to happy faces serving as no-go stimuli, with high delayers exhibiting fewer false alarms than low delayers. (The difference between the high and low delay groups was also observed when the task was performed inside the scanner; Figure 6.2 right panel.)

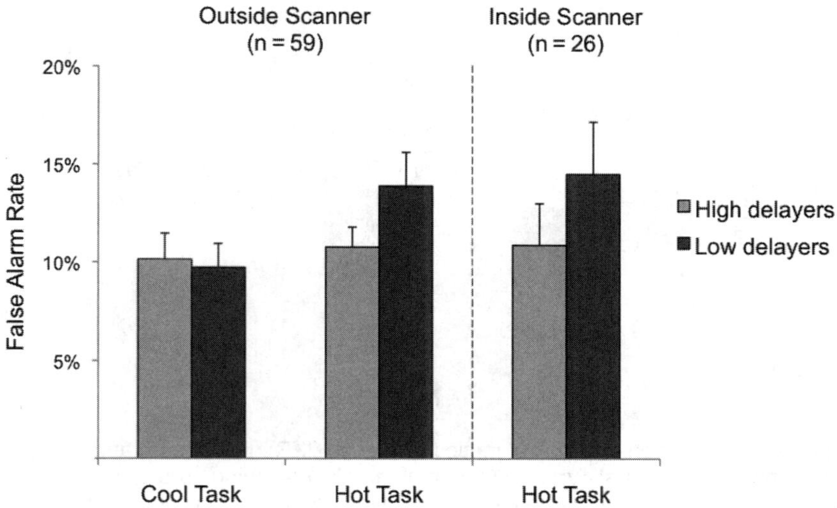

Figure 6.2. Mean false alarm rate in the behavioral study (experiment 1: left panel) and in the imaging study (experiment 2: right panel). In the go/no-go task, when the cues are "cool" (neutral facial expressions), there was no significant difference in performance between high versus low delayers. However, when the cues are "hot" (emotional faces) low delayers made more errors than did high delayers. Error bars denote 1 standard error above and below the mean. From "Behavioral and Neural Correlates of Delay of Gratification 40 Years Later," by B. J. Casey et al., 2011. *Proceedings of the National Academy of Sciences of the United States of America,* 108, p. 15000. Copyright 2011 by the National Academy of Sciences. Adapted with permission.

An investigation of the neural substrates of these differences focused particularly on the role of the IFG, a region of the PFC involved in the resolution of conflict between competing motor responses (Aron, Robbins, & Poldrack, 2004; Casey, Tottenham, & Fossella, 2002) and among competing representations in memory (Jonides & Nee, 2006). We hypothesized that in the basic task facing participants—that is, resolving the decision of whether to go or *not* to go—the IFG would be recruited more heavily, and more important, that high delayers, compared with low delayers, would recruit the IFG more heavily. Consistent with these hypotheses, as shown in Color Plate 9 (Panel A), the IFG was recruited more heavily on no-go trials compared with go trials (and so was the left motor cortex, Panel B, and cerebellum, Panel C). Moreover, as shown in Figure 6.3, compared with their low delaying counterparts, high delayers showed greater IFG activation in trials requiring the inhibition of a response (nogo trials) than trials that did not (go trials).

In addition, given that the behavioral findings showed that the two groups were statistically indistinguishable when the cues to be inhibited were neutral but differed primarily in situations in which the cues to be inhibited

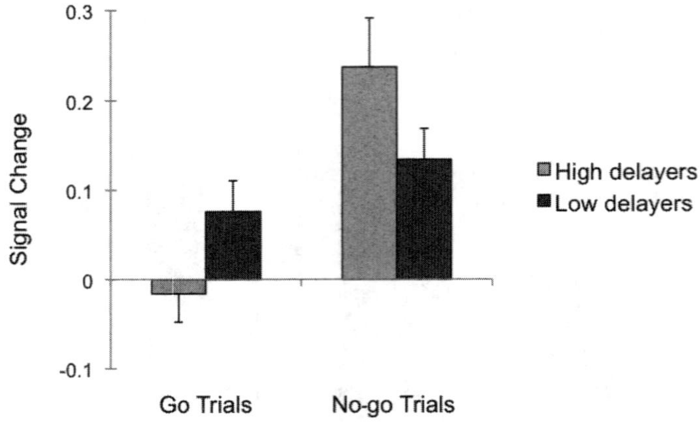

Figure 6.3. Percent change in magnetic resonance (MR) signal to go and no-go trials in the inferior frontal gyrus (IFG) in high and low delaying groups. High delay ability predicts greater recruitment of the IFG when correctly inhibiting responses to no-go trials (positive social cues) relative to go trials 40 years later.

were appetitive and prepotent, we investigated the extent to which limbic structures were recruited in the go/no-go task. We hypothesized that activation of neural regions involved in the processing of rewards, such as the ventral striatum, which is routinely involved in the processing of appetitive stimuli (Delgado, 2007), would also distinguish the two groups. As shown in Color Plate 10, the neural data indicated that the low delay group, compared with the high delay group, showed greater activation of the ventral striatum when happy faces served as no-go stimuli.

IMPLICATIONS FOR THEORY AND RESEARCH ON DELAY OF GRATIFICATION

There has been an explosion of research in cognitive neuroscience, social neuroscience, and neuroeconomics focusing on the neural structures involved in decision making, temporal discounting, cognitive control, and reward sensitivity. The emerging picture is that delay of gratification ability is affected by the interplay of limbic structures associated with the processing of tempting cues, on the one hand, and the PFC and cingulate cortex associated with the regulation of cognition, affect, and behavior, on the other (Bechara, 2005; LeDoux, 1996; McClure et al., 2004; McClure, Erikson, Laibson, Loewenstein, & Cohen, 2007; Ochsner et al., 2004; Sanfey et al., 2003, 2006; Somerville & Casey, 2010). The recent findings from our research team (Casey et al., 2011; Eigsti et al., 2006) further clarify the cognitive and neural mechanisms enabling effective delay of gratification and how these mechanisms relate to preschool delay ability assessed over two decades earlier. We discuss below how this recent work contributes to current theorizing of the neural mechanisms underlying delay of gratification.

Implications for the Cool System: The Role of Cognitive Control

The classic findings from the original preschooler delay of gratification studies and recent work utilizing behavioral and neural measures to probe cognitive control in adulthood converge to support the idea that delay of gratification requires cognitive control. To effectively wait the entire 15 minutes in the classic delay of gratification situation as well as to efficiently and correctly perform the computer-based go/no-go task, one must be able to inhibit behaviors that promote impulsive action: In the delay task, a child must inhibit the urge to eat the treat or ring the bell, and in the go/no-go task, the adult must inhibit the impulse to press a button in response to a prepotent, but task-irrelevant, cue.

Moreover, these findings indicate that individuals differ in their ability to spontaneously recruit cognitive control, and there is evidence for some remarkable stability in this ability over the life span. In the absence of any explicit instructions, in two studies with two different cohorts (Casey et al., 2011; Eigsti et al., 2006), the ability to spontaneously recruit strategies (e.g., distraction) in the delay of gratification situation in preschool predicted the ability to efficiently inhibit responses to distracting, potent cues in the go/no-go task in adulthood. Furthermore, providing more direct empirical evidence that delay of gratification requires cognitive control, in the recent follow-up (Casey et al., 2011), high delayers recruited areas of the IFG, which is involved in the resolution of conflict, to a greater extent than low delayers. This stability is impressive given the 20-year time span, the drastically different methods of assessment (behavioral vs. reaction-based computer task), and the distinct contexts and cues (food vs. happy faces).

Implications for the Hot System

In the recent imaging work (Casey et al., 2011), the low delay group (compared with the high delay group) showed greater activation of limbic-related neural structures, such as ventral striatum, involved in the processing of rewards when happy faces served as no-go stimuli. One straightforward explanation for this finding is that the representation of happy faces (a social reward) was more salient and affective for low delayers than for high delayers. This would be in line with the idea that low delayers may be more sensitive to appetitive cues (happy faces) than are high delayers, and that this sensitivity promotes greater impulsive responding and makes the task of inhibiting responses to happy faces more difficult (Herzberger & Dweck, 1978). Thus, those with poorer delay ability may have chronically overactive limbic systems that tip the relative balance of the hot/cool system.

It is worth noting that preschool delay of gratification predicted performance in the go/no-go task primarily in situations in which the cues to be inhibited were appetitive and prepotent. In the Casey et al. (2011) follow-up, the two groups were statistically indistinguishable when the cues to be inhibited were neutral. That delay ability is most clearly observed in situations that involve inhibition of affective, hot, prepotent stimuli, not just irrelevant (but cool) stimuli, supports a growing body of research distinguishing between hot and cool executive functions (Figner et al., 2009; Somerville & Casey, 2010; see also Chapter 3, this volume).

Moreover, these findings are particularly interesting in light of developmental models of cognitive control (Casey, Getz, & Galvan, 2008; Somerville & Casey, 2010; see also Chapter 4, this volume) that aim to understand the neural mechanisms that may heighten risky decision making during adolescence. From this developmental perspective, although the PFC cognitive control system matures in a relatively linear fashion, the limbic affective system is highly reactive during adolescence. Thus, the greater development of limbic structures relative to PFC-related cognitive control structures biases sensitivity to and the processing of immediate rewards (relative to delayed rewards) and leads to greater risky decision making and behaviors. Such developmental models could be fruitfully applied to understanding individual differences (Carlson, Zayas, & Guthormsen, 2009). In this view, adults with poor self-control might be viewed as developmentally less mature and similar to adolescents in possessing less mature frontostriatal circuitry that predisposes them to greater risk.

Interactions Between the Cool and Hot Systems

Increasingly, cognitive neuroscience is focusing on interactions among systems. So too did the initial conceptualization of the hot/cool framework. An underlying theme of these perspectives is the focus on the balance between the affective systems on the one hand and control systems on the other, and how the two systems continuously interact and influence one another. Thus, these approaches raise another, although not mutually exclusive, account of the recent follow-up (Casey et al., 2011). They raise the possibility that perhaps the differential activation of the ventral striatum is not simply a *cause* but also a *consequence* of differences in the ability to engage in cognitive control processes regulated by the PFC cognitive system. For example, high delayers' ability to effectively recruit cognitive control processes, and thus resolve conflict between competing representations, may have dampened the sensitivity to and processing of appetitive stimuli. Applied to Casey et al.'s (2011) findings, this reasoning suggests that the ability to efficiently resolve conflict between go responses to fearful faces and no-go responses to happy faces may have weakened the appetitive aspects of the no-go stimuli (happy faces). That is, if the conflict between the behavioral options to the stimuli is resolved quickly, then the representation of the distracting, appetitive no-go stimuli (happy faces) will be quickly expunged from working memory and be less likely to activate limbic structures involved in the processing of prepotent rewards. In contrast, if there is greater difficulty in resolving the conflict between the two behavioral options, the representation of the no-go stimuli (happy faces), which should be inhibited, will remain in working memory for a longer period of time and thus more strongly activate limbic structures involved in the processing of rewards. Thus, it is possible that high delayers' ability to engage in cognitive control decreased the salience of the appetitive stimuli and made the task of inhibiting a response less difficult.

Although further research is needed, such a possibility is evident in past work showing that an important benefit of effortful acts of control is that they make the very task of resisting temptation easier. They do so, for example, by preventing in-depth processing of the appetitive stimuli (via ignore/distraction strategies) and by dampening the appetitive and hot representations of temptations in working memory (via reconstrual). These strategies, in effect, decrease the psychological temptation, or "pull," of the situation and thus make the goal of delaying less effortful. Recent work provides additional evidence that difficulties in enacting self-control may enhance sensitivity to affective cues. Experimentally manipulating the ability to engage in self-regulation (e.g., via cognitive load manipulations) leads to more impulsive choices (Friese, Hoffman, & Wanke, 2008; Hofmann, Friese, & Strack, 2009; Shiv & Feodorikhin, 2002; Ward & Mann, 2000). Vohs, Baumeister, and Schmeichel (2012) showed that participants induced to engage in less self-regulation reported stronger emotional reactions to valenced images and film clips, stronger feelings of pain in a cold pressor task, and a greater desire to eat cookies during a tasting test. Although effortful cognitive control is a prerequisite for the enactment of self-control strategies, such acts make delaying gratification much easier. Indeed, it is ironic that to make delaying of gratification easier, and thereby lessen the need for cognitive control, one needs cognitive control.

CONCLUSION

The ability to delay gratification is necessary for achieving success in a number of life domains. A growing body of research, starting with the original delay of gratification experiments, has been identifying the psychological and neural mechanisms that enable individuals to engage in these more challenging goal pursuits. Speaking to the psychological level, this work shows that strategies such as distraction and reappraisal enable delay of gratification. Moreover, the ability to implement these strategies depends critically on cognitive control—the ability to regulate (suppress, replace, enhance, maintain) actions, thoughts, and feelings for the sake of long-term goals. Recent behavioral and neuroscientific findings are consistent with the hypothesis that those with difficulties in delaying gratification have less effective cognitive control abilities. During a task that requires inhibition of affective cues, those with difficulties delaying gratification are also more strongly affected by the appetitive aspects of immediate rewards. The cumulative effect is that those with poor delay ability are likely to place greater relative weight on the present, immediately available rewards than on the imagined, delayed rewards and decrease their ability to delay gratification (McClure et al., 2004). These recent neuroscientific findings are particularly interesting in light of models of cognitive control (Casey et al., 2008; Somerville & Casey, 2010; see also Chapter 4, this volume) and suggest that adults with poor self-control may possess less mature frontostriatal circuitry that predisposes them to greater risk.

REFERENCES

Ainslie, G. (1975). Specious reward: A behavioral theory of impulsiveness and impulse control. *Psychological Bulletin, 82*, 463–496. doi:10.1037/h0076860

Armony, J. L. and LeDoux, J. E. (1997) How the brain processes emotional information. *Annals of the New York Academy of Sciences 821*, 259–270.

Aron, A. R., Robbins, T. W., & Poldrack, R. A. (2004). Inhibition and the right inferior frontal cortex. *Trends in Cognitive Sciences*, 8, 170–177. doi:10.1016/j.tics.2004.02.010

Ayduk, O., Downey, G., & Kim, M. (2001). Rejection sensitivity and depressive symptoms in women. *Personality and Social Psychology Bulletin, 27,* 868–877. doi:10.1177/0146167201277009

Ayduk, O., Downey, G., Testa, A., Yen, Y., & Shoda, Y. (1999). Does rejection elicit hostility in rejection sensitive women? *Social Cognition, 17,* 245–271. doi:10.1521/soco.1999.17.2.245

Ayduk, O., Mendoza-Denton, R., Mischel, W., Downey, G., Peake, P., & Rodriguez, M. (2000). Regulating the interpersonal self: Strategic self-regulation for coping with rejection sensitivity. *Journal of Personality and Social Psychology, 79,* 776–792. doi:10.1037/0022-3514.79.5.776

Ayduk, O., Zayas, V., Downey, G., Cole, A. B., Shoda, Y., & Mischel, W. (2008). Rejection sensitivity and executive control: Joint predictions of borderline personality features. *Journal of Research in Personality, 42*, 151–168. doi:10.1016/j.jrp.2007.04.002

Baddeley, A. (1998). Recent developments in working memory. *Current Opinion in Neurobiology, 8*, 234–238. doi:10.1016/S0959-4388(98)80145-1

Baddeley, A. D. (1986). *Working memory*. Oxford, England: Clarendon Press.

Bantick, S. J., Wise, R. G., Ploghaus, A., Clare, S., Smith, S. M., & Tracey, I. (2002). Imaging how attention modulates pain in humans using functional MRI. *Brain: A Journal of Neurology, 125*, 310–319. doi:10.1093/brain/awf022

Barkley, R. A. (1997). Behavioral inhibition, sustained attention, and executive functions: Constructing a unifying theory of ADHD. *Psychological Bulletin, 121*, 65–94. doi:10.1037/0033-2909.121.1.65

Bechara, A. (2005). Decision making, impulse control and loss of willpower to resist drugs: A neurocognitive perspective. *Nature Neuroscience, 8*, 1458–1463. doi:10.1038/nn1584

Bishop, S. J., Jenkins, R., & Lawrence, A. D. (2007). Neural processing of fearful faces: Effects of anxiety are gated by perceptual capacity limitations. *Cerebral Cortex, 17*, 1595–1603. doi:10.1093/cercor/bhl070

Blair, C. (2010). Stress and the development of self-regulation in context. *Child Development Perspectives, 4*, 181–188. doi:10.1111/j.1750-8606.2010.00145.x

Blair, C., & Raver, C. C. (2012). Child development in the context of adversity. *American Psychologist, 67*, 309–318. doi:10.1037/a0027493

Blais, A. R., & Weber, E. U. (2001). Domain-specificity and gender differences in decision making. *Risk Decision & Policy, 6*, 47–69. doi:10.1017/S1357530901000254

Bogg, T., & Roberts, B. W. (2004). Conscientiousness and health-related behaviors: A meta-analysis of the leading behavioral contributors to mortality. *Psychological Bulletin, 130*, 887–919. doi:10.1037/0033-2909.130.6.887

Bonato, D. P., & Boland, F. J. (1983). Delay of gratification in obese children. *Addictive Behaviors, 8*, 71–74. doi:10.1016/0306-4603(83)90059-X

Booth, J. R., Burman, D. D., Meyer, J. R., Lei, Z., Trommer, B. L., Davenport, N. D., . . . Mesulam, M. M. (2003). Neural development of selective attention and response inhibition. *NeuroImage, 20*, 737–751. doi:10.1016/S1053-8119(03)00404-X

Botvinick, M. M., Braver, T., Barch, D., Carter, C., & Cohen, J. (2001). Conflict monitoring and cognitive control. *Psychological Review, 108*, 624–652. doi:10.1037/0033-295X.108.3.624

Breiter, H. C., Etcoff, N. L., Whalen, P. J., Kennedy, W. A., Rauch, S. L., Buckner, R. L., . . . Rosen, B. R. (1996). Response and habituation of the human amygdala during visual processing of facial expression. *Neuron, 17*, 875–887. doi:10.1016/S0896-6273(00)80219-6

Brown, S. M., Henning, S., & Wellman, C. L. (2005). Short-term, mild stress alters dendritic morphology in rat medial prefrontal cortex. *Cerebral Cortex, 15*, 1714–1722. doi:10.1093/cercor/bhi048

Bruce, A. S., Black, W. R., Bruce, J. M., Daldalian, M., Martin, L. E., & Davis, A. M. (2011). Ability to delay gratification and BMI in preadolescence. *Obesity, 19*, 1101–1102. doi:10.1038/oby.2010.297

Bunge, S. A., & Zelazo, P. D. (2006). A brain-based account of the development of rule use in childhood. *Current Directions in Psychological Science, 15*, 118–121. doi:10.1111/j.0963-7214.2006.00419.x

Cacioppo, J. T., & Gardner, W. L. (1999). Emotion. *Annual Review of Psychology, 50*, 191–214. doi:10.1146/annurev.psych.50.1.191

Carlson, S. M., Zayas, V., & Guthormsen, A. (2009). Neural correlates of decision making on a gambling task. *Child Development, 80*, 1076–1096. doi:10.1111/j.1467-8624.2009.01318.x

Carretié, L., Hinojosa, J. A., Martín-Loeches, M., Mercado, F., & Tapia, M. (2004). Automatic attention to emotional stimuli: Neural correlates. *Human Brain Mapping, 22*, 290–299. doi:10.1002/hbm.20037

Casey, B. J., Getz, S., & Galvan, A. (2008). The adolescent brain. *Developmental Review, 28*, 62–77. doi:10.1016/j.dr.2007.08.003

Casey, B. J., Somerville, L. H., Gotlib, I., Ayduk, O., Franklin, N., Askren, M. K., . . . Shoda, Y. (2011). Behavioral and neural correlates of delay of gratification 40 years later. *Proceedings of the National Academy of Sciences of the United States of America, 108*, 14998–15003. doi:10.1073/pnas.1108561108

Casey, B. J., Tottenham, N., & Fossella, J. (2002). Clinical, imaging, lesion, and genetic approaches toward a model of cognitive control. *Developmental Psychobiology, 40*, 237–254. doi:10.1002/dev.10030

Casey, B. J., Trainor, R. J., Orendi, J. L., Schubert, A. B., Nystrom, L. N., Giedd, J. N., . . . Rapoport, J. L. (1997). A developmental functional MRI study of prefrontal activation during performance of a go-no-go task. *Journal of Cognitive Neuroscience, 9*, 835–847. doi:10.1162/jocn.1997.9.6.835

Childress, A. R., Mozley, P. D., McElgin, W., Fitgerald, J., Reivich, M., & O'Brien, C. P. (1999). Limbic activation during cue-induced cocaine craving. *The American Journal of Psychiatry, 156*, 11–18.

Cohen, J. D., & Servan-Schreiber, D. (1992). Context, cortex and dopamine: A connectionist approach to behavior and biology in schizophrenia. *Psychological Review, 99*, 45–77. doi:10.1037/0033-295X.99.1.45

Compton, R. J. (2003). The interface between emotion and attention: A review of evidence from psychology and neuroscience. *Behavioral and Cognitive Neuroscience Reviews, 2*, 115–129. doi:10.1177/1534582303002002003

Cunningham, W. A., Johnson, M. K., Raye, C. L., Gatenby, J. C., Gore, J. C., & Banaji, M. R. (2004). Separable neural components in the processing of Black and White faces. *Psychological Science*, 15, 806–813.

David, S. P., Munafò, M. R., Johansen-Berg, H., MacKillop, J., Sweet, L. H., Cohen, R. A., . . . Walton, R. T. (2007). Effects of acute nicotine abstinence on cue-elicited ventral striatum/nucleus accumbens activation in female cigarette smokers: A functional magnetic resonance imaging study. *Brain Imaging and Behavior, 1*, 43–57. doi:10.1007/s11682-007-9004-1

Davidson, M. C., Amso, D., Anderson, L. A., & Diamond, A. (2006). Development of cognitive control and executive functions from 4 to 13 years: Evidence from manipulations of memory, inhibition, and task switching. *Neuropsychologia, 44*, 2037–2078. doi:10.1016/j.neuropsychologia.2006.02.006

Davidson, M. C., Horvitz, J. C., Tottenham, N., Fossella, J. A., Watts, R., Ulug, A. M., & Casey, B. J. (2004). Differential cingulate and caudate activation following unexpected nonrewarding stimuli. *NeuroImage, 23*, 1039–1045. doi:10.1016/j.neuroimage.2004.07.049

Davis, M., & Whalen, P. J. (2001). The amygdala: Vigilance and emotion. *Molecular Psychiatry, 6*, 13–34. doi:10.1038/sj.mp.4000812

Delgado, M. R. (2007). Reward-related responses in the human striatum. *Annals of the New York Academy of Sciences, 1104*, 70–88. doi:10.1196/annals.1390.002

Delgado, M. R., Locke, H. M., Stenger, V. A., & Fiez, J. A. (2003). Dorsal striatum responses to reward and punishment: Effects of valence and magnitude manipulations. *Cognitive, Affective & Behavioral Neuroscience, 3*, 27–38. doi:10.3758/CABN.3.1.27

Delgado, M. R., Nystrom, L. E., Fissell, C., Noll, D. C., & Fiez, J. A. (2000). Tracking the hemodynamic responses to reward and punishment in the striatum. *Journal of Neurophysiology, 84*, 3072–3077.

Demos, K. E., Kelley, W. M., & Heatherton, T. F. (2011). Dietary restraint violations influence reward responses in nucleus accumbens and amygdala. *Journal of Cognitive Neuroscience, 23*, 1952–1963. doi:10.1162/jocn.2010.21568

Desimone, R., & Duncan, J. (1995). Neural mechanisms of selective visual attention. *Annual Review of Neuroscience, 18*, 193–222. doi:10.1146/annurev.ne.18.030195.001205

Downey, G., & Feldman, S. (1996). Implications of rejection sensitivity for intimate relationships. *Journal of Personality and Social Psychology, 70*, 1327–1343. doi:10.1037/0022-3514.70.6.1327

Downey, G., Freitas, A., Michaelis, B., & Khouri, H. (1998). The self-fulfilling prophecy in close relationships: Rejection sensitivity and rejection by romantic partners. *Journal of Personality and Social Psychology, 75*, 545–560. doi:10.1037/0022-3514.75.2.545

Downey, G., Lebolt, A., Rincon, C., & Freitas, A. L. (1998). Rejection sensitivity and children's interpersonal difficulties. *Child Development, 69*, 1074–1091.

Durston, S., Thomas, K. M., Worden, M. S., Yang, Y., & Casey, B. J. (2002). The effect of preceding context on inhibition: An event-related fMRI study. *NeuroImage, 16*, 449–453. doi:10.1006/nimg.2002.1074

Durston, S., Thomas, K. M., Yang, Y., Ulug, A. M., Zimmerman, R. D., & Casey, B. J. (2002). A neural basis for the development of inhibitory control. *Developmental Science, 5*, F9–F16. doi:10.1111/1467-7687.00235

Durston, S., Tottenham, N. T., Thomas, K. M., Davidson, M. C., Eigsti, I. M., Yang, Y., . . . Casey, B. J. (2003). Differential patterns of striatal activation in young children with or without ADHD. *Biological Psychiatry, 53*, 871–878. doi:10.1016/S0006-3223(02)01904-2

Eigsti, I.-M., Zayas, V., Mischel, W., Shoda, Y., Ayduk, O., Dadlan, M. B., . . . Casey, B. J. (2006). Attentional control in preschool predicts cognitive control at age eighteen. *Psychological Science, 17*, 478–484. doi:10.1111/j.1467-9280.2006.01732.x

Eisenberger, N., Smith, C. L., Sadovsky, A., & Spinrad, T. L. (2004). Effortful control: Reactions with emotion regulation, adjustment, and socialization in childhood. In R. F. Baumeister & K. D. Vohs (Eds.), *Handbook of self-regulation: Research, theory, and applications* (pp. 259–282). New York, NY: Guilford Press.

Etkin, A., Egner, T., Peraza, D. M., Kandel, E. R., & Hirsch, J. (2006). Resolving emotional conflict: A role for the rostral anterior cingulate cortex in modulating activity in the amygdala. *Neuron, 51*, 871–882. doi:10.1016/j.neuron.2006.07.029

Evans, G. W., & Kim, P. (2013). Childhood poverty, chronic stress, self-regulation, and coping. *Child Development Perspectives, 7*, 43–48.

Everitt, B. J., Dickinson, A., & Robbins, T. W. (2001). The neuropsychological basis of addictive behaviour. *Brain Research Reviews, 36*, 129–138. doi:10.1016/S0165-0173(01)00088-1

Everitt, B. J., & Robbins, T. W. (2005). Neural systems of reinforcement for drug addiction: From actions to habits to compulsion. *Nature Neuroscience, 8*, 1481–1489. doi:10.1038/nn1579

Figner, B., Mackinlay, R. J., Wilkening, F., & Weber, E. U. (2009). Affective and deliberative processes in risky choice: Age differences in risk taking in the Columbia Card Task. *Journal of Experimental Psychology: Learning, Memory, and Cognition, 35*, 709–730. doi:10.1037/a0014983

Figner, B., & Weber, E. U. (2011). Who takes risks, when, and why? Determinants of risk taking. *Current Directions in Psychological Science, 20*, 211–216. doi:10.1177/0963721411415790

Fillmore, M. T., & Rush, C. R. (2002). Impaired inhibitory control of behavior in chronic cocaine users. *Drug and Alcohol Dependence, 66*, 265–273. doi:10.1016/S0376-8716(01)00206-X

Fillmore, M. T., Rush, C. R., & Hays, L. (2002). Acute effects of oral cocaine on inhibitory control of behavior in humans. *Drug and Alcohol Dependence, 67*, 157–167. doi:10.1016/S0376-8716(02)00062-5

Fishbach, A., & Trope, Y. (2005). The substitutability of external control and self-control in overcoming temptation. *Journal of Experimental Social Psychology, 41*, 256–270. doi:10.1016/j.jesp.2004.07.002

Francis, L. A., & Susman, E. J. (2009). Self-regulation and rapid weight gain in children from age 3 to 12 years. *Archives of Pediatrics & Adolescent Medicine, 163*, 297–302. doi:10.1001/archpediatrics.2008.579

Friese, M., Hofmann, W., & Wänke, M. (2008). When impulses take over: Moderated predictive validity of implicit and explicit attitude measures in predicting food choice and consumption behavior. *British Journal of Social Psychology, 47*, 397–419

Galvan, A., Hare, T. A., Davidson, M., Spicer, J., Glover, G., & Casey, B. J. (2005). The role of ventral frontostriatal circuitry in reward-based learning in humans. *The Journal of Neuroscience, 25*, 8650–8656. doi:10.1523/JNEUROSCI.2431-05.2005

Grillon, C., & Charney, D. R. (2011). In the face of fear: Anxiety sensitizes defensive responses to fearful faces. *Psychophysiology, 48*, 1745–1752. doi:10.1111/j.1469-8986.2011.01268.x

Gyurak, A., & Ayduk, O. (2007). Defensive physiological reactions to rejection: The effect of self-esteem and attentional control on startle responses. *Psychological Science, 18*, 886–892. doi:10.1111/j.1467-9280.2007.01996.x

Gyurak, A., Goodkind, M. S., Kramer, J. H., Miller, B. L., & Levenson, R. W. (2012). Executive functions and the down-regulation and up-regulation of emotion. *Cognition & Emotion*, 26, 103–118.

Hackman, D. A., Farah, M. J., & Meaney, M. J. (2010). Socioeconomic status and the brain: Mechanistic insights from human and animal research. *Nature Reviews Neuroscience, 11*, 651–659. doi:10.1038/nrn2897

Hare, T. A., Camerer, C. F., & Rangel, A. (2009). Self-control in decision-making involves modulation of the vmPFC valuation system. *Science, 324*, 646–648. doi:10.1126/science.1168450

Hare, T. A., Tottenham, N., Davidson, M. C., Glover, G. H., & Casey, B. J. (2005). Contributions of amygdala and striatal activity in emotion regulation. *Biological Psychiatry, 57*, 624–632. doi:10.1016/j.biopsych.2004.12.038

Heatherton, T. F. (2011). Neuroscience of self and self-regulation. *Annual Review of Psychology, 62*, 363–390. doi:10.1146/annurev.psych.121208.131616

Herzberger, S. D., & Dweck, C. S. (1978). Attraction and delay of gratification. *Journal of Personality, 46*, 215–227. doi:10.1111/j.1467-6494.1978.tb00176.x

Hinson, J. M., Jameson, T. L., & Whitney, P. (2003). Impulsive decision making and working memory. *Journal of Experimental Psychology: Learning, Memory, and Cognition, 29*, 298–306. doi:10.1037/0278-7393.29.2.298

Hofmann, W., Friese, M., & Strack, F. (2009). Impulse and self-control from a dual-systems perspective. *Perspectives on Psychological Science, 4*, 162–176. doi:10.1111/j.1745-6924.2009.01116.x

Jackson, D. C., Muller, C. J., Dolski, I., Dalton, K. M., Nitschke, J. B., Urry, H. L., . . . Davidson, R. J. (2003). Now you feel it, now you don't: Frontal brain electrical asymmetry and individual differences in emotion regulation. *Psychological Science, 14*, 612–617. doi:10.1046/j.0956-7976.2003.psci_1473.x

James, W. (1950). *The principles of psychology*. New York, NY: Dover. (Original work published 1890).

Johnstone, T., van Reekum, C. M., Urry, H. L., Kalin, N. H., & Davidson, R. J. (2007). Failure to regulate: Counterproductive recruitment of top-down prefrontal-subcortical circuitry in major depression. *Journal of Neuroscience, 27*, 8877–8884. doi:10.1523/JNEUROSCI.2063-07.2007

Jonides, J., & Nee, D. E. (2006). Brain mechanisms of proactive interference in working memory. *Neuroscience, 139*, 181–193. doi:10.1016/j.neuroscience.2005.06.042

Kaufman, J. N., Ross, T. J., Stein, E. A., & Garavan, H. (2003). Cingulate hypoactivity in cocaine users during a GO–NOGO task as revealed by event-related functional magnetic resonance imaging. *The Journal of Neuroscience, 23*, 7839–7843.

Keating, D. P., & Bobbitt, B. L. (1978). Individual and developmental differences in cognitive-processing components of mental ability. *Child Development, 49*, 155–167. doi:10.2307/1128604

Kerns, J. G., Cohen, J. D., MacDonald, A. W., III, Cho, R. Y., Stenger, V. A., & Carter, C. S. (2004). Anterior cingulate conflict monitoring and adjustments in control. *Science, 303*, 1023–1026. doi:10.1126/science.1089910

Knutson, B., Adams, C. A., Fong, C. W., & Hommer, D. (2001). Anticipation of increasing monetary reward selectively recruits nucleus accumbens. *The Journal of Neuroscience, 21*, RC159.

Konishi, S., Nakajima, K., Uchida, I., Kikyo, H., Kameyama, M., & Miyashita, Y. (1999). Common inhibitory mechanism in human inferior prefrontal cortex revealed by event-related functional MRI. *Brain: A Journal of Neurology, 122*, 981–991. doi:10.1093/brain/122.5.981

Kubzansky, L. D., Martin, L. T., & Buka, S. L. (2009). Early manifestations of personality and adult health: A life course perspective. *Health Psychology, 28*, 364–372. doi:10.1037/a0014428

LeDoux, J. (1996). Emotional networks and motor control: A fearful view. *Progress in Brain Research, 107*, 437–446. doi:10.1016/S0079-6123(08)61880-4

Lieberman, M. D. (2007). The X- and C-systems: The neural basis of automatic and controlled social cognition. In E. Harmon-Jones & P. Winkelman (Eds.), *Fundamentals of social neuroscience* (pp. 290–315). New York, NY: Guilford Press.

Lieberman, M. D., Gaunt, R., Gilbert, D. T., & Trope, Y. (2002). *Reflexion and reflection: A social cognitive neuroscience approach to attributional inference*. In M. P. Zanna (Ed.), *Advances in experimental social psychology* (Vol. 34, pp. 199–249). New York, NY: Academic Press. doi:10.1016/S0065-2601(02)80006-5

Liston, C., Miller, M. M., Goldwater, D. S., Radley, J. J., Rocher, A. B., Hof, P. R., . . . McEwen, B. S. (2006). Stress-induced alterations in prefrontal cortical dendritic morphology predict selective impairments in perceptual attentional set-shifting. *The Journal of Neuroscience, 26*, 7870–7874. doi:10.1523/JNEUROSCI.1184-06.2006

McClure, S. M., Erikson, K. M., Laibson, D. I., Loewenstein, G., & Cohen, J. D. (2007). Time discounting for primary rewards. *The Journal of Neuroscience, 27*, 5796–5804. doi:10.1523/JNEUROSCI.4246-06.2007

McClure, S. M., Laibson, D. I., Loewenstein, G., & Cohen, J. D. (2004). Separate neural systems value immediate and delayed monetary rewards. *Science, 306*, 503–507. doi:10.1126/science.1100907

McEwen, B. S., & Gianaros, P. J. (2010). Central role of the brain in stress and adaptation: Links to socioeconomic status, health, and disease. *Annals of the New York Academy of Sciences, 1186*, 190–222. doi:10.1111/j.1749-6632.2009.05331.x

McRae, K., Hughes, B., Chopra, S., Gabrieli, J. D. E., Gross, J. J., & Ochsner, K. N. (2010). The neural bases of distraction and reappraisal. *Journal of Cognitive Neuroscience, 22*, 248–262. doi:10.1162/jocn.2009.21243

Mellers, B., Schwartz, A., & Weber, E. (1997). Do risk attitudes reflect in the eye of the beholder? In A. A. J. Marley (Ed.), *Choice, decision, and measurement: Essays in honor of R. Duncan Luce* (pp. 57–71). Mahway, NJ: Erlbaum.

Metcalfe, J., & Jacobs, W. J. (1996). A "hot-system/cool-system" view of memory under stress. *PTSD Research Quarterly, 7*(2), 1–6.

Metcalfe, J., & Jacobs, W. J. (1998). Emotional memory: The effects of stress on "cool" and "hot" memory systems. In D. L. Medin (ed.), *The psychology of learning and motivation: Advances in research and theory* (Vol. 38, pp. 187–222). San Diego, CA: Academic Press.

Metcalfe, J., & Mischel, W. (1999). A hot/cool system analysis of delay of gratification: Dynamics of willpower. *Psychological Review, 106*, 3–19. doi:10.1037/0033-295X.106.1.3

Miller, E. K., & Cohen, J. D. (2001). An integrative theory of prefrontal cortex function. *Annual Review of Neuroscience, 24*, 167–202. doi:10.1146/annurev.neuro.24.1.167

Mischel, W. (1974). Process in delay of gratification. In L. Berkowitz (Ed.), *Processes in delay of gratification* (Vol. 7, pp. 249–292). *Advances in experimental social psychology*. San Diego, CA: Academic Press.

Mischel, W., & Ayduk, O. (2002). Self-regulation in a cognitive-affective personality system: Attentional control in the service of the self. *Self and Identity, 1*, 113–120.

Mischel, W., & Ayduk, O. (2004). Willpower in a cognitive-affective processing system: The dynamics of delay of gratification. In R. F. Baumeister & K. D. Vohs (Eds.), *Handbook of self-regulation: Research, theory, and applications* (pp. 99–129). New York, NY: Guilford Press.

Mischel, W., Ayduk, O. N., Berman, M., Casey, B. J., Jonides, J., Kross, E., . . . Shoda, Y. (2011). "Willpower" over the life span: Decomposing impulse control. *Social Cognitive and Affective Neuroscience, 6*, 252–256. doi:10.1093/scan/nsq081

Mischel, W., & Baker, N. (1975). Cognitive appraisals and transformations in delay behavior. *Journal of Personality and Social Psychology, 31*, 254–261. doi:10.1037/h0076272

Mischel, W., & Ebbesen, E. (1970). Attention in delay of gratification. *Journal of Personality and Social Psychology, 16*, 329–337. doi:10.1037/h0029815

Mischel, W., Ebbesen, E. B., & Zeiss, A. R. (1972). Cognitive and attentional mechanisms in delay of gratification. *Journal of Personality and Social Psychology, 21*, 204–218. doi:10.1037/h0032198

Mischel, W., & Moore, B. (1973). Effects of attention to symbolically presented rewards on self. *Journal of Personality and Social Psychology, 28*, 172–179. doi:10.1037/h0035716

Mischel, W., Shoda, Y., & Rodriguez, M. L. (1989). Delay of gratification in children. *Science, 244*, 933–938. doi:10.1126/science.2658056

Mischel, W., & Underwood, B. (1974). Instrumental ideation in delay of gratification. *Child Development, 45*, 1083–1088.

Moffitt, T. E., Arseneault, L., Belsky, D., Dickson, N., Hancox, R. J., Harrington, H., . . . Caspi, A. (2011). A gradient of childhood self-control predicts health, wealth, and public safety. *Proceedings of the National Academy of Sciences of the United States of America, 108*, 2693–2698. doi:10.1073/pnas.1010076108

Morris, J. S., Öhman, A., & Dolan, R. J. (1998). Conscious and unconscious emotional learning in the human amygdala. *Nature, 393*, 467–470. doi:10.1038/30976

Ochsner, K. N., & Gross, J. J. (2007). The neural architecture of emotion regulation. In J. J. Gross & R. Buck (Eds.), *The handbook of emotion regulation* (pp. 87–109). New York, NY: Guilford Press.

Ochsner, K. N., Ray, R. D., Cooper, J. C., Robertson, E. R., Chopra, S., Gabrieli, J. D. E., & Gross, J. J. (2004). For better or for worse: Neural systems supporting the cognitive down- and up-regulation of negative emotion. *NeuroImage, 23*, 483–499. doi:10.1016/j.neuroimage.2004.06.030

O'Reilly, R. C. (2006). Biologically based computational models of high level cognition. *Science, 314*, 91–94. doi:10.1126/science.1127242

Phelps, E. A., & LeDoux, J. E. (2005). Contributions of the amygdala to emotion processing: From animal models to human behavior. *Neuron, 48*, 175–187. doi:10.1016/j.neuron.2005.09.025

Polivy, J. (1998). The effects of behavioral inhibition: Integrating internal cues, cognitive behavior, and affect. *Psychological Inquiry, 9*, 181–204. doi:10.1207/s15327965pli0903_1

Reyna, V. F., & Farley, F. (2006). Risk and rationality in adolescent decision making: Implications for theory, practice, and public policy. *Psychological Science in the Public Interest, 7*, 1–44.

Reyna, V. F., & Rivers, S. E. (2008). Current theories of risk and rational decision making. *Developmental Review, 28*, 1–11. doi:10.1016/j.dr.2008.01.002

Rodriguez, M. L., Mischel, W., & Shoda, Y. (1989). Cognitive person variables in the delay of gratification of older children at risk. *Journal of Personality and Social Psychology, 57*, 358–367. doi:10.1037/0022-3514.57.2.358

Rothbart, M. K., Ellis, L. K., & Posner, M. I. (2004). Temperament and self-regulation. In R. F. Baumeister & K. D. Vohs (Eds.), *Handbook of self-regulation: Research, theory, and applications* (pp. 357–370). New York, NY: Guilford Press.

Rothemund, Y., Preuschhof, C., Bohner, G., Bauknecht, H. C., Klingebiel, R., Flor, H., & Klapp, B. F. (2007). Differential activation of the dorsal striatum by high-calorie visual food stimuli in obese individuals. *NeuroImage, 37*, 410–421. doi:10.1016/j.neuroimage.2007.05.008

Rowe, J. B., Toni, I., Josephs, O., Frackowiak, R. S. J., & Passingham, R. E. (2000). The prefrontal cortex: Response selection or maintenance within working memory? *Science, 288*, 1656–1660. doi:10.1126/science.288.5471.1656

Sanfey, A. G., Hastie, R., Colvin, M. K., & Grafman, J. (2003). Phineas gauged: Decision-making and the frontal lobes. *Neuropsychologia, 41*, 1218–1229. doi:10.1016/S0028-3932(03)00039-3

Sanfey, A. G., Loewenstein, G., McClure, S. M., & Cohen, J. D. (2006). Neuroeconomics: Cross-currents in research on decision-making. *Trends in Cognitive Sciences, 10*, 108–116. doi:10.1016/j.tics.2006.01.009

Sapolsky, R. M. (1996). Why stress is bad for your brain. *Science, 273*, 749–750. doi:10.1126/science.273.5276.749

Schlam, T. R., Wilson, N. L., Shoda, Y., Mischel, W., & Ayduk, O. (2013). Preschoolers' delay of gratification predicts their body mass 30 years later. *The Journal of Pediatrics, 162*, 90–93. doi:10.1016/j.jpeds.2012.06.049

Seeyave, D. M., Coleman, S., Appugliese, D., Corwyn, R. F., Bradley, R. H., Davidson, N. S., . . . Lumeng, J. C. (2009). Ability to delay gratification at age 4 years and risk of overweight at age 11 years. *Archives of Pediatrics & Adolescent Medicine, 163*, 303–308. doi:10.1001/archpediatrics.2009.12

Shallice, T. (1988). *From neuropsychology to mental structure*. Cambridge, England: Cambridge University Press. doi:10.1017/CBO9780511526817

Shiv, B., & Fedorikhin, A. (1999), Heart and mind in conflict: The interplay of affect and cognition in consumer decision making. *Journal of Consumer Research, 26*, 278–292.

Shoda, Y., Mischel, W., & Peake, P. K. (1990). Predicting adolescent cognitive and social competence from preschool delay of gratification: Identifying diagnostic conditions. *Developmental Psychology, 26*, 978–986. doi:10.1037/0012-1649.26.6.978

Smith, E. R., & DeCoster, J. (2000). Dual-process models in social and cognitive psychology: conceptual integration and links to underlying memory systems. *Personality and Social Psychology Review, 4*, 108–131. doi:10.1207/S15327957PSPR0402_01

Somerville, L. H., & Casey, B. J. (2010). Developmental neurobiology of cognitive control and motivational systems. *Current Opinion in Neurobiology, 20*, 236–241. doi:10.1016/j.conb.2010.01.006

Steinberg, L., Albert, D., Cauffman, E., Banich, M., Graham, S., & Woolard, J. (2008). Age differences in sensation seeking and impulsivity as indexed by behavior and self-report: Evidence for a dual systems model. *Developmental Psychology, 44*, 1764–1778. doi:10.1037/a0012955

Tangney, J. P., Baumeister, R. F., & Boone, A. L. (2004). High self-control predicts good adjustment, less pathology, better grades, and interpersonal success. *Journal of Personality, 72*, 271–322. doi:10.1111/j.0022-3506.2004.00263.x

Thiruchselvam, R., Hajcak, G., & Gross, J. J. (2012). Looking inwards: Shifting attention within working memory representations alters emotional responses. *Psychological Science, 23*, 1461–1466. doi:10.1177/0956797612449838

Vaidya, C. J., Austin, G., Kirkorian, G., Ridlehuber, H. W., Desmond, J. E., Glover, G. H., & Gabrieli, J. D. E. (1998). Selective effects of methylphenidate in attention deficit hyperactivity disorder: A functional magnetic resonance study. *PNAS Proceedings of the National Academy of Sciences of the United States of America, 95*, 14494–14499. doi:10.1073/pnas.95.24.14494

Vohs, K. D., Baumeister, R. F., & Schmeichel, B. J. (2012). Motivation, personal beliefs, and limited resources all contribute to self-control. *Journal of Experimental Social Psychology, 48*, 943–947.

Vyas, A., Bernal, S., & Chattarji, S. (2003). Effects of chronic stress on dendritic arborization in the central and extended amygdala. *Brain Research, 965*, 290–294. doi:10.1016/S0006-8993(02)04162-8

Ward, A., & T. Mann. (2000). Don't mind if I do: Disinhibited eating under cognitive load. *Journal of Personality and Social Psychology, 78*, 753–763.

Weber, E. U. (2001). Personality and risk taking. In N. J. Smelser & P. B. Baltes (Eds.), *International encyclopedia of the social and behavioral sciences* (pp. 11274–11276). Oxford, England: Elsevier Science. doi:10.1016/B0-08-043076-7/01782-4

Zaleskiewicz, T. (2001). Beyond risk seeking and risk aversion: Personality and the dual nature of economic risk taking. *European Journal of Personality, 15*, S105–S122. doi:10.1002/per.426

7

THE NEUROSCIENCE OF DUAL (AND TRIPLE) SYSTEMS IN DECISION MAKING

SAMANTHA M. W. WOOD AND ANTOINE BECHARA

With the emergence of functional neuroimaging and the field of neuroeconomics, the debate about "single system" or "dual system" models for valuation is beginning to intensify. Proponents of a single system for valuation maintain that one neural region is devoted to evaluating costs and rewards, while dual system models argue decision making is a balance between fast, impulsive processing and slow, reflective processes. Using evidence from the clinical side of the argument, we will argue in this chapter that not only are the traditional two processes supported by the clinical facts, but in addition the evidence points to a third process, thus calling for the notion of "triple process" models. We also will highlight the importance of a third neural system that translates homeostatic, bodily signals into feelings of craving, which in turn modifies the dynamics of the traditional dual systems.

Dual process models have had considerable influence in psychological research. In the decision-making and self-control literature, dual process models have been invoked to explain why individuals make rational,

http://dx.doi.org/10.1037/14322-008
The Neuroscience of Risky Decision Making, by V. F. Reyna and V. Zayas (Editors)

analytical decisions in some circumstances but fail to use logical reasoning in other situations (e.g., Baumeister, Masicampo, & Vohs, 2011; Chaiken & Trope, 1999; Evans, 2008; Morewedge & Kahneman, 2010; Reyna, 2004). Often referred to as *System 1* and *System 2,* the current popular conception of the dual processes posits an *intuitive system* that is quick, automatic, and emotional and a *reasoning system* that is effortful, controlled, and nonemotional. Although research on decision making has traditionally posited two psychological systems used in evaluations (System 1 vs. System 2, which we refer to elsewhere as *impulsive* versus *reflective* systems; Bechara, 2005), more recent evidence suggests that a largely overlooked structure, the insula, plays a key role in modulating the dynamics of the systems. More specifically, the insula translates bottom-up, interoceptive signals into what subjectively may be experienced as an urge or craving.[1] This craving system potentiates the activity of the impulsive system and weakens cognitive resources that are needed for the normal operation of the reflective system. Thus, when considering physiological states that involve deprivation, withdrawal of an appetitive stimulus, stress, anxiety, or any condition associated with homeostatic perturbation, a third process (governed by the insula) emerges that works to correct the homeostatic imbalance. This third process directly affects the functionality of the traditional dual systems.

In this chapter, we detail how dual process models have evolved and discuss the neural underpinnings of these systems. Finally, we outline the role of the insula in decision making and describe how the insula interacts with the other two systems to modify decisions.

HISTORY OF DUAL PROCESS MODELS

The present conception of the two systems is not a perfect reflection of how dual processes were originally conceived. Initially, dual process models were used to explain findings about how individuals process information. Psychologists in the field of vision noticed a dissociation between automatic detection and controlled-search mechanisms (Shiffrin & Schneider, 1977). Their dual process theories claimed that automatic detection requires a great deal of training and would be difficult to suppress once learned. The term *dual process* has become less popular in vision science, but the theoretical contributions from Shiffrin and Schneider still resonate in models of attention. Contemporary theories of attention still include a bottom-up automatic

[1]As we describe later in the chapter, the insula is generally responsible for internal, subjective feelings. These feelings are not limited to cravings and other homeostatic signals but can include more abstract feelings, for example, disgust, admiration, love, and indignation.

mechanism for attending to salient stimuli and a top-down voluntary control of attention (Knudsen, 2007). Notably, this initial formulation of dual process models was completely agnostic to the role of emotion. Psychologists studying vision were interested in perceptual attention cues rather than the role of emotion in attention.

Social psychologists brought dual process theories to more affective questions. They used dual process theories to address questions related to persuasion and evaluations. For example, Chaiken's (1980) heuristic-systematic model of information processing and Petty and Cacioppo's (1984) elaboration likelihood model both argued that persuasive messages could be processed heuristically by simple cues or processed systematically using effortful cognitive activity. In addition to explaining attitudes about persuasive messages, two systems were used to explain evaluations of people. Inspired by Shiffrin and Schneider's model of two systems in information processing, Devine (1989) used a similar theory to explore stereotypes. Stereotypes are well-learned and automatically activated, like automatic detection of visual stimuli; however, unlike automatic visual detection, they can be overridden by controlled processes with cognitive effort. In these earlier social psychology examples of dual process models, theories did not explicitly identify a single system as being emotional. Theories about how people and messages are evaluated assumed that both systems must handle affective content. The major distinction between the two systems was that one was automatic while the other was controlled.

Although the dichotomy between emotional and cognitive systems (or "hot" and "cool" systems, per Metcalfe & Mischel, 1999) is now commonplace in the decision making literature, this portrayal of dual processes is relatively new. The early reviews that attempted to integrate various dual process theories of reasoning into a single System 1 and System 2 framework did not include emotional components (Stanovich & West, 2000, see Figure 7.1).[2] This framework explained why judgments sometimes maximize standard expected utility, but at other times individuals rely on heuristics and biases. While intuitive judgments might violate principles of classical economics, scholars have emphasized the computational efficiency of using heuristic-based reasoning (Gigerenzer & Goldstein, 1996). By using fuzzy and intuitive reasoning rather than strict computational logic, individuals can reduce information to smaller, more manageable dimensions (Reyna, 2004). Indeed, this intuitive, gist-based reasoning is used more often in individuals

[2]Many dual process theories of decision making had been proposed prior to Stanovich and West (2000), but this is the earliest major review paper typically cited in regard to dual process theories, likely because of Stanovich and West's thorough review as well as the responses from many influential proponents of dual process theories. However, the hot/cool dichotomy does predate this work (e.g., Metcalfe & Mischel, 1999; Nisbett & Ross, 1980).

System 1 ("Impulsive")	System 2 ("Reflective")
Associative	Rule-based
Holistic	Analytic
Automatic	Controlled
Relatively undemanding of cognitive capacity	Demanding of cognitive capacity
Relatively fast	Relatively slow
Acquisition by biology, exposure, and personal experience	Acquisition by culture and formal tuition
Highly contextualized task construal	Decontextualized

Figure 7.1. Summary of System 1 and System 2 attributes (for a review of System 1 and System 2 properties, see Stanovich & West, 2000).

as cognitive development (Reyna & Ellis, 1994) or the development of expertise (Reyna, Lloyd, & Brainerd, 2003) advances.

Scholars quickly began including emotions under System 1. Emotions may also be evoked rapidly and automatically and may conflict with our analytic reasoning (Epstein, 1994). Metcalfe and Mischel (1999) hypothesized that an internal tug-of-war between emotional and cognitive processes could explain the struggle between temptation and willpower:

> We propose that there are two types of processing—hot and cool—involving distinct interacting systems. . . . The *cool cognitive system* is specialized for complex spatiotemporal and episodic representation and thought. We call it the "know" system. The *hot emotional system* is specialized for quick emotional processing and responding on the basis of unconditional or conditional trigger features. We call it the "go" system. (p. 4)

Mischel used this framework to generate strategies for improving self-control. In a series of experiments, preschool children were given the choice to eat one marshmallow now or wait for a delay period to get two marshmallows. When both the delayed and immediate rewards were placed in front of the children during the delay period, the children could only delay themselves for an average of 1 minute (Kross & Mischel, 2010). Yet, children were able to wait longer, approximately 11 minutes, if all reward stimuli were obstructed from view or the child did not attend to them (allowing the children to rely on their less impulsive system).

However, not all research on System 1 and System 2 in delayed discounting suggests that emotional cues will induce temporal myopia. Although presenting children with an actual reward reduces how long they can delay reward, presenting children with pictures of the food rewards actually increased their ability to wait (Mischel & Moore, 1973). These findings indicate that emotional cues can facilitate either System 1 (impulsive) *or* System 2 (reflective and controlled) decisions.

The intuitive separation of emotion and cognition has become typical of System 1 and System 2 descriptions. However, as we will see when examining the neurological evidence, this dissociation of emotion and cognition does not exist in the brain. Instead, the neural systems underlying System 1 and System 2 decision making are both affective.

DUAL PROCESS MODELS IN DECISION MAKING

Individuals can often maintain incongruous goals simultaneously. We can desire a piece of chocolate cake while sincerely wanting to remain successful dieters. We may crave the thrill of skydiving but still value our physical safety. Dividing evaluative processes into two systems helps researchers account for this subjective feeling that we consist of multiple selves with diverging motivations. Because of its theoretical usefulness, the concept of System 1 and System 2 has contributed to a range of findings in the psychology of decision making.

In studies of temporal discounting, participants are required to choose between a smaller but immediate reward or a larger but delayed reward. Mischel's marshmallow study (Mischel, Shoda, & Rodriguez, 1989) is an example of a temporal discounting task for children. Children have difficulty executing the self-regulatory strategies required to wait for a delayed reward. Yet, adults also choose impatiently. Paradoxically, individuals are more likely to choose $10 today over $11 tomorrow than to choose $10 in a year over $11 in a year and day (Frederick, Loewenstein, & O'Donoghue, 2002). In both choice scenarios the time delay (1 day) and the monetary increase ($1) are identical, but the delay is preferred when both payoff options are in the future. Similar time discounting patterns hold true even when the future payoffs are ensured; for example, when subjects are given post-dated checks. Dual processing may be the underlying cause of this preference reversal.

McClure, Laibson, Loewenstein, and Cohen (2004) argued that the limbic system responds to immediate rewards while another system, governed by the prefrontal cortex, responds to any abstract rewards. Individuals with more active limbic systems would have more difficulty resisting an immediate reward. Accordingly, in Frederick et al.'s (2002) temporal discounting paradigm, only the $10 today would activate the limbic system, while the other rewards ($11 tomorrow, $10 in a year, and $11 in a year and a day) would rely on the prefrontal cortex.

Reliance on the automatic and intuitive System 1 may also account for preference reversal in risk taking. In the classic Asian disease problem, participants show greater preference for a policy that will save 200 people (out of 600) with 1/3 probability than the identical policy in which 400 people (out of 600) will die with 1/3 probability (Tversky & Kahneman, 1981). Even outside of risk assessment, the way in which choices are framed can have a significant effect on our decisions. These framing effects result from using System 1 instead of the more analytical (and less context-biased) System 2.

Dual process models have even influenced theories of moral reasoning. Moral philosophers use logical, syllogistic reasoning to arrive at moral principles. However, philosophical laymen show reliance on emotional intuitions to resolve moral dilemmas, especially under conditions of cognitive load (Greene, Morelli, Lowenberg, Nystrom, & Cohen, 2008; Haidt, 2001). Greene et al. and Haidt have argued for a dual process account of moral reasoning with one system using intuitive moral reasoning fueled by emotional reactions to moral dilemmas and a second system using cognitive resources to calculate utilitarian outcomes of moral dilemmas.

NEUROSCIENCE AND DUAL PROCESSES

Clinical neuroscience provides evidence for at least two separate but interconnected brain systems involved in the evaluation of choices. The first brain region is the amygdala–striatal system. The amygdala has strong projections to the striatum (a structure that consists of the nucleus accumbens, caudate, putamen, fundus, and olfactory tubule) (Everitt et al., 1999). While the amygdala and striatum are separate structures with some dissociable functions, some scholars refer to a neural macrostructure called the *extended amygdala*, containing the nucleus accumbens shell and central nucleus of the amygdala due to similarities in connectivity and morphology (Alheid & Heimer, 1988; Koob & Le Moal, 2001). Both the striatum and the amygdala are critical pieces of the brain's reward circuitry, responding to changes in the neurotransmitter dopamine (Kelley, Schiltz, & Landry, 2005). The amygdala–striatum corresponds to the traditional System 1 because it responds quickly and automatically on the basis of innate and learned associations. These associations are relatively inflexible in that, once a stimulus value is learned, the motivational value is difficult to change (Everitt & Robbins, 2005). The amygdala responds to both conditioned (learned) and unconditioned (innately motivational) stimuli (LeDoux, 2000). Thus, the amygdala–striatal system is responsible for the expression of motivated responses (e.g., fear, Corcoran & Quirk, 2007; and reward, Everitt & Robbins, 2005), as well as transferring controlled behaviors and preferences into habits.

Clinical studies of patients with lesions of the amygdala–striatal system provide additional insights about the System 1 of dual process models. Notably, the amygdala governs the bottom-up generation of emotions in response to "primary inducers" (Bechara & Damasio, 2005; McRae, Misra, Prasad, Pereira, & Gross, 2012; Ochsner et al., 2009). Primary inducers are stimuli that are physically present in the current environment. For example, if you were out for a walk and jumped in fear upon encountering a snake in the path, then the snake would be a primary inducer. Conditioned stimuli that have been associated with a provoking unconditioned stimulus are also primary inducers. So, if the snake in our example were always under the same bench, that bench could also become a primary inducer eliciting fear.

Individuals with damage to the amygdala have a striking disruption in their primary induction of emotion. Consider one of the best-researched examples of amygdala damage, patient SM. SM has normal IQ, memory, language, and perception. Yet, SM exhibited no fear during exposure to live snakes and spiders or during a tour of a haunted house (Feinstein, Adolphs, Damasio, & Tranel, 2011). In the haunted house,

> [t]he hidden monsters attempted to scare SM numerous times, but to no avail. She reacted to the monsters by smiling, laughing, or trying to talk to them. In contrast, their scare tactics typically elicited loud screams of fright from the other members of the group. (Feinstein et al., p. 35)

These effects are not specific to SM. War veterans with focal amygdala lesions generally show fewer signs of posttraumatic stress disorder (Koenigs et al., 2008). Conversely, amygdala stimulation increases corticosterone levels and symptoms of fear, anxiety, and attention (Applegate, Kapp, Underwood, & McNall, 1983; Kapp, Supple, & Whalen, 1994; see Phillips, Drevets, Rauch, & Lane, 2003, for an excellent review).

Amygdala lesions are typically associated with impairment in evaluating negative stimuli (e.g., Berntson, Bechara, Damasio, Tranel, & Cacioppo, 2007). However, functional neuroimaging studies and single-cell recordings indicate that the amygdala is also involved in evaluating rewards (for a review, see Murray, 2007). The amygdala activates more in response to positive, negative, and unusual or interesting stimuli than in response to neutral stimuli

(Cunningham & Brosch, 2012). Its affective tuning is flexible, and participants show greater amygdala activation in response to positive stimuli when they are asked to evaluate only the positivity of the stimuli and greater amygdala activation in response to negative stimuli when they are asked to evaluate only the negativity of the stimuli (Cunningham, Van Bavel, & Johnsen, 2008). Thus, Cunningham and colleagues argued that the amygdala responds to goal salience rather than a stimulus's valence. Yet, single-cell recordings in rhesus macaques indicate that positive and negative value are encoded in distinct but spatially integrated neurons (Paton, Belova, Morrison, & Salzman, 2006). This evidence points to the amygdala's role in forming affective associations across both positive and negative valences. Finally, this system has also been shown to be critical for evaluating certain types of risky decisions using monetary gains and losses (e.g., Bechara, Damasio, Damasio, & Lee, 1999; Weller, Levin, Shiv, & Bechara, 2007).[3]

Similarly, the striatum has been implicated in reward prediction (Schultz, 2000) in tracking how actual reward receipt compares with expected reward. Thus, the striatum recognizes patterns of rewards and calculates their probability to bias behavior (Bechara & Damasio, 2005). For example, a neurological patient who had damage to the entire medial temporal lobe[4] but retained an intact striatum was able to learn the nonconscious affective value of faces despite being unable to learn overt, factual knowledge about the faces (Tranel & Damasio, 1993).

Unlike System 1, the second dual process system has been associated with prioritizing rewards that are less concrete: outcomes in the future, outcomes that affect other individuals, and outcomes that are hypothetical. Here, we refer to these outcomes as *secondary inducers*. Secondary inducers are hypothetical or remembered emotional triggers (e.g., thoughts, memories, reflections). In the example of the snake, the next time you go for a walk, you might remember the snake in your path and decide to choose a different route. In this case, the memory of the snake is a secondary inducer.

The brain region that triggers an emotional state in response to secondary inducers is the ventromedial prefrontal cortex (vmPFC).[5] The vmPFC provides a link between the amygdala and the area of the brain involved in working memory (the dorsolateral prefrontal cortex). Since secondary inducers are not present in the current environment, they must be held online in working memory. To create an emotional state, the information about the memory

[3]Weller et al. (2007) found that patients with amygdala lesions showed a deficit in risky decision making for choices involving gains but not losses. This is particularly interesting given that the majority of studies implicate the amygdala in evaluating negative rather than positive stimuli.

[4]The amygdala and hippocampus are both housed in the medial temporal lobe. The patient's lesion also encompassed a portion of the orbital prefrontal cortex and the anterior cingulate.

[5]Here, we use vmPFC to refer to the ventral medial sector of the brain as well as the medial sector of the orbitofrontal cortex. Thus, this area encompasses Brodman's areas 25; lower 24; 32; and medial aspects of 11, 12, and 10.

must be relayed to the amygdala and striatum, structures that induce somatic responses.

Accordingly, individuals with damage to the vmPFC have selective deficits for avoiding negative future consequences in personal and social matters. The classic neurological case study of vmPFC damage comes from a 19th century railroad worker named Phineas Gage (Damasio, Grabowski, Frank, Galaburda, & Damasio, 1994). While he was working, a meter-long metal tamping rod shot through Gage's skull. Miraculously, Gage survived the accident and was still able to hear, see, speak, and use all of his motor skills. Despite this apparent full recovery, his friends felt that Gage was no longer the same person. After his brain damage, Gage had trouble holding a regular job, anticipating the future, acting in socially appropriate ways, and having a sense of responsibility. Modern patients with vmPFC damage show similar impairments. They repeatedly ignore negative future consequences when making decisions and fail to learn from these mistakes. Yet, these patients have IQ scores in the normal range and show normal performance on the Wisconsin Card Sorting Test, tasks that require self-ordering, cognitive estimations, and judgments of recency and frequency (Bechara, Damasio, Damasio, & Anderson, 1994).

One task that has proven particularly effective in disentangling primary and secondary inducers is the Iowa gambling task (IGT). In this task, participants are asked to make choices from among four decks of cards. Each card choice is associated with winning some amount of money (a certain reward); however, some cards also take money away (a probabilistic loss). Unknown to the participant, two of the decks have cards that bring high rewards, but the losses are also high. Because the losses are so large, these decks actually have a negative net value. If a participant chooses only from those "disadvantageous" decks, she will lose more money than she wins. On the other hand, in the other two "advantageous" decks, each card brings only a small reward, but when there is a loss, it is also very small. Because the probabilistic losses are much smaller, the net value of these advantageous decks is positive.

When playing the IGT, both patients with amygdala damage and patients with vmPFC damage tend to perform poorly, but for different reasons. Behavioral performance for the two patient groups is nearly identical, but psychophysiological methods tell a more complicated story. Skin conductance responses (SCRs) give a measure of emotional arousal by recording the sweat secretion by eccrine sweat glands, controlled by the autonomic nervous system. A large SCR suggests that the associated stimulus has strong motivational value (Hugdahl, 1995). During the IGT, normal, neurologically healthy participants show large SCRs before choosing from a disadvantageous deck (an anticipatory response to a secondary inducer) as well as after actually receiving a reward or punishment (a primary inducer). However, patients with vmPFC lesions did not show large SCRs before choosing from a disadvantageous deck (Bechara & Damasio, 2005; Bechara et al., 1999). The secondary inducer did not produce emotional arousal when the vmPFC was damaged. These patients still responded to primary inducers by showing large SCRs in response to winning or losing money in the game. These patients had a System 1 that was intact and able to assess the motivational value of concrete rewards and losses in the here and now.

The SCRs of the patients with amygdala damage are even more revealing. One might expect a double dissociation: that amygdala patients would have high SCRs in anticipation of choosing from a disadvantageous deck (a secondary inducer), but not in response to winning or losing (a primary inducer). Instead, patients with amygdala damage did not show large SCRs in either situation (Bechara & Damasio, 2005; Bechara et al., 1999). This finding suggests that emotional responses to a secondary inducer are generated by using information from primary responses prospectively. A large monetary loss triggers an affective reaction associated with a neural pattern of activation during the game. When patients with amygdala damage imagine the outcome of choosing from that deck again, the vmPFC triggers a reactivation of that original neural pattern of activation. Thus, the vmPFC does not calculate the emotional saliency of a stimulus by itself. Instead, the vmPFC relies on the amygdala–striatal system to enact somatic changes.

In this sense, neuroscientific evidence contradicts our intuitions about self-control. Colloquialisms on self-control tend to imply that we use two completely separable systems to weigh short-term and long-term goals. We feel torn between two options; we wrestle with ourselves and listen to either the devil or the angel on our shoulder. In actuality, though, self-control is not a shouting match between two isolated brain regions. The amygdala–striatal region and the prefrontal cortex are interconnected systems. Patients with amygdala lesions are unable to produce emotional responses to primary *and* secondary stimuli, implying that the amygdala is necessary to trigger response in the vmPFC (Weller et al., 2007).

RECENT OPPOSITION

Despite the popularity of using two systems in models of decision making, dual process theories are not without opposition. Recently, the interdisciplinary field of neuroeconomics has applied the methods of neuroscience to the study of economics. With the advent of neuroeconomics, researchers began to search for a single source of valuation in the brain. In economic marketplaces, currency is useful for placing comparable values on disparate goods and services. Single process theories argue for a single neural currency for evaluating options. These attempts to uncover a single system for decision making mostly pinpointed the vmPFC as the neural correlate of value. By examining changes in vmPFC BOLD signal, researchers could predict individuals' preferences for a wide variety of stimuli including soft drinks (McClure, Li, et al., 2004) snacks (Plassmann, O'Doherty, & Rangel, 2007), car brands (Schaefer, Berens, Heinze, & Rotte, 2006), and wine (Plassmann, O'Doherty, Shiv, & Rangel, 2008).

Although these functional neuroimaging studies provide a strong argument for the vmPFC and adjacent regions as being a center of valuation, neurological evidence demonstrates that a large bilateral lesion that wipes out this area of the brain does not entirely abolish valuation. According to clinical observations, these patients do not generally make decisions that lead to concrete and immediate harm to themselves and others. Their impairments are specific to decisions about consequences that are delayed, probabilistic, and abstract (Bechara & Damasio, 2005). To illustrate, although these patients do not properly value future or probabilistic outcomes in the IGT, they still prefer high immediate gain or avoid high immediate loss, which suggests that their valuations of these immediate contingencies are not disrupted. Indeed, by the end of the IGT, many patients with vmPFC damage are actually able to report which decks were advantageous or disadvantageous when asked directly, but they persisted in choosing disadvantageous decks (Bechara et al., 1997).

ADDICTION: A CLINICAL EXAMPLE

We propose that addiction is the result of an imbalance of the two systems described above: the impulsive amygdala–striatal system and the reflective prefrontal cortex system (Bechara, 2005). Due to dysregulation of one or both of these systems, addicts behave similarly to individuals with vmPFC damage. They tend to ignore future long-term consequences and fail to learn from their past mistakes. This description of addiction is consistent with studies of structural brain abnormalities in addicts. Cocaine addicts have significantly reduced amygdala (Makris et al., 2004), striatal (Barrós-Loscertales et al., 2011), and vmPFC (Franklin et al., 2002) volume compared with healthy controls.

Furthermore, a wide range of addicts show impaired decision making as measured by the IGT. The IGT mimics real-life decisions by creating a conflict between an immediate, luring reward and a probabilistic punishment. The IGT paradigm has pointed to decision-making deficits in alcohol (Fein, Klein, & Finn, 2004), ecstasy (Hanson, Luciana, & Sullwold, 2008), cocaine (Verdejo-Garcia et al., 2007), and cannabis (Whitlow et al., 2004) abusers. This decision-making impairment is not selective to drug abuse and can also be found in behavioral addictions including pathological gambling (Cavedini, Riboldi, Keller, D'Annucci, & Bellodi, 2002) and overeating/obesity (Davis, Levitan, Muglia, Bewell, & Kennedy, 2004).

Addicts' performance on the IGT and measures of their skin conductance while playing can give us more information about the neural disruptions underlying their addictions. When Bechara, Dolan, and Hindes (2002) asked substance abusers to play the IGT, the participants fell into three categories. The first group was a minority of participants who performed similarly to normal, healthy individuals. Based on their lack of decision making impairment as measured by the IGT, this group may consist of mainly "functional" addicts. Such addicts have generally experienced minimal consequences of their drug use in their everyday life and may not be poor decision makers per se.

A second portion of the addicts played similarly to individuals with vmPFC lesions. These players showed impaired behavioral performance as well as reduced SCRs in anticipation of choosing from the disadvantageous decks. Although they still showed large SCRs in response to losing large sums of money, they did not turn these emotional responses into prospective signals of the riskiness of each deck of cards.

The final group of addicts showed a novel signature of SCRs while playing the IGT. Like the second group, these individuals showed impaired behavioral performance. However, these individuals had SCRs similar to those of normal, healthy participants, with the exception that they had heightened emotional responses (SCRs) in response to winning large sums of money. Unlike individuals with lesions to the vmPFC who display myopia for the future, these individuals seem to fail at the IGT due to a hypersensitivity to reward (for a discussion on hypersensitivity to reward in adolescence, see Chapter 3, this volume).

An open question in studying the neurobiology of addiction is the extent to which these brain abnormalities are due to genetic predisposition and neurotoxicity. Some studies suggest that individuals who have not used drugs but who are at high risk for drug abuse (e.g., a family history of alcohol abuse) are more likely than other healthy individuals to have decision-making impairments (Fein & Chang, 2008; Lovallo et al., 2006). Moreover, both drug-dependent individuals and their nonaddicted siblings have frontostriatal brain abnormalities, suggesting that these abnormalities are not caused entirely by drug use (Ersche et al., 2012). Nonetheless, because drug use cannot be experimentally manipulated in humans, animal models are typically used to separate the influences of genetics and environment. Animal studies indicate that brain abnormalities in addicts are part of a vicious circle. Rats that are bred without the dopamine D1 receptor show increased vulnerability to develop drug self-administration (Caine et al., 2007). Studies of human addicts indicate that some brain volume losses are correlated with years of use, implying that drug use also causes neurological changes (Goldstein & Volkow, 2002). Dysfunction in reward processing makes individuals more likely to use and become addicted to drugs; drug use then further disrupts reward processing.

Although we have used addiction as a case study, disruption in the prefrontal cortex and amygdala–striatal system is not unique to addiction. Dysfunction in these brain regions has been linked to impulsivity more generally. In addition to addiction, other clinical disorders have been linked to impulsive behavior, including attention-deficit/hyperactivity disorder (ADHD), mania, and antisocial behavior (Dalley, Everitt, & Robbins, 2011). For instance, ADHD is associated with hypoactivity in the frontal cortex and basal ganglia, among other regions (Dickstein, Bannon, Castellanos, & Milham, 2006). Patients with vmPFC damage show impairments in moral judgment (Young et al., 2010), pointing to a role for the vmPFC in antisocial behavior.

THE INSULAR CORTEX—A MISSING PIECE?

Dual process theories have remained popular models due to their explanatory power. However, we argue that the neuroscientific evidence points to an additional system involved in decision making. The neural basis for this third system is the insular cortex, or insula. The cognitive function of the insula is translating bodily states into conscious feelings. Although the amygdala is responsible for associative learning and emotions, the insula governs the conscious feeling of those emotions. As explained by Damasio (1994), emotions can be disentangled from the feeling of emotions. Emotions are the physical reactions to stimuli, but we may have that emotional reaction without translating the somatic reactions into a feeling. This sentiment is not unique to the modern somatic marker hypothesis; it was echoed by James and Lange decades earlier:

> Common sense says, we lose our fortune, are sorry and weep; we meet a bear, are frightened and run; we are insulted by a rival, are angry and strike. The hypothesis here to be defended says that this order of sequence is incorrect . . . and that the more rational statement is that we feel sorry because we cry, angry because we strike, afraid because we tremble . . . Without the bodily states following on the perception, the latter would be purely cognitive in form, pale, colorless, destitute of emotional warmth. We might then see the bear, and judge it best to run, receive the insult and deem it right to strike, but we should not actually feel afraid or angry. (James, 1890, p. 449–450)

The insula system adds a crucial missing element to the dual process model: a subjective feeling of craving. As we explain below, craving is the result of the brain attempting to correct an imbalance in homeostasis. Recognizing the role of the insula in decision making highlights the importance of the situational context, the way we feel in the moment of the decision. Consider the adage that one should never go grocery shopping while hungry. Hunger is associated with a dearth of insulin, which signals a homeostatic imbalance to the brain. As a result, the brain treats food as a disproportionately more valuable reward, prompting the hungry shopper to buy foods that will seem far less appetizing later.

The Insula: Anatomy and Function

We recognize five senses that are responsible for perceiving the external world. Sight, hearing, touch, smell, and taste allow us to engage in *exteroception*—awareness of stimuli outside the body. The insula is responsible for a "sixth sense," that of *interoception*—perception of what is happening inside the body.

Typically, interoception is defined as awareness of the state of one's internal organs. For example, the insula responds to changes in cardiovascular function (Critchley, Wiens, Rotshtein, Öhman, & Dolan, 2004), stimulation of the gastrointestinal tract (Aziz et al., 2000), and distention (Wang et al., 2008). Yet, the insula also translates internal bodily signals that are not specific to organs. The Valsalva maneuver (Henderson et al., 2003), sensual touch (Arnow et al., 2002), and exercise (Williamson, McColl, & Mathews, 2003) are all associated with insula activation. Clinically, there is ongoing activity in the insula in chronic pain patients (Kupers, Gybels, & Gjedde, 2000). Also, dysfunction in the insula can lead patients to feel bodily signals when none exist; patients with neuropathic pain show evoked activity in the insula (Peyron, Laurent, & Garcia-Larrea, 2000).

The insula is part of an evolutionarily old interoceptive system in the brain responsible for maintaining the body's homeostasis. Sympathetic and parasympathetic afferents are relayed from the brainstem through the thalamus to the posterior insula (Craig, 2002). These inputs are necessary for somatosensory, vestibular, and motor functions. However, these physiological states also have motivational value. Homeostatic signals are only valuable insofar as they prompt regulatory behavior to correct imbalances. According to Craig's (2002) research on insula function, the physiological states activated in the posterior insula are re-represented in the anterior insula to produce subjective feelings. To provide an example of this re-representation, Craig, Chen, Bandy, and Reiman (2000) examined activity in the insula when applying innocuous cool stimuli to subjects' right hands. Activity in the posterior insula was linearly related to the actual temperature of the stimuli. Intriguingly, activity in the anterior insula was correlated with subjects' subjective ratings of the intensity of the stimulus.

The anterior insula is a phylogenetically newer brain region that acts as a neural highway connecting interoceptive information (from the posterior insula) with information about existing motivations, reward cues, environmental stimuli, and social conditions (for a review on the evolution of insular pathways, see Craig, 2002). The anterior insula has reciprocal connections to regions including the amygdala, ventral striatum, vmPFC, and anterior cingulate cortex. Rather than merely representing the state of viscera, the translation of signals in the anterior insula represents all subjective feelings. Past studies have elicited insula activity using a variety of emotional (rather than purely somatic) feelings including "the feeling of knowing" (a subjective sense of retrievability), love, anger, fear, disgust, happiness, beauty, unfairness and indignation, social exclusion, empathy, trust, and "a state of union with God" (for an excellent review, see Craig, 2009). Patients with right insular lesions report altered subjective feelings: anergia, underactivity, and tiredness, perhaps due to the insula's connections to brain regions that are necessary for willed actions (Manes, Paradiso, & Robinson, 1999).

Craving and the Insula

Subjective feelings are a critical component of normal decision making. Cases of self-control provide a useful illustration of the role of the insula and subjective feelings in decision making. In these instances, the insula mediates a feeling of craving that can affect the reward value of stimuli.

The insula has been implicated in processing the value of a variety of rewards. Injecting a rat insula with low doses of SB-334867 (a receptor agonist that blocks activity in the insula) leads to a reduction in intake of nicotine (Hollander, Lu, Cameron, Kamenecka, & Kenny, 2008) and higher doses reduce intake of palatable, high-fat food as well as total baseline food (Nair, Golden, & Shaham, 2008; Rodgers et al., 2001). Similarly, temporarily inactivating the rat posterior insula disrupts drug seeking in amphetamine-experienced rats (Contreras, Ceric, & Torrealba, 2007). Rats lack the phylogenetically newer insular structures underlying the evaluation of interoceptive signals through re-representation in the anterior insula (Craig, 2002). Therefore, these findings suggest that reward-seeking behavior requires physical sensations of craving, but not necessarily the subjective feeling of craving. In humans, insula activity during a decision-making game can predict relapse in recovering methamphetamine addicts (Paulus, 2007). In addition, chronic cocaine users have a smaller ratio of gray to white matter in the insula (Franklin et al., 2002). The density decrease was not correlated with years of cocaine use, so the brain abnormality may have been preexisting rather than gradually induced with increased drug exposure.

Patients with insula lesions provide striking evidence that the changes in reward seeking are due to a disruption in craving. Naqvi, Rudrauf, Damasio, and Bechara (2007) examined nicotine addiction in patients who had acquired brain lesions from strokes or surgical resectioning. All of the patients had been cigarette smokers prior to their brain damage. However, patients with insula damage (compared with all other lesions) were more likely to undergo a "disruption of smoking addiction. A patient was considered to have a "disrupted" addiction if she quit smoking after the lesion and did not relapse, rated the difficulty of quitting smoking as relatively easy (less than 3 on a scale of 1 to 7), and reported no urges to smoke since quitting. Smokers with damage to the insula were nearly 8 times more likely to undergo a disruption of addiction than were smokers with damage to other brain regions. One insula patient reported that he was smoking more than 40 cigarettes per day prior to his stroke. After his stroke, he abruptly stopped smoking, explaining that, "I forgot that I was a smoker," elaborating that "my body forgot the urge to smoke." Cravings and urges are represented in the insula, so when insula function was interrupted, the nicotine addiction was as well.

ROLE OF THE INSULA: A BALANCE OF POWER

The standard account offered by dual process models suggests that there are two separate systems that compete to determine what decision will be made—favoring a concrete reward in the present or an abstract reward that is in the future, probabilistic, or benefiting someone else. However, the insula affects decision making by representing the subjective feeling of cravings and maintaining homeostasis—a role that is not accounted for in standard dual process theories. We propose that dual process models should be modified to include a third system: cravings. These cravings are elicited by the brain and body's joint efforts to correct a homeostatic imbalance.

Moreover, the neuroscientific evidence does not provide support for separate competing systems. Instead, the involved brain regions are highly interconnected and affect decision making by modifying each other's activity. These forces are sometimes depicted as conflicting parties; however a better analogy may be that of a "neural balance of power." Balance of power has been a popular model to regulate governmental decision making. The government is divided into three branches (typically legislature, executive, and judiciary); each of the branches can check the power of the other branches. For instance, the legislature can pass laws, but if those laws are

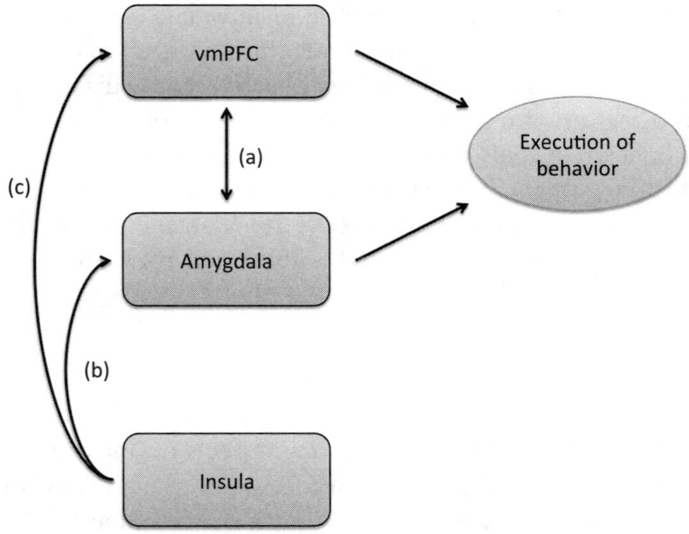

Figure 7.2. A diagram of the triple process model. The amygdala–striatal system, which we have referred to as the impulsive system or System 1, triggers emotional responses to the present environment. The vmPFC triggers responses to secondary inducers (hypothetical or remembered states). The relationship between the amygdala and vmPFC is reciprocal (Amaral, Price, Pitkänen, & Carmichael, 1992; Milad & Quirk, 2002). (a) Amygdala activation is necessary to trigger vmPFC response, but the reflective system can affect the impulsive system through several mechanisms of impulse control. During homeostatic imbalance, the insula can alter the dynamics between the amygdala and vmPFC by (b) sensitizing the impulsive system and (c) disabling the reflective system.

unjust they may be vetoed by the executive or overturned by the judiciary. The brain regions involved in decision making can also check each other (see Figure 7.2). The amygdala rapidly and automatically evaluates stimuli based on associative learning, but those evaluations can be modified by the vmPFC (based on the evaluation of the stimuli's abstract properties) and the insula (based on how the stimuli could fulfill homeostatic needs). Certainly not every decision needs to invoke the vmPFC and insula, just as not every law needs to be evaluated by the executive and judiciary. Everyday life would become too burdensome if every habit from how we brush our teeth or how we tie our shoes needed deliberation.

The prefrontal cortex modifies decision making through mechanisms of impulse control that modulate amygdala activity. For example, the ventrolateral prefrontal cortex modulates activity in the amygdala and nucleus accumbens during emotional reappraisal tasks (Wager, Davidson, Hughes, Lindquist, & Ochsner, 2008). The insula operates in a similar way. The insula modulates activity of the vmPFC and amygdala to maintain internal biological (and perhaps emotional) homeostasis. A need to restore homeostasis (e.g., due to hunger, drug withdrawal) activates the insula and is experienced as a feeling of craving. The current needs of the body outweigh long-term or abstract goals; correspondingly, the insula may inhibit activity in the reflective system (vmPFC) and increase activity in the impulsive system (amygdala–striatal). This reflects the adaptive notion that future rewards are inconsequential if the body cannot survive current situations.

CONCLUSION

The standard dual process accounts of decision making depict two competing systems: a cold and calculating system that is slow and effortful against a hot and emotional system that is quick and automatic. Based on this account, our decisions are a result of whether rational or emotional cognition prevails. Past dual process models did not always presuppose that automatic processes are emotional while controlled processes are devoid of emotions. In fact, neurological evidence indicates that both decision-making systems depend on brain regions related to emotional processing: the amygdala–striatal system and the vmPFC. Both brain regions are critical for forming somatic markers. The amygdala responds to primary inducers of emotion while the vmPFC responds to secondary inducers of emotion. However, the vmPFC evokes emotional reactions to secondary inducers by modulating activity in the amygdala. Rather than being competitive, these brain regions are highly interconnected and modulate each other's activity. One or both of these systems may be affected in cases of addiction (a clinical example of dysfunctional reward processing).

In addition to the two systems that are typically discussed, recent evidence suggests that a third system needs to be considered. This third decision-making system reflects important contextual information about someone's current state. It incorporates information about physical and emotional homeostasis, from feelings of hunger to feelings of compassion. These feelings may alter the motivational value of rewards, for example, ascribing higher reward value to food or drugs when we are hungry or going through withdrawal. The insula has been implicated in interoception, or the representation of internal, bodily signals. As a third neural system in decision making, the insula modulates activity in the vmPFC and amygdala, affecting the perceived value of rewards and costs. To give a full account of decision making, we need to go beyond dual process models to include this third system.

REFERENCES

Alheid, G. F., & Heimer, L. (1988). New perspectives in basal forebrain organization of special relevance for neuropsychiatric disorders: The striatopallidal, amygdaloid, and corticopetal components of substantia innominata. *Neuroscience, 27*, 1–39. doi:10.1016/0306-4522(88)90217-5

Amaral, D. G., Price, J. L. Pitkänen A., & Carmichael S. T. (1992). Anatomical organization of the primate amygdaloid complex. In J. P. Aggleton (Ed.), *The amygdala: Neuropsychological aspects of emotion, memory, and mental dysfunction* (pp. 1–66). New York, NY: Wiley-Liss.

Applegate, C. D., Kapp, B. S., Underwood, M. D., & McNall, C. L. (1983). Autonomic and somatomotor effects of amygdala central nucleus stimulation in awake rabbits. *Physiology & Behavior, 31*, 353–360. doi:10.1016/0031-9384(83)90201-9

Arnow, B. A., Desmond, J. E., Banner, L. L., Glover, G. H., Solomon, A., Polan, M. L., . . . Atlas, S. W. (2002). Brain activation and sexual arousal in healthy, heterosexual males. *Brain: A Journal of Neurology, 125*, 1014–1023. doi:10.1093/brain/awf108

Aziz, Q., Thompson, D. G., Ng, V. W. K., Hamdy, S., Sarkar, S., Brammer, M. J., . . . Williams, S. C. R. (2000). Cortical processing of human somatic and visceral sensation. *The Journal of Neuroscience, 20*, 2657–2663.

Barrós-Loscertales, A., Garavan, H., Bustamante, J. C., Ventura-Campos, N., Llopis, J. J., Belloch, V., & Ávila, C. (2011). Reduced striatal volume in cocaine-dependent patients. *NeuroImage, 56*, 1021–1026. doi:10.1016/j.neuroimage.2011.02.035

Baumeister, R. F., Masicampo, E. J., & Vohs, K. D. (2011). Do conscious thoughts cause behavior? *Annual Review of Psychology, 62*, 331–361. doi:10.1146/annurev.psych.093008.131126

Bechara, A. (2005). Decision making, impulse control and loss of willpower to resist drugs: A neurocognitive perspective. *Nature Neuroscience, 8*, 1458–1463. doi:10.1038/nn1584

Bechara, A., & Damasio, A. R. (2005). The somatic marker hypothesis: A neural theory of economic decision. *Games and Economic Behavior, 52*, 336–372. doi:10.1016/j.geb.2004.06.010

Bechara, A., Damasio, A. R., Damasio, H., & Anderson, S. W. (1994). Insensitivity to future consequences following damage to human prefrontal cortex. *Cognition, 50*(1–3), 7–15. doi:10.1016/0010-0277(94)90018-3

Bechara, A., Damasio, H., Damasio, A. R., & Lee, G. P. (1999). Different contributions of the human amygdala and ventromedial prefrontal cortex to decision-making. *The Journal of Neuroscience, 19*, 5473–5481.

Bechara, A., Dolan, S., & Hindes, A. (2002). Decision-making and addiction (part II): Myopia for the future or hypersensitivity to reward? *Neuropsychologia, 40*, 1690–1705. doi:10.1016/S0028-3932(02)00016-7

Berntson, G. G., Bechara, A., Damasio, H., Tranel, D., & Cacioppo, J. T. (2007). Amygdala contribution to selective dimensions of emotion. *Social Cognitive and Affective Neuroscience, 2,* 123–129. doi:10.1093/scan/nsm008

Caine, S. B., Thomsen, M., Gabriel, K. I., Berkowitz, J. S., Gold, L. H., Koob, G. F., . . . Xu, M. (2007). Lack of self-administration of cocaine in dopamine D1 receptor knock-out mice. *The Journal of Neuroscience, 27,* 13140–13150. doi:10.1523/JNEUROSCI.2284-07.2007

Cavedini, P., Riboldi, G., Keller, R., D'Annucci, A., & Bellodi, L. (2002). Frontal lobe dysfunction in pathological gambling patients. *Biological Psychiatry, 51,* 334–341. doi:10.1016/S0006-3223(01)01227-6

Chaiken, S. (1980). Heuristic versus systematic information-processing and the use of source versus message cues in persuasion. *Journal of Personality and Social Psychology, 39,* 752–766. doi:10.1037/0022-3514.39.5.752

Chaiken, S., & Trope, Y. (Eds.). (1999). *Dual process theories in social psychology.* New York, NY: Guilford Press.

Contreras, M., Ceric, F., & Torrealba, F. (2007). Inactivation of the interoceptive insula disrupts drug craving and malaise induced by lithium. *Science, 318,* 655–658. doi:10.1126/science.1145590

Corcoran, K. A., & Quirk, G. J. (2007). Activity in prelimbic cortex is necessary for the expression of learned, but not innate fears. *The Journal of Neuroscience, 27,* 840–844. doi:10.1523/JNEUROSCI.5327-06.2007

Craig, A. D. (2002). How do you feel? Interoception: The sense of the physiological condition of the body. *Nature Reviews Neuroscience, 3,* 655–666.

Craig, A. D. (2009). How do you feel—now? The anterior insula and human awareness. *Nature Reviews Neuroscience, 10*(1), 59–70. doi:10.1038/nrn2555

Craig, A. D., Chen, K., Bandy, D., & Reiman, E. M. (2000). Thermosensory activation of insular cortex. *Nature Neuroscience, 3,* 184–190. doi:10.1038/72131

Critchley, H. D., Wiens, S., Rotshtein, P., Öhman, A., & Dolan, R. J. (2004). Neural systems supporting interoceptive awareness. *Nature Neuroscience, 7,* 189–195. doi:10.1038/nn1176

Cunningham, W. A., & Brosch, T. (2012). Motivational salience: Amygdala tuning from traits, needs, values, and goals. *Current Directions in Psychological Science, 21,* 54–59. doi:10.1177/0963721411430832

Cunningham, W. A., Van Bavel, J. J., & Johnsen, I. R. (2008). Affective flexibility: Evaluative processing goals shape amygdala activity. *Psychological Science, 19,* 152–160. doi:10.1111/j.1467-9280.2008.02061.x

Dalley, J. W., Everitt, B. J., & Robbins, T. W. (2011). Impulsivity, compulsivity, and top-down cognitive control. *Neuron, 69,* 680–694. doi:10.1016/j.neuron.2011.01.020

Damasio, A. R. (1994). *Descartes' error: Emotion, reason, and the human brain.* New York, NY: Putnam.

Damasio, H., Grabowski, T., Frank, R., Galaburda, A. M., & Damasio, A. R. (1994). The return of Gage, Phineas—Clues about the brain from the skull of a famous patient. *Science, 264,* 1102–1105. doi:10.1126/science.8178168

Davis, C., Levitan, R. D., Muglia, P., Bewell, C., & Kennedy, J. L. (2004). Decision-making deficits and overeating: A risk model for obesity. *Obesity Research, 12,* 929–935. doi:10.1038/oby.2004.113

Devine, P. G. (1989). Stereotypes and prejudice—Their automatic and controlled components. *Journal of Personality and Social Psychology, 56*(1), 5–18. doi:10.1037/0022-3514.56.1.5

Dickstein, S. G., Bannon, K., Castellanos, F. X., & Milham, M. P. (2006). The neural correlates of attention deficit hyperactivity disorder: An ALE meta-analysis. *Journal of Child Psychology and Psychiatry, 47,* 1051–1062. doi:10.1111/j.1469-7610.2006.01671.x

Epstein, S. (1994). Integration of the cognitive and the psychodynamic unconscious. *American Psychologist, 49,* 709–724. doi:10.1037/0003-066X.49.8.709

Ersche, K. D., Jones, P. S., Williams, G. B., Turton, A. J., Robbins, T. W., & Bullmore, E. T. (2012). Abnormal brain structure implicated in stimulant drug addiction. *Science, 335,* 601–604. doi:10.1126/science.1214463

Evans, J. S. B. T. (2008). Dual-processing accounts of reasoning, judgment, and social cognition. *Annual Review of Psychology, 59,* 255–278. doi:10.1146/annurev.psych.59.103006.093629

Everitt, B. J., Parkinson, J. A., Olmstead, M. C., Arroyo, M., Robledo, P., & Robbins, T. W. (1999). Associative processes in addiction and reward—The role of amygdala–ventral striatal subsystems. *Annals of the New York Academy of Sciences, 877,* 412–438. doi:10.1111/j.1749-6632.1999.tb09280.x

Everitt, B. J., & Robbins, T. W. (2005). Neural systems of reinforcement for drug addiction: From actions to habits to compulsion. *Nature Neuroscience, 8,* 1481–1489. doi:10.1038/nn1579

Fein, G., & Chang, M. (2008). Smaller feedback ERN amplitudes during the BART are associated with a greater family history density of alcohol problems in treatment-naive alcoholics. *Drug and Alcohol Dependence, 92*(1–3), 141–148. doi:10.1016/j.drugalcdep.2007.07.017

Fein, G., Klein, L., & Finn, P. (2004). Impairment on a simulated gambling task in long-term abstinent alcoholics. *Alcoholism: Clinical and Experimental Research, 28,* 1487–1491. doi:10.1097/01.ALC.0000141642.39065.9B

Feinstein, J. S., Adolphs, R., Damasio, A., & Tranel, D. (2011). The human amygdala and the induction and experience of fear. *Current Biology, 21*(1), 34–38. doi:10.1016/j.cub.2010.11.042

Franklin, T. R., Acton, P. D., Maldjian, J. A., Gray, J. D., Croft, J. R., Dackis, C. A., . . . Childress, A. R. (2002). Decreased gray matter concentration in the insular, orbitofrontal, cingulate, and temporal cortices of cocaine patients. *Biological Psychiatry, 51,* 134–142. doi:10.1016/S0006-3223(01)01269-0

Frederick, S., Loewenstein, G., & O'Donoghue, T. (2002). Time discounting and time preference: A critical review. *Journal of Economic Literature, 40*, 351–401. doi:10.1257/002205102320161311

Gigerenzer, G., & Goldstein, D. G. (1996). Reasoning the fast and frugal way: Models of bounded rationality. *Psychological Review, 103*, 650–669. doi:10.1037/0033-295X.103.4.650

Goldstein, R. Z., & Volkow, N. D. (2002). Drug addiction and its underlying neurobiological basis: Neuroimaging evidence for the involvement of the frontal cortex. *The American Journal of Psychiatry, 159*, 1642–1652. doi:10.1176/appi.ajp.159.10.1642

Greene, J. D., Morelli, S. A., Lowenberg, K., Nystrom, L. E., & Cohen, J. D. (2008). Cognitive load selectively interferes with utilitarian moral judgment. *Cognition, 107*, 1144–1154. doi:10.1016/j.cognition.2007.11.004

Haidt, J. (2001). The emotional dog and its rational tail: A social intuitionist approach to moral judgment. *Psychological Review, 108*, 814–834. doi:10.1037/0033-295X.108.4.814

Hanson, K. L., Luciana, M., & Sullwold, K. (2008). Reward-related decision-making deficits and elevated impulsivity among MDMA and other drug users. *Drug and Alcohol Dependence*, 96(1–2), 99–110. doi:10.1016/j.drugalcdep.2008.02.003

Henderson, L. A., Woo, M. A., Macey, P. M., Macey, K. E., Frysinger, R. C., Alger, J. R., . . . Harper, R. M. (2003). Neural responses during Valsalva maneuvers in obstructive sleep apnea syndrome. *Journal of Applied Physiology, 94*, 1063–1074.

Hollander, J. A., Lu, Q., Cameron, M. D., Kamenecka, T. M., & Kenny, P. J. (2008). Insular hypocretin transmission regulates nicotine reward. *Proceedings of the National Academy of Sciences of the United States of America, 105*, 19480–19485. doi:10.1073/pnas.0808023105

Hugdahl, K. (1995). *Psychophysiology: The mind–body perspective*. Cambridge, MA: Harvard University Press.

James, W. (1890). *The Principles of Psychology*. (Vol. 2). New York, NY: Holt.

Kapp, B. S., Supple, W. F., & Whalen, P. J. (1994). Effects of electrical stimulation of the amygdalaloid central nucleus on neocortical arousal in the rabbit. *Behavioral Neuroscience, 108*, 81–93. doi:10.1037/0735-7044.108.1.81

Kelley, A. E., Schiltz, C. A., & Landry, C. F. (2005). Neural systems recruited by drug- and food-related cues: Studies of gene activation in corticolimbic regions. *Physiology & Behavior*, 86(1–2), 11–14. doi:10.1016/j.physbeh.2005.06.018

Knudsen, E. I. (2007). Fundamental components of attention. *Annual Review of Neuroscience, 30*, 57–78. doi:10.1146/annurev.neuro.30.051606.094256

Koenigs, M., Huey, E. D., Raymont, V., Cheon, B., Solomon, J., Wassermann, E. M., & Grafman, J. (2008). Focal brain damage protects against post-traumatic stress disorder in combat veterans. *Nature Neuroscience, 11*, 232–237. doi:10.1038/nn2032

Koob, G. F., & Le Moal, M. (2001). Drug addiction, dysregulation of reward, and allostasis. *Neuropsychopharmacology, 24,* 97–129. doi:10.1016/S0893-133X(00)00195-0

Kross, E., & Mischel, W. (2010). From stimulus control to self-control: Toward an integrative understanding of the processes underlying willpower. In R. Hassin, K. Oschner, & Y. Trope (Eds.), *Self-control in society, mind, and brain* (pp. 329–337). New York, NY: Oxford University Press. doi:10.1093/acprof:oso/9780195391381.003.0023

Kupers, R. C., Gybels, J. M., & Gjedde, A. (2000). Positron emission tomography study of a chronic pain patient successfully treated with somatosensory thalamic stimulation. *Pain, 87,* 295–302. doi:10.1016/S0304-3959(00)00295-5

LeDoux, J. E. (2000). Emotion circuits in the brain. *Annual Review of Neuroscience, 23,* 155–184. doi:10.1146/annurev.neuro.23.1.155

Lovallo, W. R., Yechiam, E., Sorocco, K. H., Vincent, A. S., & Collins, F. L. (2006). Working memory and decision-making biases in young adults with a family history of alcoholism: Studies from the Oklahoma Family Health Patterns Project. *Alcoholism: Clinical and Experimental Research, 30,* 763–773. doi:10.1111/j.1530-0277.2006.00089.x

Makris, N., Gasic, G. P., Seidman, L. J., Goldstein, J. M., Gastfriend, D. R., Elman, I., . . . Breiter, H. C. (2004). Decreased absolute amygdala volume in cocaine addicts. *Neuron, 44,* 729–740. doi:10.1016/j.neuron.2004.10.027

Manes, F., Paradiso, S., & Robinson, R. G. (1999). Neuropsychiatric effects of insular stroke. *Journal of Nervous and Mental Disease, 187,* 707–712. doi:10.1097/00005053-199912000-00001

McClure, S. M., Laibson, D. I., Loewenstein, G., & Cohen, J. D. (2004). Separate neural systems value immediate and delayed monetary rewards. *Science, 306,* 503–507. doi:10.1126/science.1100907

McClure, S. M., Li, J., Tomlin, D., Cypert, K. S., Montague, L. M., & Montague, P. R. (2004). Neural correlates of behavioral preference for culturally familiar drinks. *Neuron, 44,* 379–387. doi:10.1016/j.neuron.2004.09.019

McRae, K., Misra, S., Prasad, A. K., Pereira, S. C., & Gross, J. J. (2012). Bottom-up and top-down emotion generation: Implications for emotion regulation. *Social Cognitive and Affective Neuroscience, 7,* 253–262. doi:10.1093/scan/nsq103

Metcalfe, J., & Mischel, W. (1999). A hot/cool-system analysis of delay of gratification: Dynamics of willpower. *Psychological Review, 106,* 3–19. doi:10.1037/0033-295X.106.1.3

Milad, M. R., & Quirk, G. J. (2002). Neurons in medial prefrontal cortex signal memory for fear extinction. *Nature, 420,* 70–74. doi:10.1038/nature01138

Mischel, W., & Moore, B. (1973). Effects of attention to symbolically presented rewards of self-control. *Journal of Personality and Social Psychology, 28,* 172–179. doi:10.1037/h0035716

Mischel, W., Shoda, Y., & Rodriguez, M. L. (1989). Delay of gratification in children. *Science, 244*, 933–938. doi:10.1126/science.2658056

Morewedge, C. K., & Kahneman, D. (2010). Associative processes in intuitive judgment. *Trends in Cognitive Sciences, 14*, 435–440. doi:10.1016/j.tics.2010.07.004

Murray, E. A. (2007). The amygdala, reward and emotion. *Trends in Cognitive Sciences, 11*, 489–497. doi:10.1016/j.tics.2007.08.013

Nair, S. G., Golden, S. A., & Shaham, Y. (2008). Differential effects of the hypocretin 1 receptor antagonist SB 334867 on high-fat food self-administration and reinstatement of food seeking in rats. *British Journal of Pharmacology, 154*, 406–416. doi:10.1038/bjp.2008.3

Naqvi, N. H., Rudrauf, D., Damasio, H., & Bechara, A. (2007). Damage to the insula disrupts addiction to cigarette smoking. *Science, 315*, 531–534. doi:10.1126/science.1135926

Nisbett, R. E., & Ross, L. D. (1980). *Human inference: Strategies and shortcomings of social judgment*. Englewood Cliffs, NJ: Prentice-Hall.

Ochsner, K. N., Ray, R. R., Hughes, B., McRae, K., Cooper, J. C., Weber, J., . . . Gross, J. J. (2009). Bottom-up and top-down processes in emotion generation: Common and distinct neural mechanisms. *Psychological Science, 20*, 1322–1331. doi:10.1111/j.1467-9280.2009.02459.x

Paton, J. J., Belova, M. A., Morrison, S. E., & Salzman, C. D. (2006). The primate amygdala represents the positive and negative value of visual stimuli during learning. *Nature, 439*, 865–870. doi:10.1038/nature04490

Paulus, M. P. (2007). Decision-making dysfunctions in psychiatry—Altered homeostatic processing? *Science, 318*, 602–606. doi:10.1126/science.1142997

Petty, R. E., & Cacioppo, J. T. (1984). Source factors and the elaboration likelihood model of persuasion. *Advances in Consumer Research, 11*, 668–672.

Peyron, R., Laurent, B., & Garcia-Larrea, L. (2000). Functional imaging of brain responses to pain. A review and meta-analysis (2000). *Neurophysiologie Clinique-Clinical Neurophysiology, 30*, 263–288. doi:10.1016/S0987-7053(00)00227-6

Phillips, M. L., Drevets, W. C., Rauch, S. L., & Lane, R. (2003). Neurobiology of emotion perception I: The neural basis of normal emotion perception. *Biological Psychiatry, 54*, 504–514. doi:10.1016/S0006-3223(03)00168-9

Plassmann, H., O'Doherty, J., & Rangel, A. (2007). Orbitofrontal cortex encodes willingness to pay in everyday economic transactions. *The Journal of Neuroscience, 27*, 9984–9988. doi:10.1523/JNEUROSCI.2131-07.2007

Plassmann, H., O'Doherty, J., Shiv, B., & Rangel, A. (2008). Marketing actions can modulate neural representations of experienced pleasantness. *Proceedings of the National Academy of Sciences of the United States of America, 105*, 1050–1054. doi:10.1073/pnas.0706929105

Reyna, V. F. (2004). How people make decisions that involve risk–A dual-processes approach. *Current Directions in Psychological Science, 13*, 60–66. doi:10.1111/j.0963-7214.2004.00275.x

Reyna, V. F., & Ellis, S. C. (1994). Fuzzy-trace theory and framing effects in children's risky decision-making. *Psychological Science, 5*, 275–279. doi:10.1111/j.1467-9280.1994.tb00625.x

Reyna, V. F., Lloyd, F. J., & Brainerd, C. J. (2003). Memory, development, and rationality: An integrative theory of judgment and decision-making. In S. Schneider & J. Shanteau (Eds.), *Emerging perspectives on judgment and decision research* (pp. 201–245). New York, NY: Cambridge University Press. doi:10.1017/CBO9780511609978.009

Rodgers, R. J., Halford, J. C. G., de Souza, R. L. N., de Souza, A. L. C., Piper, D. C., Arch, J. R. S., ... Blundel, J. E. (2001). SB-334867, a selective orexin-1 receptor antagonist, enhances behavioural satiety and blocks the hyperphagic effect of orexin-A in rats. *European Journal of Neuroscience, 13*, 1444–1452. doi:10.1046/j.0953-816x.2001.01518.x

Schaefer, M., Berens, H., Heinze, H. J., & Rotte, M. (2006). Neural correlates of culturally familiar brands of car manufacturers. *NeuroImage, 31*, 861–865. doi:10.1016/j.neuroimage.2005.12.047

Schultz, W. (2000). Multiple reward signals in the brain. *Nature Reviews Neuroscience, 1*, 199–207. doi:10.1038/35044563

Shiffrin, R. M., & Schneider, W. (1977). Controlled and automatic human information processing. II. Perceptual learning, automatic attending, and a general theory. *Psychological Review, 84*, 127–190. doi:10.1037/0033-295X.84.2.127

Stanovich, K. E., & West, R. F. (2000). Individual differences in reasoning: Implications for the rationality debate? *Behavioral and Brain Sciences, 23*, 645–665. doi:10.1017/S0140525X00003435

Tranel, D., & Damasio, A. R. (1993). The covert learning of affective valence does not require structures in hippocampal system or amygdala. *Journal of Cognitive Neuroscience, 5*(1), 79–88. doi:10.1162/jocn.1993.5.1.79

Tversky, A., & Kahneman, D. (1981). The framing of decisions and the psychology of choice. *Science, 211*, 453–458. doi:10.1126/science.7455683

Verdejo-Garcia, A., Benbrook, A., Funderburk, F., David, P., Cadet, J. L., & Bolla, K. I. (2007). The differential relationship between cocaine use and marijuana use on decision-making performance over repeat testing with the Iowa gambling task. *Drug and Alcohol Dependence, 90*(1), 2–11. doi:10.1016/j.drugalcdep.2007.02.004

Wager, T. D., Davidson, M. L., Hughes, B. L., Lindquist, M. A., & Ochsner, K. N. (2008). Prefrontal–subcortical pathways mediating successful emotion regulation. *Neuron, 59*, 1037–1050. doi:10.1016/j.neuron.2008.09.006

Wang, G. J., Tomasi, D., Backus, W., Wang, R., Telang, F., Geliebter, A., . . . Volkow, N. E. (2008). Gastric distention activates satiety circuitry in the human brain. *NeuroImage, 39*, 1824–1831. doi:10.1016/j.neuroimage.2007.11.008

Weller, J. A., Levin, I. P., Shiv, B., & Bechara, A. (2007). Neural correlates of adaptive decision making for risky gains and losses. *Psychological Science, 18*, 958–964. doi:10.1111/j.1467-9280.2007.02009.x

Whitlow, C. T., Liguori, A., Livengood, L. B., Hart, S. L., Mussat-Whitlow, B. J., Lamborn, C. M., . . . Porrino, L. J. (2004). Long-term heavy marijuana users make costly decisions on a gambling task. *Drug and Alcohol Dependence, 76*(1), 107–111. doi:10.1016/j.drugalcdep.2004.04.009

Williamson, J. W., McColl, R., & Mathews, D. (2003). Evidence for central command activation of the human insular cortex during exercise. *Journal of Applied Physiology, 94*, 1726–1734.

Young, L., Bechara, A., Tranel, D., Damasio, H., Hauser, M., & Damasio, A. (2010). Damage to ventromedial prefrontal cortex impairs judgment of harmful intent. *Neuron, 65*, 845–851. doi:10.1016/j.neuron.2010.03.003

INDEX

Note: "C.P." in the index refers to Color Plates.

Abstract rewards, concrete vs., 149
ACC. *See* Anterior cingulate cortex
ACC/dmPFC BOLD signal, 22, 23, 28
Accumulator, 23–24
Adaptive adolescent period, 109
Adaptive decision making, 31
Addiction, 98, 152, 156, 187–189, 194
ADHD (attention-deficit/hyperactivity disorder), 189
Adolescence, 73–87
- adaptive adolescent period in, 109
- brain imaging and risk-taking research in, 80–84
- brain maturation in, 96–98
- cognitive development in, 99–100, C.P. 4
- defined, 73
- evidence for increases in risk taking in, 75–78
- hormonal factors during, 83–84
- juvenile justice system and developmental factors in, 107–109
- neurobiological models of risk taking during, 78–80
- neuroimaging evidence of unique reward processing in, 101–107
- peer influences in, 83–84
- phases of, 73–74
- sensation-seeking period in, 93–111
- social reorientation during, 79

Adolescents
- directions for future research involving, 85–87
- impulsivity in, 29–30
- mortality among, 74
- risk taking by, 74–75, 94–96
- ventral striatum responses to reward in, 80–83, C.P. 2

Adrenergic receptors, 97
Affective node, 79
Affective processing, and age, 124
Affective systems, framing effects and activation of, 44–45
Aging brain. *See* Older adults
Albert, D., 83, 107
Alcohol, 12, 86, 187
American Psychological Association (APA), xii
Amygdala, 21–22
- in adolescents, 78–79
- and delay of gratification, 153–156
- and dual/triple processes, 182–187, 189, 191
- fear response of, 45
- in fMRI studies, 80

Anderson, S. W., 60
Animal studies, 17, 53, 101, 103, 104, 184, 188, 191
Anterior cingulate cortex (ACC), 20, 22, 26, 60
- in adolescence, 99
- and delay gratification, 156
- dorsal, 20
- in fMRI studies, 80
- rostral, 148–149, 156

Anterior insula, 20, 28
Anterior parahippocampal gyrus, 26
Anterior temporal cortex, 79
Antisaccade (AS) tasks, 81, 103
Anxiety, 20, 22, 79
APA (American Psychological Association), xii
Asian disease problem, 44, 47, 182
Association for Psychological Science, xiii
Attention, in adolescents, 100
Attentional bias, 153
Attentional control, 149, 157–159
Attention-deficit/hyperactivity disorder (ADHD), 189
Attribute framing, 48–51
Autism, 32
Ayduk, O., 148

Bandy, D., 21, 190
Basal ganglia, 16, 189
- development of, in adolescence, 96
- orbitofrontal cortex and, 101

Basten, U., 21, 23

Bauer, A. S., 60
Bault, N., 77
Baumeister, R. F., 53
Bechara, A., 21, 60, 188
Beck, H., 57
Becker–DeGroot–Marschak method, 19
Behaviorism, 31
Betz, N., 18–19
BIAS Task, 129
Biele, G., 20–21
Bilateral caudate, 20
Bilateral hippocampus, 26
Bilateral parietal cortex, 26
Bipolar personality disorder, 156
Bird, G., 86
Bjork, J. M., 82
Blais, A.-R., 18–19
Blakemore, S. J., 77, 86
Blood oxygen dependent (BOLD) signal, 19, 22–23, 187
Body mass index, 147
Bowman, C. R., 25–26
Brain, 13. *See also specific regions*
  framing effects and activation of affective systems in, 44–45
  glucose use by, 53
  and handedness, 54–55
  maturation of, in adolescence, 96–98
  and reward/valuation, 16–19
  and uncertainty, 15
  white matter integrity, C.P. 8
Brain imaging, and risk-taking research in adolescence, 80–84
Brammer, M., 81–82
Braun, K. A., 48
Bronfenbrenner, Uri, xii–xiii
Bruine de Bruin, W., 58
Burnett, S., 77, 86

Cacioppo, J. T., 179
Cake gambling task, 81
Cannabis, 187–188
Card gambling, 77
Casey, B. J., 31, 78, 164–165
Ceci, Stephen, xii
Central executive, 153
Chaiken, S., 179
Chein, J., 83, 107
Chen, G., 82
Chen, K., 21, 190
Childhood, 73. *See also* Adolescence
Chronic pain patients, 190
Cigarette smoking, 95, 191, 192
Cingulate cortex, 162
Cingulum, 96
Circadian rhythms, 52–54
Cocaine addiction, 187, 191–192
Cognition, age-related changes in, 124
Cognitive control, 153–156
Cognitive development, in adolescence, 99–100, C.P. 4
Cognitive-regulatory node, 79
Cognitive strategies, for delay of gratification, 149–162
Cognitive theories, of decision making, 75–76
Cohen, J. D., 22–23, 182
Cohen, J. R., 105
Common-currency hypothesis, 17–18
Comparison of options, 22–23
Concrete rewards, abstract vs., 149
Conditioned stimuli, 183
Conflict between options, 23
Control
  attentional, 149
  cognitive, 153–156
  self-, 28–30, 191
Cool cognitive system, 153, 163–165, 180
Corbin, J., 57
Coricelli, G., 77
Cornell University, xiii
Cortico-subcortical connectivity, 97
Coupon redemption, 48–49
Craig, A. D., 21, 190
Craving, 191–192
Craving system, 178
Criminal behavior, 12
Crone, E. A., 76
Cue processing, 103
Cue reactivity paradigm, 155–156
Cunningham, W. A., 184

D1 receptors, 98
D2 receptors, 98
D'Acremont, M., 20
Damasio, A. R., 189
Damasio, H., 60
Davis, F. C., 53

Decision aids, for enhancement of choice, in older adults, 133–134
Decision making. *See also specific headings*
absence of global decline in, in older adults, 132–133
adaptive, 31
cognitive theories of, 75–76
dual process models of, 177–194
and handedness, 54–55
Decisions, functionally significant features of, 30–31
Decision strategies, effect of, on delay of gratification, 150
Decision value, 105
Delay of gratification, 145–166
cognitive strategies enabling, 149–162
definition of, 145
effect of decision strategies on, 150
effect of reappraisal on, 150–151
experimental findings on, 151–152
future research, directions for, 162–165
hot/cool systems approach to, 152–165
longitudinal findings on, 151
preschool, 146–149
De Martino, B., 22, 23
Dennis, N. A., 25–26
Detection node, 79
Devine, P. G., 179
Diagnostic and Statistical Manual of Mental Disorders (DSM–IV–REV), 15
Diamond, W. D., 48
Dickinson, D. L., 53
Diffusion tensor imaging studies, 96–97, 131
Distractions, 150
Distractors, 99
dlPFC (Dorsolateral prefrontal cortex), 27–30, 105–106
Dolan, S., 188
Domain-Specific Risk-Taking (DOSPERT) scale, 18
Dopamine, 97–98, 108, 131
Dopaminergic activity, 16
Dorsal anterior cingulate cortex, 20
Dorsal hypothalamic region, 17
Dorsal striatum, 16
Dorsolateral prefrontal cortex (dlPFC), 27–30, 105–106
DOSPERT (Domain-Specific Risk-Taking) scale, 18
Down-regulation, 29
Drug addiction, 187–189
DSM–IV–REV *(Diagnostic and Statistical Manual of Mental Disorders)*, 15
Dual process (term), 178
Dual process models, 177–194
addiction clinical example, 187–189
with adolescents, 78–79, 82
in decision making, 181–182
history of, 178–181
and insular cortex, 189–194
neurological evidence for, 182–186
opposition to, 186–187
Dvorak, R. D., 54

Economic approach (to defining risky decision making), 14–16
Eigsti, I.-M., 159
Einarson, A., 48
Elaboration likelihood model, 179
Emotion regulation, 22
Emotion suppression, 51–52, 62
Endocannabinoids, 97
Environmental factors, in adolescent risk taking, 95–96
Ernst, M., 83
Esctasy (narcotic), 187
Estrada, S. M., 27
EV. *See* Expected value
Executive control, in adolescents, 99, 100
Executive functions, 153
Expected utility, 14, 24–25
Expected value (EV), 14–15, 20, 24–25, 27, 75–78, 133
Experience, learning from, 23–24
Explicit memory, 131
Extended amygdala, 182
Exteroception, 190
Eye-tracking technology, 57

Faces, 184
False memory, 25
Fear, 22, 45, 58, 79
Fecteau, S., 29

Feedback, 77, 82, 127, 129
FEF (frontal eye field), 103
Fetal risk, 48
Fiebach, C. J., 21
Figner, B., 77
Firearms, 12
Fischhoff, B., 58
Fixed economy, 107
fMRI. *See* Functional magnetic resonance imaging
fMRI studies. *See* Functional MRI studies
Food rewards, money rewards vs., 18
Forbes, E. E., 84
Foster, R. G., 53
Framing effects, 26–27, 43–63
  and activation of affective systems in brain, 44–45
  attribute, 48–51
  and dual process models, 45, 182
  and emotion suppression, 51–52
  future research, directions for, 62–63
  and handedness, 54–55
  with impaired vs. unimparied older decision makers, 59–61
  with older adults, 57–61
  and physiological vs. behavioral measures, 55–57
  reflection effects vs., 46
  risky-choice, 47, 50, 52–54
  and System 1 vs. System 2 decision making, 45–46
  ubiquity of, 44
Frederick, S., 45, 182
Frontal eye field (FEF), 103
Frontal lobe hypothesis of aging, 58
Functionally significant features, of decisions, 30–31
Functional magnetic resonance imaging (fMRI), 19, 20, 60, 62, 125
Functional MRI (fMRI) studies, 80
  of reward learning, in older adults, 127
  of reward processing, 103–108
  and self-esteem/attentional control, 156
  of working memory, 99
Fusiform face area, 79
Fuzzy memory representations, 24
Fuzzy reasoning, 179
Fuzzy trace theory, 12–16, 20, 21, 24–28, 30–33, 35, 38–40, 45, 56–57, 62, 68, 76, 85, 90, 100, 118, 132, 134, 140, 152, 174, 175, 178–180, 200, 201

GABA (gamma-aminobutyric acid), 97
Gaeth, G. J., 48
Gage, Phineas, 185
Gain and loss learning, in older adults, 127–128
Gains, neural substrates differentiating losses, probabilities, and, 19–22
Gain trials, 58–59
Gallo, M., 48
Galvan, A., 81, 86
Gambling, 18, 46, 76, 81, 188. *See also* Iowa Gambling Task (IGT)
Gamma-aminobutyric acid (GABA), 97
Geier, C. F., 107
Giampetro, V., 81–82
Gianotti, L. R., 28–29
Gist-based reasoning, 56–57, 76, 134, 179–180
Gist memory representations, 23–28, 31, 133
Glimcher, P. W., 17–18
Glucose, 52–54
Glutamate, 97
Gmax, 27, 28
Goals, incongruous, 181
Goel, R., 48
Go/no-go tasks, 157–158, 160, C.P.s 9–10
Graham v. Florida, 108
Gratification, delay of. *See* Delay of gratification
Gross, J. J., 29, 51, 154
Gyurak, A., 156

Hajcak, G., 154
Halari, R., 81–82
Handedness, 54–55
Head Start, xiii
Heerkeren, H. R., 20–21
Heuristic-systematic model of information processing, 179
High temptation focus, 158
Hindes, A., 188
Hippocampus, 24, 26, 155

Homicide, 12
Hommer, D. W., 82
Hormonal factors, in adolescence, 80, 83–84, C.P. 3
Hot/cool framework (delay of gratification), 152–165
  cool cognitive system in, 153, 163
  and development, 157–159
  hot limbic system in, 152–153, 163–164
  individual differences in, 155–156
  interaction between cool and hot systems in, 164–165
  neural correlates in, 159–162
  with preschoolers, 157
  relative activation of hot and cool systems in, 153–155
Hot emotional system, 180
Hot limbic system, 152–153, 163–165
Huettel, S. A., 28, 60
Huizenga, H. M., 77
Hunt, L. T., 19
Hutcherson, C. A., 29

IFG. *See* Inferior frontal gyrus
IGT. *See* Iowa Gambling Task
Illicit substances, use of, 86
Immaturity, in adolescents, 108–109
Impaired decision making, framing effects with, 59–61
Impulse control, 157–159
Impulsive system, 178
Impulsivity, 13, 28–31, 152, 154, 189
Incarcerated youths, 29–30
Incentives, 78–79
Incongruous goals, 181
Individual differences
  in hot/cool framework, 155–156
  in older adults, 132
Inferior frontal gyrus (IFG), 153, 161, 163
Information processing
  heuristic-systematic model of, 179
  social, 79–80, 86
Inhibition, 28–30
Inhibitory control, in adolescents, 99–100, 104
Insula (insular cortex), 20–22, 28, 86, 154
  and dual process models, 189–194
  and fear response, 45
International Statistical Classification of Diseases and Related Health Problems (ICD–10), 15
Interoception, 190
Intuition, 14, 24
Intuitive system, 178
Iowa Gambling Task (IGT), 24–26, 59–60, 77, 132, 185–188

Jackson v. Hobbs, 108
James, William, 45, 189
James McKeen Catell Fellow Award, xiii
Jansen, B. R. J., 77
Jasper, J. D., 48
Jones, R. M., 78
Juvenile justice system, 107–109

Kahneman, D., 44, 45, 47, 55
Koren, G., 48
Kühberger, A., 27, 57

Laboratory experiments, 12–13, 31
Laibson, D. I., 182
Lateral parietal cortex, 25
Lateral prefrontal cortices, 58
Learning from experience, 23–24
Levenson, R. J., 51
Levin, I. P., 46, 48, 49
Levy, D. J., 17–18
Life expectancies, 49
Lmin, 27, 28
Loewenstein, G., 182
Loss anticipation, 126
Loss aversion, 15–16, 21–22, 28
Losses
  and memory representations of risk preference, 26–27
  neural substrates differentiating gains, probabilities, and, 19–22
Low temptation focus, 158
Luna, B., 107

Mackinlay, R. J., 77
Magnetic resonance imaging (MRI), 96. *See also* Functional magnetic resonance imaging (fMRI)
Magnetoencephalography, 19
Major depressive disorder, 156

Making Human Beings Human (Bronfenbrenner), xiii
Marijuana, 86
Masicampo, E. J., 53
McClelland, Peter, xii
McClure, E. B., 79
McClure, S. M., 182
McElroy, T., 53, 55, 57, 62
McMahon, A. J., 54
Medial orbitofrontal cortex (mOFC), 19, 21, 23
Medial prefrontal cortex (MPFC), 20, 25, 60, 125, C.P. 5
Medial temporal lobe (MTL), 24, 25
Memory representations, 24–28
  encoding of, 24
  of risk preference, in decision making, 26–28
Menaker, M., 53
Metcalfe, J., 180
Midbrain dopamine areas, 16
MID (monetary incentive delay) tasks, 82
Miller v. Alabama, 108
Mills, B. A., 27
Mischel, W., 180, 181
Moen, Phyllis, xii
Mohr, P. N., 20–21
Monetary gains/losses, processing of, in older adults, 125–127, C.P.s 5–6
Monetary incentive delay (MID) tasks, 82, 84
Monetary incentives, 106–107
Money rewards, food rewards vs., 18
Motivation, in adolescents, 99, 105–106
Motor response stage, 103
MPFC. *See* Medial prefrontal cortex
MRI (magnetic resonance imaging), 96. *See also* Functional magnetic resonance imaging (fMRI)
MTL (medial temporal lobe), 24, 25
Myelin sheath, 96

Naqvi, N. H., 192
Nelson, E. E., 79, 80, 86
Neural network, changes in, in older adults, 130–131
Neurochemical maturation, during adolescence, 97–98
Nicotine addiction, 191, 192
Nucleus accumbens, 16, 80, 86, 101, 153
Nystrom, L. E., 22–23

O'Brien, L., 83, 107
Occipital cortex, 26
Ochsner, K. N., 155
Oculomotor control regions, 103–104
O'Doherty, J., 19
OFC. *See* Orbitofrontal cortex
Older adults, 123–135
  absence of global decline in decision making in, 132–133
  and changes in neural network, 130–131
  decision aids for enhancement of choice in, 133–134
  framing effects in, 57–61
  future research, directions for, 135
  gain and loss learning in, 127–128
  individual differences in, 132
  processing of monetary gains/losses in, 125–127, C.P.s 5–6
  and research applicability to real-world tasks, 134
  risky decision making in, 128–130, C.P. 7
Op de Macks, Z. A., 84
Orbitofrontal cortex (OFC), 26
  in fMRI studies, 80
  in older adults, 58
  and reward processing in adolescence, 101, 105–106

Parahippocampal regions, 24
Pardo, J. V., 60
Parietal cortex, 20, 23, 24
  bilateral, 26
  lateral, 25
  posterior, 27–28
Parietal eye field, 103
Parker, A. M., 58
Payne, J. W., 49
Peer influences, 83–84
Petty, R. E., 179
PFC. *See* Prefrontal cortex
Phantom recollection, 25
Phenomenology, 25
Pine, D. S., 79
Plassman, H., 19, 29

Pmax, 27
Pochon, J. B., 22–23
Positive feedback, 127
Positivity effects, 125, 126
Posterior cingulate cortex, 17–18, 25
Posterior parietal cortex, 27–28
Posttraumatic stress disorder (PTSD), 183
Precentral cortex, 26
Prediction error, 105
Preference reversal, 181–182
Prefrontal cortex (PFC), 16, 189. *See also* Ventromedial prefrontal cortex (vmPFC)
  in adolescents, 79
  and cognitive control, 153–156, 161
  development of, in adolescents, 96–98
  functional maturation of, 58
  medial, 20, 25, 60, 125, C.P. 5
  superior, 26
Prefrontal systems, in adolescence, 99, 100
Pregnancy, 48
Preschoolers, delay of gratification in, 146–152, 157–159
Primate studies, 103, 104
Probabilities, neural substrates differentiating gains, losses, and, 19–22
Prospect theory, 56
Psychological approach (to defining risky decision making), 14–16
Psychopathy, 12
PTSD (posttraumatic stress disorder), 183
Puberty, 74, 80, 83–84, 93, 109
Public health, risky decision making as threat to, 12

rACC. *See* Rostral anterior cingulate cortex
Ralph, M. R., 53
Rangel, A., 19, 29
Reaction times (in choice selection), 23
Real-world risky behaviors, 13
Real-world tasks, research applicability to, in older adults, 134
Reappraisal, effect of, on delay of gratification, 150–151
Reappraising, 149–150
Reasoning system, 178
Reconstruing, 149–150
Reflection effects, 46
Reflective system, 178
Reiman, E., 21, 190
Rejection sensitivity (RS), 148
Response preference, 23–30
  and impulsivity/inhibition of responses, 28–30
  and memory representations, 24–28
Reward(s)
  concrete vs. abstract, 149, 151
  and expected value, 14
  neural substrates of, 16–19
  representation/remembrance of, 13
Reward accrual, 103
Reward anticipation, 82
Reward circuit (of brain), 16, 22
Reward prediction, 184
Reward processing
  in aging brain. *See* Older adults
  neuroimaging evidence of, in adolescence, 101–107, C.P. 1
Reward receipt, ventral striatum and, 81–83
Reward sensitivity, 13, 31, 76, 103, 107, 162
Reward types, risk preferences across, 17
Reyna, V. F., 27, 76
Rhesus macaques, 184
Right anterior insula, 20
Riis, J., 22–23
Risk attitude, 14, 16, 18
Risk aversion, 12–17
Risk perception, 13
Risk preference, 13, 14
  across reward types, 17
  memory representations of, in decision making, 26–28
  in older adults, 129
Risks, defined, 74
Risk taking
  by adolescents, 74–87, 94–96
  healthy vs. unhealthy, 15
Risky-choice framing, 47, 50, 52–54
Risky decision making, 152
  economic vs. psychological approaches to defining, 14–16
  in laboratory vs. real world, 12–13
  in older adults, 58–59, 128–130

Roper v. Simmons, 108
Rostral anterior cingulate cortex (rACC), 148–149, 156
RS (rejection sensitivity), 148
Rubia, K., 81–82

Samanez-Larkin, G. R., 126
Sanfey, A. G., 22–23
Sanyal, A., 48
Satisficing, 133
SB-34867 receptor agonist, 191
Scheel, M. H., 54
Schneider, W., 178
Schonberg, T., 29
Schott, B. H., 126–127
SCN (suprachiasmatic nucleus), 52–53
SCRs (skin conductance responses), 185–186, 188
Secondary inducers, 184
Self-control, 28–30, 191
Self-esteem, 156
Sensation seeking, 13, 16, 18, 76, 84
Sensation-seeking period, adolescent, 93–111
  and adaptive adolescent period, 109
  and brain maturation, 96–98
  and cognitive development, 99–100
  and juvenile justice system, 107–109
  and neuroimaging evidence of unique reward processing, 101–107
  and risk taking, 94–96
Serotonin, 97
Seta, J., 55
Sexual risk taking, 74, 76, 86, 146
Shannon, B. J., 29
Shiffrin, R. M., 178
Single process theories, 186–187
Skin conductance responses (SCRs), 185–186, 188
Smith, A. B., 81–82
Smith, A. R., 82
Social information processing model, 79–80, 86
Social reorientation, during adolescence, 79
Society for Neuroeconomics, xii
Society for Research in Child Development, xii
Socioemotional selectivity theory, 125–126
Somerville, L. H., 78, 79, 83
Stanovich, K. E., 45–46, 49, 179, 180
The State of Americans (Bronfenbrenner et al.), xii–xiii
Steinberg, L., 83, 107
Stereotypes, 53, 179
Striatum, 22, 182–186. *See also* Ventral striatum (VS)
  in cocaine addicts, 187
  in common-currency hypothesis, 17
  dorsal, 16
  and reward processing in adolescence, 105, 106
  underrecruitment of, in middle adolescence, 82
Stroke, 192
"Strong-handedness," 55
Subcortical brain, 58, 78
Superior longitudinal fasciculus, 96
Superior parietal cortex, 26
Superior prefrontal cortex, 26
Superior temporal sulcus, 79
Supplementary eye field, 103
Suprachiasmatic nucleus (SCN), 52–53
Sustained attention tasks, 81–82
Synaptic pruning, 96
System 1 decision making, 45–46, 62, 178–183
System 2 decision making, 45–46, 52, 62, 178–181

Tanner, C., 27, 57
Teens, homicide among, 12
Temporal discounting, 81, 152, 181
Temporal lobe, medial, 24, 25
Temporal sulcus, superior, 79
Temptation, 146–150
Temptation focus, 158
Testosterone, 84, C.P. 3
Thalamus, C.P. 8
Thiruchselvam, R., 154
Thompson, S., 86
Transmagnetic cranial stimulation (TMS), 29
Triadic model, 79
Triple process model, 79, 192–194
True memory, 25
Tversky, A., 44, 47, 55

Uckert, K., 83, 107
Uncertainty, 15–16
Uncinate fasciculus, 96
Unique reward processing, neuro-imaging evidence of, in adolescence, 101–107
Up-regulation, 29
Urie Bronfenbrenner Award for Lifetime Contribution to Developmental Psychology in the Service of Science and Society, xiii
U.S. Supreme Court, 108

Valuation, neural substrates of, 16–19
Vandekar, S. N., 25–26
van Duijvenvoorde, A. C. K., 77
van Leijenhorst, L., 76, 81
Variance, 14
Venkatraman, V., 27, 28
Ventral striatum (VS), 16
  in adolescents, 78, 80–83, C.P. 2
  and anticipation of monetary losses, in older adults, 125, C.P. 5
  and available reward processing studies in adolescence, C.P. 1
  in fMRI studies, 80
  and "hot system," 153
  responses of, to reward, in adolescents, 80–83
  and reward processing in adolescence, 101–105, 108
  and reward processing in older adults, 127
  and risky decision making, in older adults, 130
Ventromedial prefrontal cortex (vmPFC), 16, 28
  and amygdala, 22, 30
  in cocaine addicts, 187
  in common-currency hypothesis, 17, 18
  and down-/up-regulation, 29
  and dual processing, 184–188
  and fear response, 45
  fMRI studies, 19
  and IGT performance, 60
  and reward processing in adolescence, 105–106
  in triple process model, 193–194
Verbatim memory representations, 24–28, 56, 134
Vigilance, 22, 160
Visser, I., 77
Visual cortex, 26, 96
vmPFC. *See* Ventromedial prefrontal cortex
vmPFC/mOFC signal, 19, 21, 23
Vohs, K. D., 165
VS. *See* Ventral striatum

Wang, X. T., 54
Weber, E. U., 18–19, 77
Weller, J. A., 58, 184n3
West, R. F., 45–46, 49, 179, 180
Westenberg, P. M., 76
Wethington, Elaine, xii
Wheel of fortune task, 81
White matter integrity, C.P. 8
Wilkening, F., 77
Wisconsin Card Sorting Test, 185
Wood, S. M. W., 21
Working memory
  fMRI studies of, 99
  inferior frontal gyrus and, 153

Zanolie, K., 81

ABOUT THE EDITORS

Valerie F. Reyna, PhD, is director of the Human Neuroscience Institute at Cornell University and former president of the Society for Judgment and Decision Making, professor and codirector of the Center for Behavioral Economics and Decision Research at Cornell University, and codirector of the Cornell University Magnetic Resonance Imaging Facility. She is a developer of fuzzy trace theory, a model of memory, decision making, and development that is widely applied in law, medicine, and public health. Her recent work has focused on numeracy, medical decision making, risk perception and risk taking, neurobiological models of development, and neurocognitive impairment and genetics. Dr. Reyna has been a leader in using memory principles such as accessibility and mathematical models of memory to explain judgment and decision making. Among her theoretical proposals, she is particularly well known for a model of intuition that places it at the apex of judgment and decision making, rather than treating it as a developmentally primitive process. She also helped to initiate what is now a burgeoning area of research on developmental differences in judgment and decision making. Her research supports an evidence-based explanation of neural and psychological processes of risk taking in adolescence and adulthood, which predicts real-world behaviors. The author of more than 175 publications that have been cited more than 8,000 times, Dr. Reyna is a fellow of numerous scientific societies and has served on scientific panels of the National Research Council, the National Science Foundation, the National Institutes of Health, the MacArthur Foundation, and the National Academy of Sciences.

Vivian Zayas, PhD, is an associate professor of psychology at Cornell University. Her research examines the cognitive and affective processes involved in delay of gratification and the interplay between attachment and affiliative processes, on the one hand, and self-control processes, on the other, using theoretical frameworks and methods that cross traditionally defined boundaries between social and personality psychology and cognitive psychology and cognitive neuroscience and developmental psychology. Her research has appeared in journals such as *Psychological Science*, the *Journal of Personality and Social Psychology*, *Proceedings of the National Academy of Sciences*, *Personality and Social Psychology Bulletin*, *Child Development*, *Nature Neuroscience*, and the *Journal of Personality*. She has received funding from the National Science Foundation and the National Institutes of Health.